D1505453

"How did we get the church calendar? How did the season of Advent evolve? Where did Christmas customs like candles, trees, Santa Claus, mistletoe, holly, poinsettias, and exchanging gifts originate? The answers to these and hundreds of other questions about the church year, Sunday observance, the week, the seasons, holy days, Halloween, Thanksgiving, Mary, the saints, purgatory, and sacramentals are all here in this popular, indexed guide.

"Fascinating to browse through, the book is a goldmine for anyone, from parish minister to parent, who wants to keep the best of the traditions alive and pass on their story and meaning to a new generation."

Jim Scully
The Pecos Benedictine

"This book by Greg Dues is most timely, given the fact that many young and less-young adults who are members of the Catholic church do not seem to be familiar with 'customs and traditions' that other generations have grown up knowing and living. The volume should prove to be an important one for Catholics who so frequently ask, or are expected to be able to answer, questions about what Catholics do in their devotional life and why they do them."

Agnes Cunningham, SSCM
Mundelein Seminary

"This book can help those who want to teach catechumens or neophytes about Catholic customs, who would like to explain certain traditions to their children, and who want to promote faith among their family members....You will not regret purchasing this little encyclopedia."

Jovian Lang, OFM
Modern Liturgy

REVISED AND UPDATED

CATHOLIC CUSTOMS

& TRADITIONS

a popular guide

GREG DUES

TWENTY
THIRD 23rd
PUBLICATIONS

PB: Ninth printing of revised edition 2009
Hardcover edition 2009

TWENTY-THIRD PUBLICATIONS
A Division of Bayard
One Montauk Avenue, Suite 200
New London, CT 06320
(860) 437-3012 or (800) 321-0411

ISBN 978-0-89622-515-2 (PB)
Library of Congress Catalog Card Number: 92-80801 (PB)

ISBN 978-1-58595-771-2 (HC)
Library of Congress Catalog Card Number: 200993552 (HC)

Printed in the U.S.A.

To my parents Joseph (d. 1986) and Mary (d. 1983)

my brothers and sisters: Genevieve, Harold (d. 1986),
Wilfred (d. 1992), Joseph (d. 1985), Stanley, Wilma,
Helen, Maria, Lowell,
Jeanette, Marilyn, and MaryAnn

my wife: Barbara Walkley

my daughters: Francisca and Elena

CONTENTS

Introduction   1

Part One—Religious Traditions

1. The Nature of Religious Traditions   6
    Human and Limited • Subject to Change • Effective • Cyclic
    •Based on Real Life • Earthiness • Religious Persecution
    • Traditions in a Technological Age

Part Two—The Church Year

2. The Church Year   14
    Calendars • Church Year • Ancient Christian Centers • Evolution
    of the Church Year • Annual Pascha • Christmas Cycle
    • Temporal Cycle • Sanctoral Cycle • Devotional Feasts

3. Sunday   19
    Most Ancient of Traditions • First Day of the Week • From
    Sunday Evening... • ...to Sunday Morning • Agape Meals
    • Blessing of Lights • Lord's Day • Sunday • Sunday Themes
    • Sunday Assembly • Sunday Obligation • Day of Rest • Servile
    Work • Blue Laws • Contemporary Observance of Sunday

4. Weekdays   29
    Origin of the Week • Private Prayer • Public Prayer • Liturgical
    Hours • Origin of the Rosary • Revival of the Liturgy of the
    Hours • Family Prayer • Meal Prayer • Bedtime Prayer • Fasting
    • Friday Abstinence • Daily Mass • Daily Themes

5. Seasons   37
    Cycle of Seasons • Ember Days • Rogation Days

Part Three—The Temporal Cycle

6. Advent   42
   Beginning of Church Year • Theme • Origin • Penitential Theme
   • Mixed Theme • Advent Wreath • Jesse Tree • Advent House
   • Advent Calendar • Manger • Advent Colors

7. Christmas   49
   Origin of Christmas • Date of Christmas • Non-Christian
   Influence • Popularity of Christmas • Secular Christmas
   • Christmas in North America • Sacred and Secular • Christmas
   Candle • Window Lights • Luminaries • Hanukkah • Kwanzaa
   • Nativity Scene • Las Posadas • Oplatek • Christmas Tree
   • Christmas Carols • Mistletoe • Holly • Poinsettia • Christmas
   Cards • Christmas Pageants • Exchanging Gifts • Kriss Kringle
   • Santa Claus

8. Christmastime   63
   Twelve Days of Christmas • Feast Days of Martyrs • Holy Family
   • January 1 • New Year's Day • Epiphany • Magi • Blessing of
   Homes • Candlemas • Annunciation

9. Lent   70
   Origin • Lent and Baptism • Penitential Theme • Forty Days
   • Mardi Gras • Paczki • Shrove Tuesday • Ash Wednesday
   • Lenten Atmosphere • Fasting and Abstinence • Popular
   Penances • Stations of the Cross • Pretzels • Hot Cross Buns
   • Recent Trends

10. Holy Week   78
    The Pascha, or Passover • Holy Week • Sacred Triduum • Palm
    Sunday • Palms • Preparation Days • Easter Duty • Spring
    Cleaning • Holy Thursday • Washing of Feet • Chapel of
    Adoration • Stripping the Altar • Forty Hours Devotion
    • Chrism Mass • Seder • Good Friday • Veneration of the Cross
    • Mass of the Pre-Sanctified • Fasting • Tre Ore • Hot Cross Buns

11. The Easter Vigil   89
    Easter Vigil • Easter Fire • Easter Candle • Holy Saturday
    Morning Liturgy • Renewal of Easter Vigil • Blessing of Easter
    Baskets

12. Easter   94
    Date of Easter • Fertility Theme • Name of Easter • Easter
    Sunday Mass • Easter Duty • Sunrise Services • New Easter
    Clothes • Easter Parade • Easter Lamb • Easter Ham • Easter
    Eggs • Easter Bunnies • Easter Lilies • Mystagogia • Pentecost

13. Ordinary Time   101
    Trinity Sunday • Corpus Christi • Corpus Christi Procession
    • Benediction • Feast of the Sacred Heart • Christ the King

                    Part Four—The Sanctoral Cycle

14. Communion of Saints   106
    Martyrs and Persecution • Confessors • Other Saints • Spread of
    Devotion to Saints • Abuses • Communion of Saints
    • Remembering the Saints • Patron Saints • Holy Days • Feast
    Days • Relics • Images • Praying to Saints • Litanies • Feast of
    All Saints • Canonization • Halo

15. Mary   118
    Hyperdulia • Early Cult • Intercessory Role • Modern Devotion
    • Cautions • Little Office of Our Lady • Hail Mary • Rosary
    • Antiphons • Saturday • May and Mother's Day • Month of the
    Rosary • Marian Litanies • Angelus • Apparitions • Images
    • Scapular • Blessing of Flowers and Herbs

16. Purgatory   128
    Purgatory • Prayer for the Dead • November 2 • Indulgences
    • Stipends • Visiting Graves • November • Black as Liturgical
    Color

17. Popular Saints and Legends   136
    St. Christopher • St. Nicholas • St. Valentine • St. Patrick

                Part Five—Sacraments and Sacramentals

18. Sacraments   144
    Principle of Sacramentality • Origin of Catholic Sacraments
    • *Baptism:* An Initiation Process • Baptistries • Private Baptism

• Renewal of Baptism • *Confirmation* • Order of Initiation
Restored • *Eucharist* • Eucharistic Sacrifice • Distancing from
Laity • Deterioration of Meaning and Practice • Renewal of
Eucharist • *Reconciliation* • Sin: Human Experience • Gospel of
Reconciliation • Beginnings of Ritual Penance • Public Penance
• Private Penance • Purgatory and Indulgences • Contemporary
Practice • *Anointing of the Sick* • Transition to Anointing of the
Dying • Current Practices • *Marriage* • A Problem with Sex
• Marriage Becomes Sacrament • Current Thinking and Practice
• *Orders* • Origin of Catholic Priesthood • Ordination Process
• Expanding Orders of Clergy • Presbyters Become Priests • A
Different Lifestyle • Post-Reformation Priesthood • Current
Trends • Priest Garb

19. Sacramentals   171

Definition • Popular Devotions • Principle of Sacramentality
• St. Blaise and Blessing of Throats • Gestures and Bodily
Positions • Standing • Facing East • Kneeling • Prostration
• Genuflecting • Bowing • Sitting • The Raising of Eyes and
Hands • Laying on of Hands •Folding Hands • Striking the Breast
• Sign of the Cross • Music • Ritual Words • Litanies • Altar
• Lights • Candles • Votive and Vigil Lights • Holy Water
• Vestments • Bells • Medals• Miraculous Medal • Incense
• Colors • Symbols • Crosses

Part Six—Special Days

20. Halloween   192
21. Thanksgiving   195
22. Memorial Day   198

Selected Bibliography   200
Index   203

INTRODUCTION

There was total silence among the 100 or more adult parishioners. Enthusiastic discussion and testimony had filled the hall just minutes before as these parents shared memories of religious traditions popular in their homes when they were children. Their remembrances were filled with nostalgia and some laughter. Then they were asked, "What will your children remember?" Silence.

Stories not told are soon forgotten and the truth they kept alive is eventually lost. The practice and celebration of religious traditions tell stories. They tell of faith. Another generation hears the religious story by continuing the traditions.

Some parishioners lost a chapter in the story in the 1960s as religious traditions began to fade in practice and promotion. No malicious conspiracy on the part of church leaders or parents was responsible for this change in popular faith. Pastors did not announce: "From now on, do not observe any religious traditions other than what we do here in church on Sunday." Parents did not deliberately cancel prayer at table and special lenten practices in the family.

The 1960s witnessed the beginning of profound changes in how people live. These changes touched every aspect of human life: economics, politics, education, social structures, family life, *and religion.* This had happened many times in history. The cause is usually some broad upheaval in society. Each time there is such an upheaval, security in doing what has always been done, *because it had always been done,* no longer sways people as in "the olden days." Old traditions begin to fade as a primary motivation for current practices and future planning. A transitional period of re-adjustment—and sometimes chaos—occurs as old traditions are transformed or abandoned, and new ones adopted.

The Second Vatican Council (1962-1965) assembled at the beginning of this time of upheaval. It called for a long overdue renewal and reform in how people live their faith in practical ways. A challenge to the validity of many old traditions was a side effect. Cleansing reli-

gion of centuries of excesses, misplaced emphases, and even superstition, seemed at first to sanitize it of all popular traditions and folk-
lore. These reform efforts sometimes created a religious vacuum in
homes and parishes. People began to feel that their popular traditions
were no longer important. Many parish leaders, wanting people to
believe, to pray, and to worship "correctly" and according to new
forms, often ignored the more human and less manageable elements
of popular faith. Some religious educators allowed new insights into
faith development and principles of catechetics to overshadow the
value of popular customs and rituals in faith development. An important dimension of religion was threatened. A part of people's religious story was no longer told.

Now, over a generation later, religious traditions are seen in better
perspective as supporting the living faith of people. These traditions
have always been an important dimension of celebrating faith and of
passing it on to another generation. Parents and parish leaders are
looking back, not to repeat the past, but to learn from it. They remember that Catholics, generation after generation, found mystery in
down-to-earth religious traditions. They do not feel they have to "re-
invent the wheel"; it just needs some redesigning to support personal and community faith.

Each age is a time of special grace, including our age of high technology in a society and culture that seem to ignore tradition. Within
this real-life situation our challenge is to revive or renew those religious traditions that anchor and support our quest for mystery.
Catholic Customs and Traditions: A Popular Guide encourages readers to
respect, enjoy, and, we hope, to practice those traditions that are in
keeping with our contemporary Catholic church, liturgy, and spirituality. This book cannot deal in an exhaustive way with almost twenty centuries of accumulated traditions among peoples of different cultures, languages, nationalities, and races. Attention is limited to those
popular practices that have particular meaning for North American
Catholics of the Roman Rite.

These traditions are discussed within the context of the church
year. With few exceptions, religious traditions have no meaning outside of the cyclical unfolding of the liturgical seasons and the church's
great variety of festivals and rituals. This context will help readers to
live their faith in practical ways as the year unfolds.

In some cases there are different explanations for the origins of certain traditions and different dates of origin. Using contemporary
scholarship, an attempt has been made to record the more likely ori-

gins and dates. In many cases, details of interest only to scholars have been omitted.

I have written this book for a broad audience of readers: parish teams and catechists responsible for promoting practical faith in families, catechumens and neophytes who want to understand Catholic customs better, and parents who want to clarify their motives for preserving certain traditions. This book is intended also for adults in special formation programs, such as lay ministers and students in college religious studies.

Catholic Customs and Traditions has six parts. Part One discusses the nature of religious traditions. Part Two gives an overview of the church year, which is the context of most religious traditions. It also serves as an introduction to the temporal cycle (Part Three) with its rich variety of customs associated with the seasons of Advent, Christmas, Lent, Holy Week, and Easter; and the sanctoral cycle (Part Four), which puts into perspective the Catholic tradition of honoring Mary and the saints and praying for the souls in purgatory. Since Catholicism embraces the principle of sacramentality, Part Five discusses customs and traditions associated with the seven sacraments, and with the signs, symbols, sacramentals, and popular devotions that make this principle practical in the lives of people. A brief Part Six discusses traditions not directly associated with the church year, for example, Halloween and Thanksgiving.

Most of the chapters follow a similar pattern. First there is a brief overview of the theme, the meaning, and the practice of particular traditions. This, along with a more extensive treatment of their origins or histories, puts traditions in perspective. Then there is a description of how these popular customs have been observed and, in some cases, how current trends relate to the centuries-old traditions. Actual rituals and prayers have not been included in the text. Readers who would benefit from them are encouraged to read Kathleen O'Connell Chesto's *Family Prayer for Family Times* (Mystic, Connecticut: Twenty-Third Publications, 1995) and *Catholic Household Blessings and Prayers* (Washington, D.C.: United States Catholic Conference, 1988).

On a practical note, a family that has lost almost all practice of religious traditions might find their renewal or revival awkward at first. A simple guideline is helpful: A few things done well, freely, and with enthusiasm are always more effective than many things done poorly or out of compulsion. It will have been worth writing *Catholic Customs and Traditions* if Catholics continue to incarnate their faith with effective, enjoyable, and creative religious practices grounded in our long faith-tradition.

PART ONE
RELIGIOUS TRADITIONS

1

THE NATURE OF
RELIGIOUS TRADITIONS

Jacob, a son of Isaac, was fleeing into exile after having alienated his twin brother, Esau. One night he had a dream of the Lord blessing him and of angels going up and down a stairway to heaven, an experience popularly called "Jacob's ladder." When he awoke he reflected on his religious experience: "Truly, the Lord is in this spot...how awesome is this shrine! This is nothing else but an abode of God, and that is the gateway to heaven!" Then Jacob took the stone that had been his pillow, set it up as a memorial stone, and poured oil on top of it. He called the site Bethel: the "house of God" (Genesis 28:1–19).

Religious traditions are like memorial stones that mark the spot of people's own Jacob's ladder. They mark a particular place, moment in time, or part of human life made sacred by the meeting of the mystery of God with the mystery of the human creature. People remember this meeting and repeat it by visiting sacred places, keeping certain times holy, saying prayers, observing rituals, eating special foods on certain days, and using particular colors to highlight religious themes.

The most important religious traditions are the church's public rituals and all the features connected with them. Some traditions have become closely associated with the church's discipline, such as going to church on Sunday and fasting during Lent. Others are more private and function unofficially alongside of the church's official rituals and disciplines, such as burning a candle before a sacred image and other private devotions. Whatever their form, these traditions give visibility to what otherwise might be theoretical religious teachings and abstract theologies. Repeated with some regularity, they become an important part of people's religious story and identity.

Human and Limited
Religious traditions are like the people who keep them alive: human and limited in scope. From wearing religious symbols to putting up a Christmas tree, they are neither the whole nor final answer to the

practice of faith. They evolve naturally among real people in particular places and at particular points in history.

In their origin religious traditions were neither planned nor carefully thought out. Nor were they mandated by church authorities. Some of them, such as the veneration of saints, eventually did became part of universal church teaching. Some of them disappeared into history and trivia, such as giving milk and honey to the newly baptized. Others evolved into new forms, such as the color for funerals. And still others, often in a renewed form, such as the Easter Vigil, are as fresh today as during the generation they were born.

Subject to Change

Because religious traditions are a human dimension of faith, they are subject to change. This process may be so subtle that it is not noticed in any one particular generation. Sometimes, however, the change is dramatic. The 1960s, for example, witnessed the beginning of a profound change in how Catholics live their faith. The cause of this dramatic change in the 1960s, as many times before in the history of the church, was a broad upheaval in society. It had happened when Christianity became allied with and even synonymous with the Roman Empire in the 4th and 5th centuries. Beginning about the same time, and continuing for centuries, "barbarian" tribes began moving against the boundaries of the Roman Empire and eventually swept over them. This caused such an upheaval in both the state and church that it has been called the "dark ages" (565-1095). Another upheaval happened in the Middle Ages when the peoples of Europe entered the Age of Feudalism with its small principalities and highly structured ranking among kings, princes, lords, knights, and serfs. These upheavals continued with the emergence of nations, the Protestant Reformation, colonization, revolutions promoting democracies, and finally, world wars and a nuclear age.

Upheavals in society always affect the traditions of Christians. The church adopted structures (for example, dioceses) and court etiquette (for example, genuflecting) from the civil Roman Empire. It also adopted many of the earthy religious practices of the "barbarian" tribes when these people became Christian. The church became monastic during the so-called dark ages, feudalistic with clearly defined roles for clergy and laity during the Age of Feudalism. In modern times the church functioned monarchically with highly concentrated central authority, much as kings ruled nations. And, finally, today it struggles with tendencies toward democracy.

To reiterate an important point made in the introduction, the security that comes from doing something because "it has always been done" no longer influences people as it had in decades or even centuries past. The old traditions no longer function as motives for present practices and future planning. Readjustment takes place—sometimes amid chaos—as old ways are changed or dropped and new ways adopted.

The upheaval in the society of the 1960s, with echoes today, was not caused by any one particular event. It is associated more with a change in attitude—a challenging of authority. On a popular level there was the "hippie movement" and the challenging of the validity of certain features of such institutional structures as education, government, and the military. Another cause of the upheaval was rapid advances in communication systems. People became exposed to ways of living and thinking, once foreign to them, by way of a mushrooming electronic media. They began to live differently, often without traditions to guide them.

The Second Vatican Council assembled at the beginning of this time of upheaval. Probably no event in the church's history has had such a widespread effect on religious traditions as did this council. It re-introduced the ancient tradition of worship in the language of the people. As a result, the church's public worship once again was available as the center of people's spirituality. Popular devotions, which had by necessity claimed this position for a millennium, have had to be refocused. The council reformed the seasons of the church year so that important religious traditions associated with them might be practiced with even greater faith. This conciliar reform has continued with periodic instructions that clarify the church's age-old traditions. In 1966, for example, Paul VI issued an apostolic constitution, *Poenitemini*, which limited obligatory abstinence to Ash Wednesday and all Fridays of Lent and the discipline of fasting to Ash Wednesday and Good Friday. While the tradition of "no meat on Fridays" no longer characterizes Catholics, the U.S. bishops have encouraged us to abstain from meat on Fridays.

Effective

Religious traditions are effective for several reasons. They are in tune with people's religious needs. They are cyclic, repeating on a regular basis and, therefore, serving as a reinforcement mechanism for faith. They take their shape from the real stuff of people's lives, cultures, and experiences. Finally, they are effective because they are earthy in the sense that they promote a religion of the heart, body, senses, environment, intuition, and imagination.

Cyclic

Religious traditions are cyclic, repeating on a regular basis. They may be observed daily (daily Mass, liturgy of Hours, mealtime and bedtime prayers), weekly (customs surrounding Sunday observance of worship and resting from work), monthly (First Friday customs), or seasonally (customs associated with Advent, Christmas, Lent, Easter).

This cyclic or repetitive nature of religious traditions reinforces what is important to believers. Popular religious traditions gradually introduce the young to sacred mysteries and support their growing faith on a regular basis. Until recent centuries, they served as the church's ordinary faith formation or religious education system. They can make the same important contribution today.

Based on Real Life

Religious traditions originate and are formed from people's daily lives, cultures, and experience. It is natural that Christians stay close to the cycles, events, and symbols of their real world as they practice their faith. Local pre-Christian customs, for example those associated with the mysteries of marriage, pregnancy, and childbirth were continued with some modifications called for by Christian faith. It was not unusual for Christians to become homesick for pagan celebrations enjoyed before conversion. They found ways of modifying them or substituting similar traditions. The December 25 date for a Nativity festival, for example, coincided with a pagan sun-worship festival. This contributed nuances of light versus darkness symbolism to this Christian festival. A springtime religious procession, the major Rogation Day on April 25 (discontinued in 1969), began as a substitute for a pagan procession in Rome that pleaded with the gods to prevent mildew on the grain crops. People have always loved a parade! And a procession is a form of parade. Numerous Christian traditions associated with evergreen trees and Christmas lights originated in pre-Christian Germanic lands. The name "Sunday" comes from pagan sun worship among Germanic peoples.

Many religious traditions originated and grew in popularity when church and state were closely aligned and culture was saturated with Christianity. This condition no longer exists. Popular culture, however, still influences religious customs today. Religious elements associated with Thanksgiving Day in the United States are an example. So, too, are many of the seasonal decorations used in churches and homes.

Popular traditions sometimes happen by accident. In the Middle Ages traveling actors and troubadours visited villages and acted out popular Bible stories, morality plays, and mystery plays. The prop from one of these, a "paradise tree" in a skit about Adam and Eve on their December 24 feast day, mixed with a still popular pre-Christian winter solstice festival of lights. This combination gave rise to the Christmas tree in the land of the Germans.

Traditions sometimes straddle the worlds of acceptable church doctrines and pre-Christian customs. A pre-Christian ritual popular among the Celtic Druids of Gaul and the British Isles encourages people to play out their earthy fears of the mystery of death and agents of evil roaming about: witches, goblins, demons, ghosts. This popular ritual received a new name, "Halloween," from the eve of a Christian holy day, Feast of All Saints, which had come to be celebrated on November 1. Halloween as such, however, never really received a new meaning and continues today with many of the same traditions.

Earthiness

The most effective feature of religious traditions is their concreteness, or earthiness. They promote a religion of heart, body, senses, environment, culture, intuition, and imagination. They promote human contact with the sacred through things experienced in real life. They prevent religion from becoming a "head trip." Religious traditions celebrate mystery moments where the human person is most at home—on earth.

There has always been an earthiness to religious traditions. Bits and pieces known about ancient times, substantiated in recorded history, remind us that people routinely celebrated a mystery dimension of life. Their religious traditions evolved around hunting, sexuality, birth and death, coping with the environment, observing the change of seasons, surviving the perils of human life, ritualizing answers to "the big unknown," or just enjoying life. There was a blending of magic, mystery, and real life.

This earthiness was part of Christianity from the beginning. Jesus and his disciples were faithful Jews. They celebrated their relationship with God in a springtime ritual of Passover, in harvest festivals of Pentecost and Tabernacles, and other cyclical feasts. Their religious traditions included sacred places, burnt offerings, scapegoats, pouring of oil, lighting of lamps, blessing of bread and cups of wine, and ascending incense.

Followers of Jesus did not "re-invent the wheel" as they discovered their separate religious identity as church. They did not dream up new religious forms. In the beginning they continued familiar Jewish ones but experienced them as brimming with new meaning. Through purifying waters and sweet-smelling oil they committed themselves to Christ and to a new life. Through the touch of the community's outstretched hands they experienced anew the excitement and enthusiasm of the outpouring of spirit on Pentecost, which was a Jewish harvest festival of "First Fruits." They remembered their Lord by sitting weekly in his presence at table on Sabbath night as they shared a ritual of holy bread and cup. Early conflicts among Christians revolved around the question of observing inherited Jewish religious traditions such as circumcision and dietary laws.

Religious Persecution
Intermittent religious persecutions during the early centuries (67-313) influenced Christians to develop new traditions identified with a veneration of martyrs and with earthy places, made sacred with the blood or burial of these saints. They identified themselves with earthy signs of the cross and fish. Symbols and images were scratched on tombs and catacomb walls. Religious icons became popular. These signs and images told a story without words.

People began to depend ever more on their earthy and popular religious traditions as the church drifted away from its biblical center. This situation was compounded as official worship evolved into a stylized liturgy in a language that was becoming foreign to the laity, conducted by ranks of clergy in front of them and without their active participation. Relics of saints—verified or not—became a focal point of popular devotions. Eventually people felt more comfortable with religious practices associated with "lesser gods" like Mary and the saints. Feast days dedicated to saints began to fill the calendar, eclipsing the more fundamental themes of Christianity. These feast days were enlivened with processions (parades), dancing in the village square, eating and drinking. It is not surprising that a multiplication of blessed objects would eventually stir the soul more than consecrated oils, water, bread, and the cup of official worship.

There is always the possibility that religious traditions and the truly awe-filled moments of earthy religion, in the sense of mystery moments, will deteriorate into superstition. An awe-filled moment finds mystery as a dimension of some human experience.

Superstition attempts to create mystery. Often there is a hint of confusion between these two in the history of religious traditions. Those
who are old enough have memories of this, proof that the experiences
were effective, though questionable. There was hint of "superstition"
in doing a religious activity a certain number of times and in a certain
way to obtain some favor. So, too, with the use of some sacramentals.
A statue on the dashboard was considered by many as guaranteed
protection regardless of circumstances of one's own or another's driving. This tendency toward superstition was due in part to fifteen centuries of separation between many popular religious practices and
the church's official liturgy. Popular traditions on the whole took their
own course.

Traditions in a Technological Age

This earthy dimension of religious traditions becomes especially
important today. We live in an age of high technology in school,
employment, and family life. This is not an evil situation. The basic
symbols and forms of religion, however, will always be much slower
and more simple. The more culture moves away from earth, the more
we need to make deliberate efforts to keep our feet on it, since it is on
earth that faith takes on flesh.

Finally, it is the nature of religious traditions that many of them
disappear into history and into trivial pursuits. The pages that follow
tell the story of those which still have value today, at least potential-
ly in renewed forms. The story is important only if it encourages people to enjoy religious traditions as an important feature of their practical faith.

PART TWO
THE CHURCH YEAR

CHURCH YEAR

SUNDAY

WEEKDAYS

SEASONS

2

THE CHURCH YEAR

Primitive humans marveled at the grand lights in the sky. The greater one ruled the day and the lesser one ruled the night (Genesis 1:16). They noticed the regular cycle of these two lights: the moon and the sun. Guided by the lights' regular appearances, they remembered and celebrated exceptional events that had happened in their clans or tribes.

There is no particular religious significance to the cycle of the sun and moon, nor to the calendar year with its smaller pieces of seasons, months, weeks, and days. Humans, however, have always added a religious dimension to these cycles of time. The Hebrews, for example, found special meaning in the Sabbath, or seventh day of the week. Christians created their religious life around Sunday, or the first day of the week. The natural seasons of the year—spring, summer, fall, winter—and especially their transition points of solstices and equinoxes contributed important nuances to religious traditions. Features of the Jewish springtime Passover, for example, would cross over into the Christian Holy Week. The spring equinox was celebrated with New Year festivities among many peoples until modern times. Preoccupation with the winter solstice would influence Christmas traditions.

Calendars

The calendar year, often called the solar year, is simply a practical means of measuring the passage of time. In antiquity, a regular sequence of seasons in nature governed the lives of people because the seasons determined food supplies and movement of the herds and flocks. Calendars were useful in preparing for critical transitions in nature: a time to plant and a time to reap and a time to move on to new places. These crude calendars relied on natural time keepers: the sun, the moon, and the stars. The sun provided the smallest unit: the solar day. The seasons gave rise to the solar year. The interval between full moons determined the month.

The Roman Emperor Julius Caesar promulgated a new solar calendar in 45 Before the Common Era (B.C.E.), known as the Julian calendar. It had twelve thirty-day months, with five extra days scattered during the year, and a leap year day every four years, inserted after February 23. The early Christians followed this calendar. Today, most people of the Western world use the Gregorian calendar, which was worked out by Pope Gregory XIII in 1582. It corrected the extra annual eleven minutes of the Julian calendar and is considered accurate to within one day in 20,000 years.

Church Year
The church year, or liturgical year, is one of the ways Christian people have made a fundamental part of creation, time, sacred. It is regulated in part by the sun and moon. Immovable feasts, such as Christmas and the feasts of saints, are based on the solar, or secular, calendar. Christmas, for example, is always on December 25. Movable feasts, on the other hand, are determined by seasonal changes and phases of the moon. Easter, for example, occurs on the first Sunday following the first full moon after the spring equinox. Counting back, this date then determines Ash Wednesday and the beginning of Lent. A considerable part of the church year, therefore, fluctuates each year. The Catholic church has gone on record supporting a worldwide immovable date for Easter, provided that the seven-day week is preserved.

Unlike the secular calendar, the church year has no exact beginning or end. It is like a circle. Advent comes first only in a popular sense. Until the late Middle Ages there was not even agreement in Christian countries about the beginning of the secular year. When Julius Caesar created the Julian calendar, he shifted the beginning of the Roman year from March 1 to January 1. Until the 700s in the Frankish kingdom and the late 1700s in Venice, March 1 continued to be observed as the beginning of the year. Until the 15th century in France, the beginning of the year was Easter, and until the 16th century in Scandinavia and Germany it was Christmas. The church year was never intended to coincide with the secular calendar nor to depend on it for its beginning, unfolding, or end.

The church year was never planned. The first Christians had a personal and detailed experience of the Jewish calendar of feasts which remembered and celebrated God's saving actions. It was only natural that after experiencing the saving action of Christ they would understand their previous celebrations in a new light. Jesus himself had asked for a new remembering: "Do this in remembrance of me" (1 Corinthians 11:24).

Ancient Christian Centers

The primary features of the church year evolved during the first centuries of Christianity around ancient major Christian centers. In the East these were Byzantium (Constantinople), or Istanbul, in present-day Turkey, Jerusalem in Palestine, Antioch in Syria, and Alexandria in Egypt. This area of the church would eventually come to be known as the Eastern church. In the west the main center of Christianity was Rome. Others were Carthage in North Africa, Toledo in Spain, Tours in Gaul (western Europe), and monasteries in Britain and Ireland. These centers would become the leaders of the Western church.

At first, the influence of Rome on the evolution of the church year and the way local churches celebrated its cycle of feasts was limited pretty much to the civil diocese of the district of southern Italy and the three islands of Sicily, Sardinia, and Corsica. Later, from the late 6th century until the end of the first millennium, the deterioration in the Roman liturgy was so pervasive that Rome could not influence other churches. This situation changed in the late Middle Ages as the authority of the papacy increased.

There was, therefore, no one centralized church authority that influenced liturgical practices or religious traditions during the early history of Christianity. Variations in celebrating the church year were common. Secondary features of the church year, popular religious traditions, continued to evolve in the west among emerging peoples, such as the Anglo-Saxons, Germans, Franks, Slavs, and Celts, who would become the ancestors of modern Europe.

Evolution of the Church Year

For the first thousand years of Christianity the church year did not have the structural unity so evident today. This evolved gradually and naturally around a remembrance of the greatest moment: the resurrection of Jesus. First came a weekly memorial of the resurrection called the Lord's Day or Sunday, the weekly Pascha. Throughout Christian history Sundays would be the primary vehicle for the unfolding of the church year and Christianity's core religious themes.

Annual Pascha

From the beginning there was also an annual memorial of Christ's resurrection, an annual Pascha, later to be called Easter among

English-speaking people. Easter in turn evolved into a Holy Triduum (Latin, "three days"), the Friday, Saturday, Sunday of the Pascha with Holy Thursday added later. Then came a Holy Week which commemorates the passage of Jesus through death to a new life: the Paschal Mystery. And Holy Week eventually was preceded by the season of Lent, six weeks of preparation for Easter. Fifty days of rejoicing after the Pascha, or Easter, were celebrated already by the early Christians just as the Jews observed a fifty-day festival following their Passover. This season ended with Pentecost, a harvest festival and memorial of the covenant for the Jews, and for Christians the memorial of the outpouring of the Spirit.

Christmas Cycle

Only later did other pieces of the church year fall into place. There were some annual feasts commemorating martyrs already in the 2nd century.

The feast of Christ's nativity, or Christmas, became popular in the late 3rd or early 4th century, its preparation season of Advent in the late 5th century, and finally a Christmas cycle and annual feasts honoring Mary. By the end of the 6th, the church year was complete in the essentials we know today.

Temporal Cycle

The church year unfolds through two cycles. The temporal cycle (Latin *tempus*, "time," "season") is the more important one. It consists of the seasons of Advent, Christmas, Lent, Holy Week, Easter, and Ordinary Time. Sundays are the primary vehicle by which this temporal cycle unfolds.

Sanctoral Cycle

Simultaneous with the temporal is the sanctoral cycle (Latin *sanctus*, "holy," "saint"). At first, yearly anniversaries of the death, or martyrdom, of saints were celebrated only locally where the person was known or died. In the 4th century, after the end of persecutions of Christians, local churches began to borrow saints from each other. The feast days of the saints spread and became part of the church year and eventually were celebrated universally.

There were some feasts days honoring Mary in the early centuries, such as the Dormition (Latin, "sleeping") and Assumption. Such feasts began to multiply after the Middle Ages. Until the reform of Vatican II, there were more Marian feasts than those celebrating the mystery of Christ. Hundreds of saints canonized by the church also took their places on the calender.

In 1969, the church reformed its calendar. Once again, the temporal cycle with its Christ-centered mysteries was clearly emphasized. Now in the sanctoral cycle a distinction is made between the calendar for the whole church and local, particular calendars, such as those for areas of common language (for example, English-speaking peoples), regional church structures (for example, dioceses), and religious communities (for example, Franciscans).

Devotional Feasts
In the Middle Ages a new kind of feast, focusing on a particular religious truth or devotion, was inserted in the church's calendar. These included the Feast of the Trinity, Corpus Christi, the Sacred Heart, Christ the King, the Precious Blood, the Holy Name, and the Immaculate Conception. Some of these, for example, the feast of the Precious Blood on July 1 (incorporated into the Feast of the Body and Blood of Christ, formerly called Corpus Christi) and the Motherhood of Mary on October 11, were dropped in 1969 or limited to local calendars.

The days and seasons of the church year have given rise to an abundance of popular religious traditions. They reflect the infinite richness within the mystery of God and specifically the mystery of Christ. It is impossible to exhaust the experience of revealed mysteries in just one celebration. A repetition or cycle is necessary so that people can come closer and closer to the saving mystery of Christ. An important dimension of faith missed one year can be enjoyed and celebrated in another.

Finally, the church year is not just a record of past events. The Christ-events are still present through the unfolding of sacred seasons and feasts and through the religious traditions that surround them. The liturgical year, therefore, revolves around the person of Jesus Christ. Even those days of the year devoted to Mary and to the other saints are related to the mystery of Christ, in whom they have their meaning and glory.

Religious traditions associated with the church year will be found in their proper places in the pages that follow.

3

SUNDAY

Years ago, and still today in many parishes, the ringing of church bells called people together on Sunday. Responding to this distinctive sound, usually beginning with a half-hour warning, the faithful streamed to their local churches. The tradition of calling people together by ringing bells began in the 6th century. This was necessary because of the absence of convenient clocks. Their graceful booming announced more than the time. It was a convincing call to the ready and to the lazy: "Come! Come!" It was a melodic invitation to individuals and families to assemble as one people to meet with their God, with Christ as Lord, and with one another as God's holy people. (In my case, this ringing of church bells is a fond memory because my family were the sextons, or bell ringers, in our country parish.)

Most Ancient of Traditions
The celebration of Sunday goes back to the very earliest years—and even possibly months and weeks—of Christianity. It is the oldest and most fundamental of all Christian activities. It is sad, therefore, that this most basic of all religious traditions is being dropped by almost half of Catholic families. At the same time it is understandable. Parishioners' motives for assembling on the Lord's Day are in transition. Before the mid-1960s a very powerful motive was the common teaching—or threat—that an unexcused absence was tantamount to serious sin. This was accompanied in previous generations by social or community pressure in smaller, self-contained, ethnic parishes. The original motive of the early Christians is yet to be recovered in the case of many parishioners today.

Sundays evolved around assemblies on the weekly anniversary of Christ's resurrection. They were called the weekly Pascha, a weekly commemoration of the Paschal Mystery. Sundays kept alive his memory and presence. They are the foundation and nucleus of what would become the church year, serving eventually as pivotal points for the unfolding of the tradition-rich seasons of Advent, Christmas,

Lent, and Easter. Sunday traditions feature an assembly for Eucharistic worship with a cycle of Scripture readings, official prayers, and seasonal themes. They also keep alive a special respect for the holiness of the day, usually by way of some kind of resting from ordinary work.

The first followers of Jesus were Jews. For a while they continued to observe Sabbath (Hebrew *shabbat,* to "leave off" or "to rest") traditions. They dedicated this seventh, or last, day of the week to the one God, Yahweh, in accord with the Genesis creation story (Genesis 2:1–3) and the Third Commandment: "Remember to keep holy the Sabbath day" (Exodus 20:8). The Jewish Sabbath provided a regular rhythm to life with traditions that emphasized rest or absence of work and physical activities. It was also a day of assembly and a feast day. Special sacrifices were offered in the temple at Jerusalem. During the centuries preceding Christianity, attendance at local synagogues, which had come into existence during the Exile, became a popular practice. There the people prayed and listened to readings of holy writing, or Scriptures, and instruction. This one day of the week also sanctified the home life of the Jews with detailed ceremonies surrounding the Sabbath meal.

First Day of the Week

From the very beginning those who believed Jesus was the Christ gathered together weekly on the first day of the Jewish week, the anniversary of his being raised from the dead. This fundamental theme of Sunday as the first day of the week runs counter to our popular cultural thinking that Sunday is part of the weekend, an ending introduced by "Thank God, it's Friday," rather than an all-important beginning.

This special day was reckoned by early Christians from sunset to sunset, as were all days according to Jewish custom. The first Christian assemblies were, therefore, most probably in the evening of the Sabbath Day.

From Sunday Evening...

Soon, however, Christians had their own special day—the first day of the week (Acts 20:7). On Sunday evening of the first day of the week and the end of a regular workday, those who believed Jesus was the Christ would gather in one of their homes, a primitive house-church, for a full meal (1 Corinthians 11:17–22). A ritual of blessing a Eucharistic cup and bread highlighted this meal. In this way Christians kept alive the memory and presence of Christ as he had requested (Luke 22:19; 1 Corinthians 11:23–26). This ritual was familiar to them because the weekly Sabbath meal, as also the annual Seder meal of Passover, included a special blessing of bread and cup. The Acts of the Apostles provides a delightful account of one such assembly and meal—and a teenager who fell asleep (20:7–12).

It is clear from the apostle Paul's letters that in some places extraordinary gifts of the Spirit were evident in the assemblies: speaking in tongues, interpreting tongues, prophesying, and healing (see 1 Corinthians 14:1–40). Mention is also made of a collection of funds, or alms, for the needy (1 Corinthians 16:2).

...to Sunday Morning

In the early 2nd century, this Eucharistic ritual was moved to before dawn on Sunday, the first day of the week. This change may have been caused by persecution. A decree of Emperor Trajan forbade suspicious gatherings in the evening. A time before dawn was necessary because Sunday was still an ordinary workday.

This Sunday morning assembly combined features that may have been separate: (1) singing hymns and psalms, prayers, reading of the Hebrew and new Scriptures, some form of preaching or instruction, very possibly some form of testifying, and (2) the Eucharistic ritual. The Service of the Word could now serve as an introduction to the Eucharistic ritual. This new arrangement was possible because the Eucharist had been separated from a regular meal as a result of abuses (1 Corinthians 11:17–22) and because it was transferred from Sunday night to Sunday morning. By the year 165, this Sunday ritual already had a form that would be recognized by Catholics today as Sunday Mass. Afterwards people went about their daily work and chores. During the first centuries of Christianity the notion of resting on this special day was unheard of.

Agape Meals

The separation of the Eucharist from a regular, though sacred, meal resulted in a transitional practice called the "agape" meal, or "love feast" (Greek *agape*, a special kind of Christian love). This agape tradition did not survive except as an occasional charity meal for widows and the poor and possibly for fellowship within the Christian community.

Blessing of Lights

Another religious tradition was influenced by the separation of the

Eucharist from a meal. It was a Jewish custom to bless special lights or lamps in the evening as part of the ceremonial meals. This continued in the Christian Eucharist (Acts 20:8). For Christians this ritual took on a special meaning, a reflection on the light of Christ among them. When the Eucharist was no longer celebrated at night, this special blessing of the lamps continued as a separate ritual called *Lucernare* (Latin *lux*, "light"). It eventually evolved into a daily prayer service called Vespers and finally, in the Middle Ages, gave rise to the blessing of the Easter Fire and Paschal Candle.

Lord's Day

The importance of Sunday is captured by the name given to it before the turn of the first century. In Revelation 1:7 it is called "the Lord's Day." This title does not dedicate the day to God in some general sense but precisely to the resurrected Christ whose proper title now is "Lord." The day belongs to the Lord. This title had a special ring to it for Christians of those first generations. It called to mind Christ's kingly glory earned through death and resurrection. In using this title for the day, Jesus was being defined as victor over the other "lords" of those times, specifically the Roman emperors who claimed divinity and were persecuting Christians. It also associated the day with the Lord's Supper.

The Lord's Day remains the church's official title for Sunday. Its Latin form, *dies dominica* or *dominicum*, is the origin of the title still used in the Romance languages: *domenica* in Italian, *domingo* in Spanish and Portuguese, and *dimanche* in French.

Sunday

The popular title, "Sunday," is a contribution from the Germanic peoples and is an example of how culture and pagan traditions influenced Christian religious traditions. This title comes from pre-Christian worship of the sun. Christians, in tune with symbolism, were comfortable with this descriptive title for the most sacred of their days. From the beginning Christ had been identified as "the light of the world" (John 8:12, 9:5, 12:46), "light of revelation to the Gentiles" (Luke 2:32), "true light" who "enlightens every person" (John 1:9). This association of the Christians' greatest day with the sun is also fitting because the sun is life-giving and never defeated, an annual lesson experienced on the occasion of the winter solstice.

Sunday Themes

Sundays had no particular themes in early Christianity until the seasons of the church year evolved. Now Sunday themes unfold in a rather elaborate way through cycles of readings from both the Hebrew and Christian Scriptures, through the official prayer formulas of the day, the homily preached, the songs sung, the colors used, rituals emphasized, and decorations hung. These themes carry the momentum of the year through the liturgical seasons of the Advent, Christmas, Lent, Easter, and the 33 or 34 weeks of the Ordinary Time.

When the process of initiating adult candidates into the church became more organized, some Sundays of Lent became associated with preparation rituals. Baptism itself has always been connected with Sundays, primarily with the annual Pascha, or Easter, Vigil, which celebrated a sharing in Christ's resurrection and new life. A second Sunday, Pentecost, also became a popular baptism day because of the theme of re-creation through the Spirit.

Two kinds of traditions evolved around the celebration of Sunday: (1) assembling or gathering together to share the Word and Eucharist and in doing so, keeping alive the presence and memory of Jesus, and (2) resting or avoiding unnecessary work and physical activity to keep the day holy. These traditions came to be known as Sunday observance or more negatively as Sunday obligation.

Sunday Assembly

Believing and assembling go together. It is unheard of in the recorded history of religion that believers worship only privately as individuals. The religious needs of humans are no different from their other needs. Social creatures need contact with one another to accomplish tasks and to fulfill needs. It was natural, therefore, that from the beginning, and still today, Christians joined one another in a group ritual. In assembly they faced the age-old questions of life and death, and handed on religious values, memories, stories of religious experiences, and beliefs. In assembly they experienced themselves as "a chosen race, a royal priesthood, a holy nation, a people God claims for God's own to proclaim the glorious works of the One who called you from darkness into marvelous light" (1 Peter 2:9). Christians felt a need, therefore, to meet with God as a group on a regular basis or according to some kind of calendar.

Followers of Jesus took it for granted that all the baptized would participate in the Sunday Eucharistic assembly. In the earliest years, while they were still considered a sect within the broader Jewish tradition, this separate assembly identified them. Later, after the church became gentile in membership, this weekly coming together on

Sunday continued to be expected of the baptized. An early Christian writing (*Didache*, c. 100) says: "On the Lord's day come together and break bread and give thanks, after confessing your sins that your sacrifice may be pure."

This kind of holy assembly, evident in all religions of recorded history, was very pronounced in the tradition of the Hebrew people, from whom Christianity developed its earliest liturgical traditions. Assembling also gave to Christianity its word "church." It happened in this way: The Hebrews called their assemblies *qahal Yahweh* or *edah Yahweh*, in English, an "assembly of God" in the sense of being called together by God. There were extraordinary assemblies, for example those called by God through Moses. Others, in later history, were assemblies according to a regular calendar of festivals. Some of these, called pilgrim festivals, required that the population journey to the holy city of Jerusalem (see Luke 2:41 ff). During these assemblies God spoke through anointed leaders and through the reading of holy writings, which would become the Hebrew Scriptures of our Bible. These channels of God reminded those assembled of the great things done for them by God, encouraged them to greater faithfulness, and persuaded them to know themselves as a special people in covenant with God.

Qahal Yahweh was translated into Greek as *ekklesia*. This term, which translates as "church," was used by the followers of Jesus to describe their own community assemblies devoted to prayer, instruction, singing of hymns, breaking of bread, and sharing of cup. Just as in the assemblies of old, God spoke to the people through anointed leaders. During the first generations of Christianity there were apostles, elders, and presbyters. God continues to speak today through bishops, priests, deacons, other specially assigned preachers, and lectors. There is evidence that in some early church communities, God spoke to the people also through extraordinary gifts of prophecy, tongues, and interpretation of tongues by participants under the influence of the Spirit (1 Corinthians 14). God also spoke through sacred writings inherited from the old covenant and through new holy writings passed from assembly to assembly, writings that would become the Christian Scriptures.

When persecution of Christians stopped in the early 4th century, and even earlier during lulls in persecution, it became customary to hold these religious assemblies in a fixed place or building instead of in house-churches of community members. In the Greek language this fixed building was called *Kyriake*, or "(house) belonging to the

Lord." This Greek term appeared in Anglo-Saxon as *circe*, in Germanic tongues as *kirche*, in Middle English as *chirche*, and finally as our *church*. The term points to the mystery of a holy place, but always first of all to the holy community of believing people who meet there.

Sunday Obligation

For the first three centuries no particular church discipline enforced participation in the Sunday assembly, or Mass. Enthusiastic weekly assembly was motivated by deep devotion to Christ's resurrection and expectation that this Christ would return shortly in glory. This motivation eventually waned. Already in the Letter to the Hebrews, about 96 of the Common or Christian Era (C.E.), there is mention of this: "Let us hold unswervingly to our profession which gives us hope. ...We must consider how to rouse each other to love and good deeds....We should not absent ourselves from the assembly, as some do, but encourage one another; and this all the more because you see the Day draws near" (Hebrews 10:23, 25).

At the beginning of the 4th century in Spain, even in the midst of a final persecution of Christians, the Council of Elvira declared that persons were to be excommunicated for a short time if they lived in the area and yet neglected Mass for three Sundays. This tendency to view presence at Sunday Mass as a serious matter seems to be connected to an identification of the Christian Sunday with the Jewish Sabbath. This was a popular, though not at first an officially accepted, application of the Third Commandment and therefore divine law to the physical observance of Sunday. By the 13th century it had become a common law of the church that all Catholics, seven years of age and older, must attend Mass on Sunday unless dispensed or excused for a serious reason. This attendance became a universal obligation only with the 1917 Code of Canon Law.

The present law of the church regarding Mass attendance reads: "On Sundays and Holy Days of Obligation the faithful are bound to participate in the Mass..." (Canon 1247). There is a big difference in the spirit of this current church law promulgated in 1983 and that of the old law (1917-1983). In the old law, the faithful were bound only to be physically present at Mass, "to hear" Mass. The new law, in using the words "to participate in the Mass," encourages active presence. On July 7, 1998 Pope John Paul II reaffirmed in an apostolic letter (*Dies Domini*, The Day of the Lord) the obligation of Catholics to attend Mass. He emphasizes the positive nature of this obligation, saying that the Lord's Day is "not just a matter of community religious discipline, but a defining and indelible expression of our relationship with God."

Day of Rest

A second major theme surrounding the weekly celebration of Sunday is that it is a day of rest. Around this theme another host of religious traditions evolved. During the first three centuries of Christianity there was no particular tradition or discipline of avoiding work and other activities on Sunday. Not all the baptized in the early church were free from obligations of work on Sunday, at that time still an ordinary weekday. Many were of the lower classes and some were even slaves. It became popular to observe Sunday as a day of rest only as the economic situation of Christians improved. Furthermore, the Sunday Eucharistic ritual evolved into a much longer assembly and the obligation to attend increased. By the middle of the 3rd century we have this admonition: "Make not your worldly affairs of more account than the word of God; but on the Lord's day leave everything and run eagerly to your church" (Teaching of the Apostles, 23).

A weekly day of rest was also linked to a human need, recognized by Roman civil authority, for a regular "break" from the monotony of work. On March 3, 321, Emperor Constantine ordered a weekly holiday on the "venerable day of the Sun." His motive, however, was probably based more on his devotion to the cult of the sun, as his father before him, than on Christian conviction. His decree did give this special Christian day the same privileges enjoyed by pagan feast days scattered through the year.

The motive for assembling for worship on Sunday, as we have seen, was not linked at first to the Jewish Sabbath and the Third Commandment. Nor was the motive refraining from physical work on Sunday. When early Christian writers interpreted the Third Commandment for the baptized, they counseled abstinence from sinful activity on Sunday and all days. St. Jerome and later the Council of Orleans (538) condemned any connection between Jewish Sabbath laws of rest and the Christian Sunday. It became increasingly common, however, to understand the Ten Commandments with a Christian content. A church discipline enforcing Sunday rest became common as a result. In 589, the Council of Narbonne called for severe punishment including whipping, for anyone who worked on Sunday. In 789, Emperor Charlemagne forbade all work on Sunday as a violation of the Third Commandment. This prohibition eventually crossed over into universal church law.

There never was consensus on the kind of work and activity forbidden on Sunday. Generally it was that kind which was unnecessary, or which prevented attendance at Mass, or disturbed the holiness of the day. The emphasis was on physical work. The present law of the church is very positive: "On Sundays and Holy Days of Obligation the faithful are bound...to abstain from those labors and business concerns which impede the worship to be rendered to God, the joy which is proper to the Lord's Day, or the proper relaxation of mind and body" (Canon 1247).

Servile Work

Beginning in the 16th century and continuing until recent times, the kind of work forbidden on Sunday was described as servile (Latin *servus*, "slave"). This was mechanical, arduous, physical sort of work, the kind that would be left to slaves or servants if that were possible.

Blue Laws

Early Christian writers emphasized an abstaining from "sinful" activities on Sunday. This eventually was applied to common forms of recreation or leisure activities. More than a thousand years later this interpretation contributed to a strong Puritan reaction in some Protestant countries, especially in England and Scotland, against all forms of recreation and frivolous behavior on Sunday. This was a form of Sabbatarianism, which sometimes also insisted on worship on Saturday rather than Sunday. This attitude came to the American Colonies with the Puritans in the 1600s. It continued with the publishing of blue laws in Connecticut in 1781 (called "blue" because of the paper they were bound in). These were local civil ordinances forbidding, among other things, what church leaders considered frivolous activities. Violators were usually punished by having to spend time in public stocks. Laws and local ordinances curtailing or forbidding certain activities on Sunday, such as athletic events and liquor sales, are still popularly called "blue laws."

Contemporary Observance of Sunday

The Second Vatican Council reemphasized the sacred meaning of Sunday popular from the beginning of Christianity: "For on this day Christ's faithful should come together into one place so that, by hearing the word of God and taking part in the Eucharist, they may call to mind the passion, the resurrection, and the glorification of the Lord Jesus, and may thank God....Hence the Lord's day is the original feast day, and it should be proposed to the piety of the faithful and taught to them in such a way that it may become in fact a day of joy and freedom from work" (Constitution on the Sacred Liturgy, 106).

More and more families today are making deliberate efforts to achieve what in earlier times was supported by society and culture: a family day of rest, worship, and recreation. Scattered during the week by busy schedules related to employment and school, many families celebrate this special time together with Mass, brunch at home or in a restaurant, and recreational activities. In his apostolic letter, "The Day of the Lord," Pope John Paul II emphasizes people's right to a day of rest, for example after-Mass excursions to favorite places.

Parishes have introduced fellowship or community-building elements to Sunday worship to recapture what came naturally in small ethnic or rural parishes of generations ago. Emphasis now is placed on the ministry of hospitality, opportunity for strangers to be introduced and made to feel welcomed, and coffee and donuts after Mass as a continuing sign of what took place during the liturgy.

With the reform of the church's liturgy after the Second Vatican Council came the popularity of Mass on the eve of Sunday after 4 P.M. Unfortunately, this has come to be considered as Saturday evening Mass. In reality, it is the vigil of Sunday Mass. This is in harmony with the practice of early Christians, who like the Jews reckoned their days from sunset to sunset.

4

WEEKDAYS

In homes of most parishioners, Monday begins another week of school, work, and ordinary family activities. There might be prayer at mealtime and possibly a goodnight kiss, prayer, and blessing. Some Catholics will pray a morning offering and possibly the rosary later in the day. Except for some religious traditions associated with the liturgical seasons of Advent and Lent, many contemporary homes are rather empty of external forms of religion during the week.

In most parish churches there is an opportunity for daily Mass on weekdays, a rather quiet ritual attended by a few people. In some parishes people attend a revived version of the ancient custom of morning prayer and evening prayer in place of or as an option to a Eucharistic liturgy. Traditional customs associated with private devotions on weekday evenings still take place in some parishes. Parish calendars are full of scheduled meetings related to a multitude of ministries. Young people and adults participate in faith formation sessions. Friday is still a popular day of voluntary abstinence from meat. First Friday of the month is observed in many parishes as a day for communion calls and special Masses.

Despite these examples, weekdays have little religious significance in themselves. In the history of Christianity there were efforts to give each day of the week special meaning, but no particular pattern emerged.

Origin of the Week
The week of seven days originated several thousand years ago among Semitic peoples of the Near East. It was based on a natural quarterly subdivision of the 28 days of the lunar month. The Book of Genesis in the Hebrew Bible presumes a seven-day week. From these Semitic people the week entered the Greek culture in Egypt. There the days were named after the sun and the moon and the five planets visible to the eye. These heavenly bodies were considered in the pagan culture to have divine power and were honored as deities. These

names of the week were later adopted throughout the Greco-Roman world.

When the Germanic peoples gained influence in the Roman Empire, they renamed four weekdays after their own gods. These names remain today among people whose language derives from ancient Germanic tribes, including English-speaking people:

Sunday—day of the sun
Monday—day of the moon
Tuesday—Tiw's day, god of war
Wednesday—god Woden's day
Thursday—god Thor's day
Friday—Frigg's day, goddess of love
Saturday—day of Saturn

Early Christianity emphasized only the observance and celebration of the first day of the week, the Lord's Day, or Sunday. Around this day evolved an elaborate ritual of Scripture reading, prayer, hymns, and the Eucharistic memorial of bread and cup. Wednesday and Friday also had special symbolic meaning for early Christians because they were related to the suffering and death of Jesus. Wednesday was the anniversary of Judas's betrayal of Jesus. Friday was the weekly memorial of Jesus' death. These two days were observed as days of fast, or station days (Roman military term for "keeping watch"), at the end of the first century. This tradition continued for several hundred years and eventually became part of the lenten discipline. There is a possibility that this custom of fasting on Wednesday and Friday began in opposition to the Jewish practice of fasting on Tuesday and Thursday.

Religious traditions associated with weekdays evolved around three activities: prayer (either private or in assembly with other parishioners in primitive Christian house-churches), fasting, and daily Mass with a seasonal theme or celebrating the life of a saint or and some devotional theme.

Private Prayer
Prayer is one of the earliest Christian traditions associated with weekdays. Daily prayer was the pattern observed by Jesus himself. It is a way of sanctifying both day and night just as the Jews did "in the evening, and at dawn, and at noon" (Psalm 55:17). Early in the 2nd century the Didache says that Christians should pray the Our Father

privately early in the morning, in the afternoon, and in the evening. An early popular tradition was to associate these prayer times with meditations on events in Jesus' suffering and death, which occurred at the same time of the day. While praying these, early Christians signed themselves on the forehead with the cross frequently as a remembrance of their baptism.

Public Prayer

Even by the early 3rd century it was recommended that the clergy—bishops, priests, and deacons—assemble the people each morning and evening in house-churches for prayer services. The morning service consisted of instruction based on a reading from Scripture, prayer, and a fellowship gesture such as a kiss of peace. The evening community prayer seems to have grown out of a ritual of blessing lights or lamps needed to read by, with the nuances of light-darkness symbolism. This ritual, called the *Lucernare* (Latin *lux*, "light"), was sometimes followed by an agape or special fellowship meal.

Liturgical Hours

After Christianity gained legal status in the Roman Empire in the early 4th century, these group prayer services continued in local churches on weekdays. There was a morning prayer, eventually called Lauds (Latin, "praise"), and an evening prayer, eventually called Vespers (Latin *Vesper*, "evening star") These prayer services consisted of Scripture readings, singing of psalms and hymns, and prayers.

When monastic life became popular in the 5th century, monks assembled at these prayer times. These twice-daily prayer services later increased to seven in monasteries: Matins, originally a sort of night vigil, and Lauds; prime (first hour, or 6 A.M.); Terce (third hour, or 9 A.M.); Sext (sixth hour, or noon); none (ninth hour, or 3 P.M.); Vespers (when the evening star appeared); and compline (just before retiring). Their workday unfolded in relation to these liturgical prayer services, or hours. These prayers of the hours, along with their content, came to be called the Divine Office, indicating that it was a duty or function of the clergy. A popular term in modern times for the book was Breviary (Latin *breviaria*), "short lists" of Scripture readings, psalms, and prayers.

Secular clergy continued to meet with their people in local churches for Lauds and Vespers. These services were conducted in Latin. They became less popular, therefore, when people whose language was evolving into new vernacular languages no longer spoke or understood Latin. During the 7th and 8th centuries, these services were gradually replaced with a daily morning Mass for ordinary parishioners.

Origin of the Rosary

People who could not read continued to observe the traditional prayer times with private devotions of their own. They began to substitute memorized private prayers for the Scripture readings and psalms of the liturgical hours prayed by monks and clergy. Soon it became popular to pray 150 Our Fathers each day in place of the 150 psalms. Later these 150 Our Fathers were substituted with the more simple Hail Marys, spaced with meditations on mysteries related to Jesus and Mary. These mysteries are divided into three groups of five each: the Joyful mysteries (Annunciation, Visitation, Nativity, Presentation in the Temple, Finding in the Temple); the Sorrowful mysteries (Agony in the Garden, Scourging, Crowning with Thorns, Carrying of the Cross, Crucifixion); the Glorious mysteries (Resurrection, Ascension, Descent of the Holy Spirit, Assumption of Mary into heaven, Mary is crowned Queen of Heaven). Some of these mysteries were borrowed from the ancient crowning of Mary prayer services. In this way the rosary (from the Latin, *rosarium*, rose garden) evolved in the Middle Ages. According to legend St. Dominic (d. 1221) spread its popularity through his preaching. The rosary received its final form in the 16th century and continues to be a popular private weekday prayer of many parishioners. Ordinarily only one-third of the rosary, five decades, are prayed at any one time. Beads are merely a system of counting and have been used to count prayers from pre-Christian times.

Revival of the Liturgy of the Hours

The chanting of Vespers in Latin continued down through the ages in some parish churches, usually on Sunday afternoon. In recent years parishes have begun to re-introduce, at least several times weekly, the more ancient daily prayer services of song, communal prayer, and Scripture: Lauds, or Morning Prayer, and Vespers, or Evening Prayer. These weekday prayer services, often led by lay ministers, are now called the Liturgy of the Hours to emphasize that they are part of the church's official liturgy. They usually replace a daily Mass. This renewed tradition carries out what Vatican II encouraged: "Pastors of souls should see to it that the chief hours, especially Vespers, are celebrated in common in church on Sunday and the more solemn feasts.

And the laity, too, are encouraged to recite the Divine Office, either with the priests or among themselves, or even individually" (Constitution on the Sacred Liturgy, 100).

Family Prayer
There has always been a tradition of family prayer in Catholic homes. For many generations it was popular to pray the rosary together. In recent years some families have begun reading Scripture as a family. Many families continue to pray at table, either in the form of a spontaneous prayer or a more formal prayer ("saying grace"). At bedtime many parents bless their children and pray with them. Catholic homes are also graced with the use of sacramentals on a daily basis, especially the burning of a candle and use of holy water.

Meal Prayer
Unfortunately, two very important weekday religious traditions are fading in contemporary homes: praying at table and blessing children, especially at bedtime. The tradition of praying at table before meals is an ancient practice inherited from the Jews. This saying of grace (Latin *gratiae*, "thanks") can be considered either a blessing or thanksgiving. Jews considered food blessed precisely because they had thanked God for it. Early Christians retained this ancient Jewish understanding of blessing. This blessing-thanksgiving was done over the two key foods on the table: bread and cup of wine. On special occasions such as the annual Seder the blessing-thanksgiving ritual was more elaborate. From these ritual table prayers of the Seder and Sabbath meals evolved our Eucharistic Prayer (Greek *eucharistos*, "grateful").

Bedtime Prayer
Another religious tradition is associated with liturgical rituals. This is the blessing of children, especially at bedtime. When infants are baptized they are marked on the forehead with a cross, today not only by the priest but also by parents and godparents. This ritual is a sign that the child is now dedicated to the Lord and to the wonders of Christian faith. Some ethnic groups, for example, the Hispanics, have continued this practice of blessing their children with, among some, a special blessing when their children marry.

Fasting
Fasting has always been a companion of prayer in the history of Christian spirituality. As mentioned above, for the first three cen-

turies a popular tradition was to observe a memorial fast until 3 P.M. on all Wednesdays (the day of Judas's contract to betray Jesus) and Fridays (the day of Jesus' death). Several major fasts each year gave weekdays a nuance that they do not have today. These were associated with the six weeks of Lent, the weeks of Advent, Ember Days during each of the four seasons, and Rogation Days. The contemporary notion of fasting is that only one main meal is eaten, with two smaller ones, combined not exceeding the main meal. Only two mandatory fast days continue, Ash Wednesday and Good Friday, for adults from ages eighteen through sixty.

Friday Abstinence

The church discipline of abstinence, refraining from eating meat on all Fridays of the year, remembers the suffering and death of Jesus on the original Good Friday and serves as a popular form of personal penance. Until recent times this religious tradition was considered a very serious obligation. It was so faithfully practiced that it was a distinguishing mark of Catholic identity and even influenced the menus of restaurants. Pope Paul VI's instruction, *Poenitemini,* relaxed the severity of abstinence in 1966. Some form of Friday penance is still encouraged but abstinence, except for Fridays of Lent and Ash Wednesday for Catholics who have completed their fourteenth year, is no longer binding by church law. U.S. bishops have encouraged the practice of Friday abstinence for world peace.

Daily Mass

By the late 4th century it had become popular to celebrate Mass on Wednesdays and Fridays of Lent, days originally made holy by fasting. Later the practice spread to other days of the week. These weekday Masses often were votive Masses to obtain a special favor or to remember the dead. Centuries would pass, however, before daily Mass became a common tradition. The custom spread during the Middle Ages (500-1450). At first these daily Masses were associated with monasteries where there was an abundance of ordained monks. Soon, however, they became a normal practice in parish churches.

These daily Masses were popular because the intention or purpose of the Mass could, in popular thinking, be determined by the offering of an individual parishioner. Common intentions were the asking for or giving thanks for recovery from illness, safe childbirth, and the welfare of the "souls" in purgatory. They came to be known as private Masses because of this practice of private donation and limited intention. The donation or gift came to be known as a stipend. These Masses were considered private also because of the number of people present and the absence of any participation such as singing.

The meaning of worship deteriorated with this custom of daily Mass. Worship is by nature communal and happens best when a participating community is present. Daily Mass also led to abuses in the Middle Ages with priests celebrating several Masses each day. Authorities in the church spoke out frequently against these abuses. Until recent times it was expected that all priests celebrate Mass daily even if no people were present.

Until the reforms of Vatican II it was common that weekday Masses were Masses for the dead, celebrated in black vestments with other funeral accouterments visible such as a catafalque (representing a coffin in the absence of a body) surrounded by unbleached beeswax candles.

Daily Themes

There were frequent attempts by spiritual writers to promote a special theme for each day of the week. These efforts never became popular among the people. Some themes, however, did establish a pattern with special Mass formulas, called Votive Masses. Monday was devoted to the Trinity; Tuesday, to the angels; Wednesday, to the apostles, St. Joseph, and Saints Peter and Paul; Thursday, to the Holy Spirit, the mystery of the Eucharist, and the priesthood of Christ; Friday, to the Precious Blood and the Sacred Heart of Jesus. Saturday became Mary's day. Some Votive Masses are still celebrated today at the discretion of the priest.

One weekday devotion that received a popular following honors the Sacred Heart of Jesus on Fridays. After private revelations to St. Margaret Mary Alacoque (1673-75), it became popular to devote the first Friday of each month to the Sacred Heart of Jesus. Parishioners would participate in Mass and receive communion (even during years when frequent communion was rare) on nine consecutive Fridays out of special devotion, in reparation to the Sacred Heart, and to receive special indulgences. It also became common for parishioners to have an image of the Sacred Heart enthroned in their homes and to burn a candle before it on Fridays. Some parish calendars still reflect these customs; for example, it is common that communion calls for shut-ins are made on the First Friday of the month.

Another devotion associated with Friday is to honor the Precious Blood of Jesus shed on the first Good Friday. Like devotion to the

Sacred Heart, it has its own litany and other prayers. This devotion was the private devotion of Pope John XXIII and received special attention during his papacy (1959-1963).

Christians in ancient times considered Friday an especially serious day to remember the suffering and death of Jesus with fasting, prayer, and private devotions. It was expected that everyone avoid frivolous activities. Those who violated this tradition did so with the possibility of evil consequences. This contributed to the popular notion that Friday, especially Friday the 13th, is an unlucky day.

5

SEASONS

Petitions to saints addressed in Latin floated in the early morning breeze on the three days before Ascension Thursday. The litany procession moved slowly around the parish grounds or even out to the fields in rural areas. The response of the laity was simple: *Ora pro nobis* ("Pray for us") if the petition was to a single saint, and *Orate pro nobis* if more than one. It was time for the spring Rogation Days (Latin *rogare*, "to ask for").

Rogation Days and Ember Days are related to the seasons of the year. Ember Days evolved around a tradition of seasonal fasting common in early centuries. Rogation Days originated as a substitute for a popular pagan prayer procession to ask the gods for protection of crops.

Cycle of Seasons
Humans have always been sensitive to the cycle of seasons connected with the relationship of the sun to Earth. Ancient people's survival depended upon this observed phenomenon. They saw a direct connection between the sun's cycle and the availability of foods they could gather and the movement of animals they hunted. Later, when settled tribes depended upon planting and harvesting of crops, the cycle of seasons continued to be an essential part of human experience.

The cycle of seasons was so important that people associated divine mystery with it. Good gods and goddesses guided the planting and from their graciousness provided a harvest. Evil ones interfered, sending bad weather and plant diseases. People prayed, offered sacrifices, and celebrated the bounty.

The agricultural season was so important that the ancient Roman lunar calendar provided months only for that particular time of the year. The rest of the year was not even computed.

In the northern hemisphere the cycle of seasons is very pronounced. The long daylight hours and heat of summer gradually change into harvest time during autumn and a dying process during early winter. Nights become long, dark, and cold. Then, a rebirth is experienced as late winter turns into springtime with delightful signs of the rebirth of light, warmth—and life itself.

The influence of seasons on religious traditions increased when the Jewish lunar calendar gave way to the secular solar calendar. This happened after 70 C.E. when Jerusalem was destroyed and the Jewish people scattered. Christianity became increasingly gentile in membership, no longer bound to the traditions from which, as a religious group, Christians had originally arisen. The Jewish lunar calendar lost its influence among them, and the church soon traded it for the Julian calendar popular throughout the gentile Greco-Roman world. This calendar was based on the solar year rather than the lunar month. As a result, the summer and winter solstices and spring and fall equinoxes, along with the seasons they introduced, became more evident in the religious life of Christians.

Ember Days
Current scholarship today challenges the presumption that the seasonal Ember Days were Christian substitutes for popular pagan agricultural festivals. The probable origin lies rather in an ancient Christian tradition of seasonal fasting. Christianity always had a religious discipline of spiritual renewal through prayer, fasting, and almsgiving. By the late 4th century, a special fasting was observed at the approximate beginning of the four seasons of the year. These came to be known as Ember Days (German *Quatember,* a corruption of the Latin expression, *quattuor tempori anni,* "four seasons of the year").

At first local churches determined the severity of discipline and choice of days. At a Roman synod in 1078 they were fixed on the Wednesday, Friday, and Saturday of the first week of Lent (springtime), the week following Pentecost (summer), the week following the feast of the Holy Cross on September 14 (fall), and the feast of St. Lucy, December 13 (winter). Until 1966 the custom of fasting and partial abstinence was observed in Catholic homes on these days.

From the late 5th century, Ember Days took on an additional theme that local parishioners were usually unaware of; namely, a time for the examination, or "scrutiny," and ordination of candidates for the priesthood. Today, national bishops' conferences determine the scheduling and themes of Ember Days. In many countries Ember Days have become days of prayer for vocations to the priesthood and religious life.

Rogation Days

Another seasonal religious tradition, the Rogation Days, does have a direct connection with pagan agricultural festivals. This is one of the clearest examples of how closely religious traditions are entwined with the real life and culture of people. The first Rogation Day of the year was originally called the Major Litany. It fell on the feast of St. Mark (April 25) but had nothing to do with this saint. It was a Christian prayer-procession substituted for a pagan Roman prayer-procession called the "Robigalia" in honor of the god Robigus ("mildew") or the goddess Robigo ("rust"). The purpose of this annual pagan procession was to ask that the grain crops be protected from the blight of mildew. The Christian substitute even followed the same route in Rome.

Three other Rogation Days with a litany procession occur on the three days before the feast of the Ascension. They were originally called days of "lesser litanies." They were introduced as days of fast in southern Gaul in the mid-400s, apparently at a time of famine and other natural disasters.

Rogation Days of fasting and prayer have always been associated with the Litany of Saints as a form of supplication, prayed usually in some kind of procession. These processions were associated with the Rogation Days to such an extent that in the Middle Ages the word "litany" meant "procession of supplication."

Rogation Days are still part of the church's seasonal calendar, except for the one on April 25, which in recent years has been removed from the church's calendar. Since 1969, however, they may be celebrated at any time of the year. Unfortunately, most parishes are unaware of this freedom to reschedule rogation days. Along with the Ember Days, they are a time to thank God and to pray for good crops. This latter motive has influenced some parishes, especially in rural areas, to revive the tradition of processions to local fields. Some farmers nail a wooden cross on fences at this time of the year.

The use of purple vestments for both the Rogation Days and Ember Days highlights their penitential theme.

PART THREE
THE TEMPORAL CYCLE

ADVENT

CHRISTMAS

CHRISTMASTIME

LENT

HOLY WEEK

THE EASTER VIGIL

EASTER

ORDINARY TIME

6

ADVENT

Daylight grows shorter. The dark of night grows longer and more intense. In this cold dark, with some first signs of snow in the north, lights begin to shine. They were not there before. They are on trees and in windows. It is as if people are afraid of the dark and all it symbolizes.

A spirit of expectation begins to pick up momentum: shopping trips, gift wrapping, parties, a different kind of music and song, and an avalanche of decorations. It is obvious that something wonderful is about to happen.

In the midst of this swelling excitement throughout contemporary society and culture, worshippers in churches are reminded to be watchful, to repent, to do penance. This gospel message parallels a secular song heard occasionally during this time of the year: "You better watch out, you better not cry, you better not pout, I'm telling you why: _____is coming to town!"

Purple inside churches clashes with red, green, and sparkling silver and gold everywhere else. Young and old alike prepare to celebrate Christmas by taking part in a great variety of traditions, some of them only remotely associated with preparation for the Christian mystery of the Messiah's birth.

Yes, someone "is coming to town." Prepare the way of the Lord!

Beginning of Church Year

Advent, with its many emotional overtones, ushers in the most popular season of the year. At first, from the early 4th century, the feast of the Nativity on December 25 began the church year at Rome. When Advent evolved, it took this position, and since the 900s has been considered the beginning of the church year. This does not mean that Advent is the most important time of the year. The Easter cycle has always had this honor. The distinction happened from the practice of placing the liturgical texts for Advent at the beginning of hand-copied books used for Mass. They had to begin somewhere.

The beginning of Advent always falls on the Sunday nearest the feast of St. Andrew the Apostle, November 30. As a preparation season, like Lent, it has no meaning in itself. It looks forward to the annual celebration of Jesus' birth, both the historical event itself and the saving event of the coming of God in flesh.

Theme

Advent has always been somewhat confused. It blends together a penitential spirit very similar to Lent, a liturgical theme of preparation for the Second and Final Coming of the Lord, called the Parousia, and a joyful theme of getting ready for the Bethlehem event. Religious traditions associated with Advent give expression to all these themes.

The word Advent (Latin *adventus*, "coming") originally described the whole mystery of the Incarnation. The conception of Jesus was an Advent, but so was his birth and what will be his final coming at the endtimes. In a more popular sense, Advent was first associated with the time of the year now called Christmastime and finally with the weeks of preparation for Christmas.

Origin

Once Christmas had become a popular feast throughout the church after the 4th century, it did not take long for Advent to evolve as a distinct liturgical season. In ancient times, people tended to precede a time of feasting with a time of fasting. There are hints of a penitential season at this time of the year in the late 5th century in Spain and especially in Gaul (roughly, today's France and the Lowlands). These parts of Europe had close links to the Eastern church, which celebrated its main Nativity feast on January 6, called Epiphany. They approached this feast with forty days of fasting and penance, very similar to Lent, possibly because Epiphany had taken on a baptismal theme just as was true of the Easter Vigil. Among those people Saturdays and Sundays were excluded from fasting, just as they were during Lent. In Gaul, to maintain forty days of fasting, Advent began on November 11, the feast of St. Martin. There, at one time, Advent was known as St. Martin's Lent.

The season of Advent as we know it probably had a different origin. By the mid-6th century, the church in Rome had begun to focus on the December Ember Days that occurred on the Monday, Wednesday, and Saturday after the feast of St. Lucy (December 13). These days, a week before the Nativity on December 25, had a distinct penitential theme. The reason lay in a five-day pagan harvest festival of Saturnalia, from December 17-23. On December 17, sacrifice was offered to Saturn, god of agriculture. The days following were filled with gift exchanges, feasting, and excesses. It seems that the church tried to offset the influence of this popular pagan festival with days of fasting, prayer, and penance as it looked ahead to the feast of Nativity on December 25.

There is evidence for this short "Advent" coinciding with the pagan Saturnalia. There is an ancient tradition of singing the O Antiphons during the Liturgy of Hours on precisely the same days as the pagan Saturnalia. The singing of these O Antiphons, always an Advent tradition, is still popular today, and they have become the Alleluia verses for December 17-23:

(O Sapientia)	Come, Wisdom of our God...
(O Adonai)	Come, Leader of Ancient Israel...
(O Radix Jesse)	Come, Flower of Jesse's Stem...
(O Clavis David)	Come, Key of David...
(O Oriens)	Come, Radiant Dawn...
(O Rex Gentium)	Come, King of all Nations...
(O Emmanuel)	Come, Emmanuel...

By the end of the 6th century, during the reign of Pope Gregory the Great (590-604), a short preparation season of four weeks had evolved in the Roman church. Sunday themes looked ahead to the joyful remembering of Jesus' birth on December 25. The penitential theme, popular generations before, faded.

Penitential Theme

Historical conditions in both the church and among emerging peoples in western Europe finally determined the length and spirit of the season of Advent. In Gaul an Advent theme, separate from that of Rome, evolved under the influence of missionaries from Ireland. They promoted a penitential spirit, emphasizing not Jesus' first coming in the Incarnation, but rather his final coming in judgment at the endtimes. Purple was used for vestments, and the Alleluia and Glory to God were omitted from the Mass.

The evolution of Advent was also influenced by traditions in the monasteries of Gaul. In 567, a synod at Tours, France, clarified the monastic practice of fasting on all Mondays, Wednesdays, and Fridays, with a greater intensity during Lent, the week following

Pentecost, and the month of December up to Christmas. Fifteen years later this same tradition of fasting was ordered for the laity from the Feast of St. Martin (November 11) until Christmas.

Mixed Theme

An accident of history contributed to the final development of the season of Advent as we know it today. For years some outlying churches in the Frankish territory of Gaul had begun to use liturgical books from Rome. These had probably traveled northward across the Alps with monks and pilgrims impressed with the way things were done in Rome.

Carolingian rulers set in motion a Romanizing process in their kingdom for both political and religious reasons. In 754, Pepin, the predecessor of Charlemagne, was crowned king of the Frankish territory by Pope Stephen. In honor of the occasion Pepin ordered that the liturgical books used throughout his kingdom be replaced by those from Rome. As a result, the shorter and non-penitential Roman Advent began to spread throughout Gaul. Because the books from Rome had to be copied by hand, there was a long period of time when a mixture of liturgies was common. Some of the penitential themes of Advent in the north were mixed with the more joyful themes of the shorter Advent from Rome.

Charlemagne, who, like his father was impressed with everything Roman, continued the effort. He borrowed books from Rome for his library in Aachen. There they served as models for copying. The books he borrowed, unfortunately, described the elaborate papal liturgy rather than that of ordinary Roman parish churches. Charlemagne's advisor, Alcuin, designed substitutes for missing parts with the king's authority. The end result was a continuation of a mixture, neither Frankish nor Roman.

In the 10th century, the church in Rome suffered a serious decline and a period of chaos because of abuses in leadership. Clergy and people lost interest in the liturgical life of the church. Only the new cluniac monasteries were able to keep alive a religious spirit associated with the church's worship. Eventually, at the end of the 10th century under orders from the Roman emperors Otto I, II, and III, the church of Rome began to reform its weakened liturgical practices by borrowing liturgical books from monastic centers up north.

The liturgical books that had traveled northward hundreds of years before were not the same as those that returned. The new liturgy, however, was soon considered authentically Roman. Eventually, it became the liturgy of the whole medieval Latin church. In this way, an Advent of four weeks, with a confused theme of penance and joy, eventually spread from Rome to the universal church.

The somber theme that colors the first Sundays of Advent is a fitting continuation of the themes of Sundays immediately preceding Advent and concluding the church year. On these Sundays there is an emphasis on the endtimes and the consummation of all history. The First Sunday of Advent continues this emphasis. Then, on the Second and Third Sundays of Advent, John the Baptist, the Advent prophet, issues a call to penance. On the Fourth Sunday of Advent, the Incarnational theme finally begins to unfold with the account of the Annunciation.

A penitential theme during Advent was more evident until recent times. A tradition of fasting continued until the Code of Canon Law of 1917-1918. Musical instruments were discouraged during Mass, the color purple was used in vestments and decorations, the Glory to God was dropped but the Alleluia kept, and weddings were prohibited. With some modifications these traditions continue today but without a serious penitential spirit.

Some religious traditions during the month of December are directly associated with the themes of Advent. Others are already part of the celebration of Christmas but are anticipated during the weeks of Advent.

Advent Wreath
Advent traditions reflect a spirit of expectation and, therefore, unfold gradually. Probably the most popular tradition today is the lighting of candles on an Advent Wreath in both churches and homes. This custom originated among Lutherans in Germany in the 16th century and quickly became popular in other areas. Along with the Christmas tree, it is probably an example of Christianizing practices popular from pre-Christian times. There had always been a festival of burning special lights and fire at the end of November and beginning of December in Germanic lands as the darkness of winter becomes more severe. This tradition continued into modern times. In the 1500s, it took on a distinct Christian symbolism as the Advent Wreath, first among Lutherans in eastern Germany and then among all German Protestants and Catholics. This tradition came to America with German immigrants. It was popularized among Catholics with the liturgical movement in the mid-1900s.

The Advent Wreath, which may be of any size, is made of evergreens and is placed on a table or suspended from the ceiling. There are four candles, one for each week of Advent. The color of the candles is not an essential factor because the symbolism is primarily in the flame. It is popular, however, that three of them be violet or purple, the traditional color of Advent. One is rose, the traditional color of the Third Sunday of Advent, originally called Gaudete ("Rejoice") Sunday from the first word of the entrance antiphon for Mass.

After the wreath is blessed on the first Sunday of Advent, a prayer is prayed and a candle lit. This ceremony repeats on each of the following three Sundays. Light increases, pushing out darkness, with another candle lit until all four are burning.

Wreaths have always been symbolic of victory and glory. The basic symbolism of the Advent Wreath goes beyond this. It lies in the tension between darkness and light. It represents the long time when people lived in spiritual darkness, waiting for the coming of the Messiah, the light of the world. Each year in Advent people wait once again in darkness for the coming of the Lord, his historical coming in the mystery of Bethlehem, his final coming at the end of time, and his special coming in every moment of grace.

Jesse Tree
Biblical persons associated with the gradual coming of the Messiah are represented by the Advent tradition of the Jesse Tree, named after the father of David. Symbols are gradually added to the tree or branch. These symbols can be drawn, cut out, found, or purchased. They represent ancestors of Jesus, either in faith or bloodline, such as Adam, Noah, Abraham, Isaac, Jacob, Moses, Jesse, David, Solomon, Joseph, and Mary.

Advent House
A popular variation of the Jesse Tree is the Advent, or Christmas, House, usually purchased in a religious goods store. One of many windows is opened each day to display still another feature of the coming of Jesus. On December 24 the door is opened, revealing the Nativity scene.

Advent Calendar
The four weeks before Christmas can be designed into a special Advent calendar of personal preparation. The days are marked with goals toward personal conversion or service to be done for others.

Manger
An Advent tradition that combines a spirit of conversion and the coming of Jesus is the practice of having children prepare the manger for the family Nativity scene. Each night, children are invited to place in the manger one piece of straw for each good deed done that day.

Advent Colors
The traditional color of Advent is purple or violet. It symbolizes a penitential spirit that has been associated with this season. Liturgists and other church leaders have begun clarifying the theme of Advent, emphasizing that it has its own distinct theme and is not a "little Lent." Some liturgists have promoted a new, or renewed, Advent color: a dark blue. While at first a little shocking to parishioners, this color has foundation in the evolution of Advent. In northern European countries and England there was a tradition to use for Advent a shade of violet different from that used for Lent. It tended more toward dark blue because of the kind of dye used. This color seems proper also because of the role of Mary in the mystery of the Christmas event.

Traditionally on the third Sunday of Advent, rose-colored vestments have been used. This color anticipates and is symbolic of the Christmas joy announced in the first word of the Entrance Antiphon: "Rejoice" (Latin, *Gaudete*).

7

CHRISTMAS

Beginning earlier and earlier each year, now before Thanksgiving, a Christmas mood begins to appear everywhere. Decorations of artificial snow, candles, and red and green wreaths cover street lights and are evident in every public display area. Elaborately decorated and lighted Christmas trees can be seen through windows of homes. The outsides of houses and trees in the yard are also decorated with bright lights. Music and song tell of Christmas cheer mixed with the Bethlehem story and cartoon characters. Stores are filled with shoppers. Little children write letters to Santa Claus and dream of presents under the tree.

This saturation of cheer and good will seems at first to contradict the Christian mystery that is still unfolding in churches. Parish Advent liturgies continue to develop a prophetic theme of preparation: a waiting for the final coming of the Lord at the end of time and a call to conversion. While these themes unfold, most families are involved in the hectic pace of Christmas preparations, often centered around decorating and making or purchasing gifts for family and friends.

Christmas, therefore, is no longer just a Christian liturgical feast. Over the centuries it has become a seasonal mood, not limited to believers who prepare for and rejoice over the birth of Jesus. Almost every aspect of society celebrates the season in some way. Jews celebrate their ancient Feast of Lights, or Hanukkah, about the same time. Non-believers participate fully in secular expressions of cheer and good will. The commercial world promotes the season for financial profit in such a persuasive way that Christian movements counter with organized efforts to "put Christ back into Christmas."

Despite the secular overtones of the season, the word "Christmas" underscores its profound Christian and spiritual significance. It has been used in English-speaking countries since the Middle Ages; the word was derived from the Old English *Cristes Maesse*, or "Mass of Christ." Over the centuries it has become a comprehensive word. It includes religious traditions which celebrate the history-shaking mystery of God coming to live among human creatures: "The Word became flesh and made his dwelling among us, and we have seen his glory: The glory of an only Son coming from the Father, filled with enduring love" (John 1:14). It also includes all the secular traditions associated with the season.

With the Father's gift of Jesus as a model, Christmas also celebrates the mystery of giving—and receiving—both with and without Christian faith. Finally, Christmas incorporates numerous pre-Christian traditions concerning the winter solstice along with the legends of St. Nicholas that gave rise to the modern creation of Santa Claus.

Origin of Christmas

The primitive church seems to have had little or no interest in the actual date or circumstances of Jesus' birth. A higher priority was their expectation of an immediate consummation of history and a final coming of Christ. They celebrated the mystery of his resurrection weekly and annually a few hundred years before a tradition of commemorating his birth became popular. Martyrs and saints were honored with annual anniversary festivals before the anniversary of the Lord's birth became a tradition. Eventually, the church's desire to live out liturgically the entire Christ mystery led to a Nativity festival. Another possible reason is the church's response to the influence of early heresies, especially Docetism, that denied the human nature of Jesus.

The actual date of Christ's birth is unknown. The gospels do not record it, nor is there any early tradition to identify it. Modern scholarship identifies only the approximate year, probably 8-6 B.C.E. with adjustments to our modern calendar taken into consideration. There are two traditional dates: December 25 in the Western church and January 6 in the Eastern church. Both have been celebrated by the church as memorials of Jesus' birth, the latter becoming the feast of Epiphany. Neither of them, however, is recognized as the actual date today.

Date of Christmas

Rome had a Nativity festival by 336 and probably a generation or so earlier. There is still disagreement among scholars concerning the reason why these early Christians of the late 3rd and early 4th century chose to celebrate Jesus' birth on December 25. Theories, still popular today, are based on three tendencies of the early Christians: their high respect for symbolism, their natural tendency to borrow from the real world around them, and their attempts to offset the influence of pagan festivals.

Earthy symbolism is very powerful at this time of the year in the northern hemisphere. Each year Christians, along with the general population, noticed that beginning with the fall equinox, the darkness of night began creeping up on daylight as days became shorter and nights longer. At the winter solstice this situation changed and the light of day began once again to defeat the darkness of night. The winter solstice occurred on December 25 on the Julian calendar and became the popular date for Christmas. As noted in the origin of Advent, a five-day pagan harvest festival of Saturnalia devoted to Saturn, the god of agriculture, occurred shortly before the winter solstice. It was celebrated with gift exchanges, feasting, and excesses. Did Christians turn their hearts to the mystery of Christ's birth to offset this pagan celebration?

Non-Christian Influence

Mithraism, a pagan sun cult popular in the Roman Empire during primitive Christianity, promoted this natural symbolism. Devotees of Mithra, a Persian deity, celebrated the birthday of their sun god with a festival called *dies natalis Solis Invicti* (Latin, "birthday of the unconquered sun") at the winter solstice. In 274, Emperor Aurelian proclaimed this Sun god the principal divine patron of the Roman Empire. He promulgated the feast throughout the empire in an effort to promote unity by way of a uniform religious monotheism.

This sun cult, or mystery religion, became a threat to Christianity. The two religions shared some religious discipline, doctrine, and symbolism in common, such as initiation, fasting, immersion, a sacred meal of bread and wine mixed with water and honey for new initiates, fellowship gestures, and belief in the immortality of the soul. One theory is that Christians began to celebrate the birth of Jesus on December 25 when this festival of the sun became popular in Rome. Christianity would have been comfortable with the symbolism because its own gospel speaks of light, or sun, as a symbol for the presence and meaning of Christ. The adoption of this date for the birthday of Jesus would have challenged people to turn from adoration of the material sun to adoration of Christ, the truly unconquered light of the world (John 8:12).

With the promulgation of the Edict of Milan in 313, Constantine became the benefactor and protector of Christianity. Consequently, pagan cultural features of sun-symbolism were no longer threatening. They could be freely absorbed by the church. The church, with its Nativity date of December 25 already in place, did precisely this. It promoted comparisons between the birth of Jesus and the winter solstice.

Once the December 25 date became popular, efforts were made to argue that it was the historical birthday of Jesus. These arguments were based on assumptions surrounding gospel events rather than on historical evidence. They do, however, take into account a growing preoccupation with the solar year and the cycle of seasons. The main assumption is that Zechariah the priest was ministering in the Holy of Holies on the Day of Atonement, which falls approximately on September 25 (fall equinox). His son, John the Baptist, would have been born on June 24 (summer solstice): "Your wife Elizabeth shall bear a son whom you shall name John" (Luke 1:1–25). Jesus would then have been conceived on March 25 (spring equinox) and born nine months later on December 25 (winter solstice): "Know that Elizabeth your kinswoman has conceived a son in her old age; she who was thought to be sterile is now in her sixth month, for nothing is impossible with God" (Luke 1:26–38).

Popularity of Christmas
Regardless of the actual reasons for the choice of the December 25 date, a Nativity festival quickly became popular. By the 5th century it marked the beginning of the church year. Later, when the preparation season of Advent received a definite shape after the 900s, it replaced Christmas as the beginning of the church year.

During the Middle Ages, Christmas exploded in popularity. So did religious traditions associated with it. Christmas competed with the more important celebration of the Paschal Mystery at Easter, and in popular practice began to outshine it. New peoples from the barbarian tribes of Europe took to the feast wholeheartedly. They added elements from their own pre-Christian winter traditions, putting their stamp on Christmas traditions that continue today.

In the 16th century, the Protestant Reformation in some countries challenged the excessive celebration of Christmas, since much of it was not at all connected directly with the mystery of Jesus' birth. Puritans in England, for example, condemned all celebration of Christmas as pagan. After they came to political power, they outlawed through Parliament in 1643 any observance of Christmas (along with Easter, Pentecost, and saints' days) under pain of punishment. This Puritan attitude came to the American colonies in the 17th century.

Secular Christmas

The Puritans lost their political power and the monarchy was restored. The celebration of Christmas returned in England but in a new form. Religious features were reserved to churches. In homes the celebration took on a secular party atmosphere of cheer, drinking, eating, and good will but with no reference to the birth of Jesus. This type of Christmas was immortalized by Charles Dickens in *A Christmas Carol.* It continues today as the only kind of Christmas celebrated by many people.

Early immigrants brought their different Christmas traditions and attitudes to America. Catholic Spaniards and French continued to celebrate Christmas with elaborate liturgies in church and religious traditions brought with them from their homelands. Puritans continued to obey a prohibition against any Christmas celebration in colonies that would become the New England states. This policy continued until the 19th century. Christmas was an ordinary workday in Boston until 1856. Public schools there held classes as usual on December 25 until 1870. Factory workers and students were disciplined if absent. By the end of the century, however, all states had granted legal recognition to Christmas Day.

Christmas in North America

The seeds of our contemporary Christmas traditions were planted in North America in the mid-19th century in the wake of the immigration waves from Ireland and central Europe. Germans brought the Christmas tree. The Irish contributed Christmas lights in windows of homes. With the Catholic immigrants came the popularity of a Midnight Mass, or at least a Mass before dawn and a religious atmosphere provided by the Nativity scene, or crèche. All denominations contributed to the composing and singing of religious Christmas carols. Soon citizens of all nationalities and faiths were enjoying Christmas festivities, many of them borrowed from each other.

Sacred and Secular

A mixture and even confusion of the sacred and secular characterizes the Christmas season today. Most people are comfortable with this situation, as Silent Night alternates with Rudolph, the Red-Nosed

Reindeer. Some popular Christmas traditions are considered religious but are only indirectly so. They reflect a Christianization of pre-Christian customs, especially traditions related to the winter solstice and the symbolism of light and dark in the northern hemisphere. This is the case with Christmas trees and Christmas lights of all shapes, sizes, and colors. Other Christmas traditions, for example Christmas liturgies and Nativity scenes, are strictly religious in nature. They are associated with the historical birth of Jesus and the mystery of the Incarnation. Finally, there are traditions associated with the veneration of saints during this time of the year, especially St. Nicholas on December 6. Even this bishop received a secular reincarnation in the evolution of Santa Claus.

Christmas Candle

The most obvious feature of the Christmas season is the popularity of special lights. At one time, all lights were burning flames in the form of wicks and candles and have always been popular religious symbols. The religious use of a special candle, called the Christmas Candle, is an ancient tradition. Some place it in the middle of the Advent Wreath, whose symbolism is now completed with the coming of Christ: The light has succeeded in pushing away the darkness of sin and religious ignorance. Others place it in some obvious place in the home. Originally it was a huge candle burned along with a Yule log, representing the light of Christ that came into the world during this season.

Window Lights

Other forms of Christmas lights are also popular during this festive season. The custom of putting a candle in the window comes from 19th-century Irish immigrants. It, too, seems to have had its origin in the Yule candle. It represents a beacon to light the way for Mary and Joseph and the coming of the Christ Child. It is possible, however, that its origin lies in a time of suppression of Catholicism in Ireland. The candles attracted fugitive priests to safe houses. This Christmas tradition spread throughout the country after being popularized by carolers in Boston a century ago.

Luminaries

In the Southwest there is a custom among Hispanics of placing luminaries, or burning candles, in paper sacks filled with sand. These decorate sidewalks and fronts of homes. This tradition has spread to non-

Hispanic areas throughout the country. Luminaries symbolically light the way for the Christ child.

Hanukkah

The Jewish Festival of Lights, Hanukkah ("dedication"), fits into the atmosphere of this season. It begins on the 25th day of the lunar month of Kislev, usually falling in December. The festivities continue for a full week with a growing crescendo of light: an additional candle is lit each night on a seven-branched menorah from one main candle until all are burning. This ritual is accompanied by singing Psalm 13, playing games, and offering gifts.

This Jewish festival of lights commemorates the saving of the Jewish faith in 165 B.C.E. Under the leadership of Judas Maccabee, a small Jewish guerrilla army defeated a much greater Syrian military force that had tried to destroy Judaism. After the victory the Temple in Jerusalem was purified of pagan profanation and rededicated. The Syrian king, Antiochus the Great, had dedicated the Temple to the Greek god Zeus, with statues to this deity and himself. Jewish monotheism was saved through this victory and rededication. From this monotheism, Christianity and, later, Islam would be born.

Kwanzaa

Another festival that begins on Dec. 21 and fits into the broad Christmas atmosphere is the relatively new African-American celebration of Kwanzaa. It evolved in 1966 under the influence of Maulana Ron Karenga, an American graduate student, in the wake of the Watts riots.

Kwanzaa, ("first fruits" in Swahili) has seven principles: Unity, Self-determination, Collective Work and Responsibility, Cooperative Economics, Purpose, Creativity, and Faith. These principles are symbolized by straw mat, candle holder, ears of corn, gifts, unity cup, flag of the black nation, and the seven candles of Rindra.

Nativity Scene

The tradition of having some kind of Nativity scene, also known by its French name (*crèche*), in churches and homes evolved during the Middle Ages, first in churches as a prop for Nativity plays associated with Mass. A crèche is a reproduction of the cave in Bethlehem with the principal characters: Mary, Joseph, the infant Jesus in a manger, shepherds, angels, and animals. St. Francis of Assisi popularized this custom with a living Nativity scene at Greccio, Italy, in 1223. These scenes, constructed from every sort of material, spread throughout Christendom.

Las Posadas
Among Hispanics it is popular to tell the story of Mary and Joseph's search for room in an inn by way of a ritual called *las Posadas*. A procession of families with "Mary" and "Joseph" approaches a designated home, the "inn," and sings out for a place for Mary who is pregnant. From inside the home the excuses of having no room is sung. This ritual is repeated on a series of nights until finally the "seekers" are invited in for a party.

Oplatek
Among people of Slavic ancestry and still today among many Poles in the United States, the father of the family solemnly breaks a Christmas wafer made of wheat flour, *oplatek* (Polish, "thin wafer"), on Christmas Eve. He distributes it to those present as a symbol of love and peace. These pieces are then shared with wishes for luck, health, and happiness. Pieces are also shared with friends and neighbors, a symbol of unity in the human family.

Christmas Tree
Next to the Nativity scene, the most popular Christmas tradition is to have a Christmas tree in the home. This custom is not the same as bringing a Yule tree or evergreens into the home, originally popular during the month of the winter solstice in Germany. The word "yule" seems to have come from the Anglo-Saxon *geol,* a word for feasting and drinking. The Yule tree reflected a longing for "green things"during the cold, dark winter. This tradition became so popular that "Yule" eventually became a substitute name for Christmas. The burning of a Yule log was adapted from an ancient Scandinavian practice of lighting bonfires in honor of the winter solstice.

Most Christmas traditions associated with evergreens and trees are related somehow to pre-Christian practices. The use of evergreens and wreaths as a symbol of life was popular already among the ancient Egyptians, Chinese, and Hebrews. Teutonic and Scandinavian peoples worshiped trees and decorated houses and barns with evergreens at the new year to scare away demons.

The Christmas tree, as did so many other Christmas traditions, originated in Germany. There it was first called the Paradise Tree. The

Christmas tree seems to have resulted from the combination of two traditions: a prop from a popular morality or mystery play of the Middle Ages with a festival of lights from pre-Christian times.

In the Middle Ages, traveling actors and troubadours visited villages and acted out popular Bible stories and morality plays in the village square or in the local church. One of these was a skit about Adam and Eve with a message promising that a Messiah would come. December 24 was observed as the feast of Adam and Eve. The prop of this skit was a Paradise Tree, a fir tree decorated with the traditional apple. Children were so delighted with this tree that parents were persuaded to have one in the home, especially when these plays were forbidden in churches because of abuses. The Paradise Tree, decorated with apples, other fruit, and pastries soon became a family tradition.

Another tradition was popular at the same time and place as the Paradise Tree. As the winter solstice approached, Germanic peoples celebrated a festival of lights as they had done ever since pre-Christian times centuries before. After their conversion these people re-interpreted the solstice lights, or candles, as symbolic of the light of the Messiah, Christ, shining in the darkness of sin and spiritual ignorance. These candles were placed each year on steps or shelves in the shape of a pyramid, decorated with evergreens and the Star of Bethlehem at the top. In the early 17th century, these two traditions seemed to have merged, probably out of convenience. The Christmas lights or burning candles and the Star of Bethlehem were attached to the Paradise Tree of the same shape as the Christmas pyramid. This gave rise in the land of the Germans to the Christmas tree.

The Christmas tree as a widespread tradition is relatively recent. By the beginning of the 19th century it had become popular throughout Germany and from there it spread to Slavic nations and France. Only in the mid-1800s was the custom introduced into England. About the same time, it was popularized in the United States by German immigrants. On a limited basis it had first been introduced in the American colonies by Hessian soldiers during the American Revolution, and even earlier by the German Moravian church.

At first, Christmas trees in this country were small table trees decorated with homemade ornaments from needlework, pastries, and ribbon. By the end of the last century, floor-to-ceiling trees were common, decorated with homemade and commercially manufactured decorations, and wrapped in tinsel garland. In the late 1930s the light-bulb-blowing process was adapted to Christmas tree balls.

Christmas trees appear in numerous forms today, including artificial ones. For many people they are merely a holiday decoration. They preserve, however, rich Christian symbolism: the green of hope at a time of dying, the burning light of Christ at a time of spiritual darkness, and the fruits of paradise.

Christmas Carols

Today, Christmas songs are usually called carols (Old English *carolen*, "to sing joyfully," which in turn came from the Greek *choraulein*, a ring dance with flutes). Originally, even in the 5th century, carols were Latin hymns. Christmas carols in a modern sense became popular in Italy in the 13th century under the influence of St. Francis of Assisi and spread throughout Europe. Carols sung today come from both Protestant and Catholic composers of recent centuries. French composers gave us "Angels We Have Heard on High," Germany, "Silent Night," "Lo, How a Rose E'er Blooming," and America, "O Little Town of Bethlehem" and "It Came Upon a Midnight Clear." The tradition of going Christmas caroling was introduced in the American colonies by the English. Later, late in the 19th century, it was popularized in the Beacon Hill district of Boston. In St. Louis at the turn of the 20th century, carolers would sing at homes decorated with a candle in the window. Today this custom continues throughout the United States, often with groups paying special attention to shut-ins.

Mistletoe

What has become an occasion of affection and even merriment, a kiss under the mistletoe, was a serious tradition in pre-Christian times. Among the Druids, a pre-Christian religious group in Gaul, Ireland, and Britain, mistletoe was considered a sacred plant with powers to heal and to protect. Because it was so sacred, enemies who met under it were expected to pledge themselves to a truce. From this came the custom of placing it over a doorway as an invitation to peace, good will, and hospitality. After Britain became Christian, the use of mistletoe was forbidden because of pagan practices associated with it. For a while, however, it became a symbol of Christ at Christmas in Britain because of its reputation of healing powers.

Holly

The use of holly as a religious tradition and Christmas decoration originated in northern Europe, where it was called the "holy tree." Because of its appearance it became associated with the burning bush of Moses and Mary's burning love for God. The red berries and prickly points also became symbolic of the crown of thorns and the bloody death that the Christ Child would eventually suffer.

Poinsettia
The poinsettia with its scarlet leaves, now of many hues, came from Mexico where it grows as a shrub. It blooms at Christmastime, and Mexicans called it "flower of the Holy Night." It was brought to the United States by the first U.S. ambassador to Mexico, Dr. Joel Roberts Poinsett (1779-1851) who had them grown in his greenhouse in South Carolina. Eventually, they were named after him. Only since 1920 have they become potted plants. Poinsettias are now associated as much with Christmas as lilies are with Easter.

Christmas Cards
Christmas cards with a seasonal greeting and message became popular late in the 19th century. The first is believed to have been designed in England by John Calcot Horsley. Today their theme varies from classical religious art emphasizing the birth of Jesus to winter scenes and holiday humor without any particular religious meaning. Billions are mailed each year.

Christmas Pageants
Probably no parent has escaped at least one Christmas pageant featuring their child! In early centuries visual aids were limited to stained glass windows, and books were non-existent. Acting out the mysteries in the life of Jesus was very important for the edification and education of people. One of these played out the story of the Nativity and was at times connected with public worship or Mass.

Widespread abuses and exaggerations caused these mystery plays to be prohibited in churches by church authorities by the 15th century. In a "cleaned-up" form they survived outside of church buildings. Three hundred years later, a simple form of the ancient Nativity play became popular again in Germany and came to the United States with immigrants. Some features of this drama have become part of Christmas services in both Protestant and Catholic churches, with children in costumes representing Mary, Joseph, shepherds, and angels. Sometimes just a single element is featured, for example, carrying a statue of the Christ Child in procession to the church's Nativity scene.

It is common that even public schools schedule some form of Christmas pageant. This tradition, however, along with displays of the Nativity scene on public property, has been challenged in courts on the constitutional grounds of separation of church and state.

Exchanging Gifts

It is understandable that a time of good will and high emotion became the occasion of exchanging gifts with family and friends. This has become one of the most popular features of the Christmas season. This custom is actually older than the feast itself. The Roman festival of Saturnalia, which occurred about the same time, included merriment and gift exchanges.

Kriss Kringle

An important traditional dimension of this gift-giving is that it be secret, especially for children. At a time when the celebration of Christmas was entirely religious, children were told that the Christ Child had brought them gifts. He also provided the other details of the Christmas celebration such as decorating the tree and completing the Nativity scene. Until recent times this tradition continued in most countries. "Christ Child" is *Christ Kinder* in German, later deteriorating into Kriss Kringle. In this form the custom was popularized by the German settlers in Pennsylvania.

Santa Claus

A concern of many parents is how to deal with the popularity of this Christmas character among young children and in society generally. The origin of this tradition is a fascinating and deliberate mixture of a bishop-saint, Father Christmas, Christmas Man, and the Norse mythological god Thor.

The veneration of saints was abolished in most Protestant areas soon after the Reformation. Banned, too, were the religious traditions associated with these saints. Banned, therefore, was St. Nicholas (Latin, *Sanctus Nicolas*). St. Nicholas had been the bishop of Myra in present-day Turkey. He was venerated as a confessor because he suffered imprisonment for his faith (d. 350). Legends tell of his practice of giving presents secretly. A feast in his honor was celebrated on December 6 and included the popular custom of a visit from St. Nicholas. This visitor in bishop's robes and a long white beard questioned young children about their behavior, encouraged them to prepare for the coming of the Lord at Christmas, and distributed simple gifts of candy, fruit, or toys. Sometimes this visit was secret during the night, and shoes put out by children were filled with gifts. In some form this tradition continued among Catholics.

Only Dutch Protestants after the Reformation kept the ancient tradition of a visit from St. Nicholas on December 6, in their language, *Sinter Klaas*. They brought this tradition and name to the American colonies. Their first church in New York City was named after him. The Dutch, however, lost control of their colony to the English. English-speaking Protestant children envied their Dutch friends' gifts from *Sinter Klaas*, which they pronounced as Santa Claus. Their parents, however, did not want to cooperate with a tradition that involved a Catholic saint, and a bishop at that.

A curious solution evolved. The secret visit with gifts was transferred from the eve of December 6 to Christmas Eve and absorbed into traditional Christmas festivities. And the good saint was replaced, except for his name, by an entirely new character. This new creation was a mixture of Father Christmas, popular in England, with some features from the Christmas Man, the mythical god Thor, and a little bit of St. Nicholas. Santa's colors of red and white, for example, were the colors of St. Nicholas's vestments and the Norse god of the north, Thor.

The Christmas Man, part of the evolution of Santa Claus, was created in some of the European countries where the Protestant Reformation had banished St. Nicholas. This character took his place as a secular symbol in some places. Details such as the sleigh, reindeer, and chimney visits may have come from this tradition. In England, St. Nicholas was replaced with the secular Father Christmas.

The Santa Claus we know today is, therefore, a "manufactured" but delightful character. In 1809, Washington Irving, in his *Knickerbocker's History of New York*, contributed to Santa's evolution by describing St. Nicholas as a heavy-set Dutchman, smoking a pipe, riding over rooftops in a wagon and dropping presents from his pockets down chimneys. These details were further expanded and St. Nicholas, now Santa Claus, became "a jolly old elf" in 1822 with Clement C. Moore's popular poem which begins with "'Twas the night before Christmas...." Final details were made popular by cartoonists in the late 19th century, especially by Thomas Nast. He put the finishing touches on the Santa Claus of today by way of a series of drawings to lighten the mood of people during the Civil War.

The work of these cartoonists also echoes details from mythology about the Norse god Thor: elderly, jolly (though god of war), with white hair and beard, friend of the common people, living in the north land, traveling through the sky in a chariot pulled by goats, and as god of fire, partial to chimneys and fireplaces.

There does not seem to be any harm done to the faith of children by cooperating with the tradition of Santa Claus. Acquaintance with myths is an important part of children's emotional development.

8

CHRISTMASTIME

Not many religious Christmas traditions—or secular ones—continue after December 25 in the typical family in the United States. Christmas holidays with school vacation, visiting and partying with family and friends are popular for a week. Christmas decorations stay up for a while, but much of life quickly settles into an ordinary routine.

The church, however, is not finished with Christmas yet. Christmas songs during liturgies remain popular until the feast of Epiphany on January 6, now celebrated on the Sunday between January 2 and 8. The feast of the Holy Family is celebrated on the Sunday between Christmas and January 1. December 26 commemorates the first martyr, St. Stephen; December 27, the evangelist St. John; and December 28 (the feast of the Holy Innocents), recalls the gospel story of events surrounding the birth of Jesus. January 1, New Year's Day, is the octave of Christmas and in ancient times a sort of repeat of Christmas. Finally, the feast of Epiphany, in ancient times a major Christmas celebration, and the feast of the Baptism of the Lord, close out Christmastime. Afterwards, the figurines in the Nativity scene are packed away along with other decorations that gave the previous weeks such an exciting atmosphere.

All major religious feasts used to be extended for at least a week, a sign that church and people were reluctant to say goodbye to it. The celebration a week later was called the octave (Latin, "the eighth day"). Festivities, sometimes elaborate, continued during the days in between. This weeklong celebration of core mysteries of Christianity was possible at a time when people were more free of exactly scheduled employment responsibilities, and family life included festivities provided by the local church.

Twelve Days of Christmas

The celebration of Christmas was stretched even further than a week. The twelve days of Christmas, secularized in a popular song, was an ancient sacred and festive celebration of Christmastime. The twelve days began on December 25, Christmas, and ended on January 6, the feast of the Epiphany, which is still a major feast of the Incarnation.

Feast Days of Martyrs

It is difficult today for people to appreciate a time when there was no pervading Christmas mood, neither religious nor secular. There was such a time. The celebration of feast days of martyrs evolved before there was a Christmas season. Three of them are celebrated as feast days immediately following Christmas. They remain on the church's calendar and are celebrated with liturgy in local churches. Popular religious traditions associated with these feasts, once widespread in Europe, have not survived among people in the United States.

These feasts of martyrs during Christmastime represent three kinds of martyrdom common during the centuries of persecution: those who went to their death willingly (St. Stephen), those who were willing to die but were not put to death (St. John), and those who were put to death without their choice (Holy Innocents).

A festival remembering St. Stephen is celebrated on December 26. Traditionally he is considered the first of Jesus' followers to die in testimony to his faith. The New Testament describes him as one of the original deacons serving the needs of the Greek-speaking Christian Jews in Jerusalem. He was arrested by the synagogue in a dispute between Christians and Jews and, after a spirited testimony, was stoned to death (see Acts, chapters 6 and 7).

The feast of St. John the Evangelist is celebrated on December 27. This disciple is traditionally remembered as the one "whom Jesus loved" and who traditionally is mentioned as the author of the last gospel and the Book of Revelation. He was an apostle in Ephesus until exiled to the island of Patmos. An unusual tradition in some parts of the world is still associated with this feast day: the blessing and distribution of St. John's wine. This tradition seems to have begun with a legend that John once drank poisoned wine and was not harmed.

Unlike these saints, the selection of December 28 for the feast of Holy Innocents was a direct spinoff from the celebration of Christmas. As part of the larger story of Jesus' birth, the gospel according to Matthew (2:13–19) tells of the massacre of innocent boys two years old and younger at the order of King Herod. The story ends with the Holy Family's flight into Egypt. These gospel stories reflect what history has recorded of Herod's tendency to execute anyone whom he considered a threat to his power, including members of his own family. Matthew probably included this story to put Jesus' birth into a broader theological context: just as the chosen people came out of Egypt to create Israel, the Jewish nation, so the chosen one, the Messiah, would come out of Egypt to create the New Israel, the church.

Holy Family

The feast of the Holy Family has been celebrated by the universal church only since 1920. Originally celebrated on the third Sunday after Epiphany, it is now observed on the Sunday between Christmas and January 1. Devotion to the Holy Family became popular after the 16th century. The theme of family, and this feast dedicated to it, is of special importance today in face of challenges to the contemporary family. Many parishes offer families an opportunity to renew their love for each other as part of the liturgy.

January 1

The celebration of a New Year's Day on January 1 with a special theme is not a universal tradition. Different people began their secular calendar on different days. It was common to observe it on March 25, the vernal, or spring, equinox. Such was the case in England until the mid-18th century. New Year's Day was celebrated on March 1 until the 8th century in the Frankish empire, on Easter in France until the 15th, and on Christmas until the 16th in Scandinavia and Germany. A January 1 date was set for the Roman Empire in 45 B.C.E. by Julius Caesar with the creation of the Julian calendar. In 1582, Pope Gregory XIII sponsored a reform of the Julian calendar. This was accompanied by a method of calculating and dividing the year still in force today. This Gregorian calendar reinstated January 1 as New Year's Day. Protestant countries rejected this calendar and therefore the January 1 observance of New Year's Day until 1700 in Germany, 1752 in Great Britain and the American colonies, and 1753 in Sweden.

January 1 has had many religious themes in Christian history. None of them are associated with the secular understanding of New Year's Day so popular in our society today. At first the day was celebrated as special because it was the octave of Christmas and, so to speak, a repeat of that day and theme. The church promoted penitential liturgies and fasting to offset the influence of pagan New Year's boisterous practices. In 567, the Second Council of Tours prescribed a three-day fast to correspond with the first days of the new year.

The church never succeeded in curtailing boisterous New Year's

Eve celebrations with its penitential emphasis. Therefore, other religious themes evolved for this day. The first one was a Marian theme because on this day the papal liturgy was held at the oldest church dedicated to Mary, St. Mary Beyond the Tiber. At first it celebrated the birthday of Mary (later moved to September 8) who gave birth to Jesus, continuing a Christmas theme.

In Spain and Gaul during the 6th century the church began to dedicate January 1 to the mystery of the circumcision of Jesus. This was in accord with the Scriptures that this event took place on the eighth day after Jesus's birth (Luke 2:21). This theme spread to Rome only in the 13th century and was added to the celebration of the Octave of Christmas and the feast of Mary.

Today January 1 continues to be a holy day in the United States. It combines a number of themes: the Octave of Christmas; Mary, the Mother of God; and, more recently, the theme of peace in the world. The theme of Jesus' circumcision was dropped in 1969. A Christmas theme continues by way of songs, music, and decorations.

New Year's Day
The theme of January 1 as New Year's Day has never been part of the church's celebration, although this theme is frequently heard in homilies. Most traditions related to this theme are secular in nature rather than religious. The tradition of drinking and partying as the old year gives way to the new goes back to ancient times and is a secular remnant of what had originally been pagan religious rites. It was a popular way of saying goodbye to the old and greeting the new: ringing out the old year and ringing in the new. Ancient pagan religious rites included a form of confession and satisfaction for the previous year's failures and evil, lighting of new fires, and some kind of communion with the dead. Loud noises from horns, drums, and shouting drove away evil spirits that were especially active at this time of the year. This may sound a little like Halloween. The end of October was New Year's Day among the Celts who gave us our Halloween customs.

Epiphany
Epiphany is celebrated on January 6 and with special solemnity in churches in the United States on the Sunday between January 2 and 8. Epiphany comes from the Greek *epiphanein*, a "showing, appearance, or revelation." It was used to describe the appearance of a god among the people, a theophany, or a visit from some civil dignitary. The Greek-speaking church of the East found it natural to use the word to

describe the appearance of the true God in flesh. Consequently, some churches in that part of the world celebrated a festival on January 6 recalling Jesus' baptism in the Jordan and his Cana miracle; others celebrated a festival commemorating his birth, and eventually a combination of the two.

Evidence of a Nativity festival in Egypt and in the churches of the Near East is very ancient, possibly beginning before the 3rd century. Theories of why a January 6 date was chosen by the Eastern church parallels the arguments for the December 25 date in the west. A popular theory, challenged by more recent research, presumes that the winter solstice occurred on January 6, according to the calendar used in that part of the world. On that day pagans celebrated with nuances of wine, water, and light, the appearance ("epiphany") of Aion, god of time and eternity, among the people. Christians, as the argument goes, adopted this day as their feast of the Incarnation, incorporating into the liturgy the gospel stories of Jesus' "epiphanies" at his birth, on the occasion of the visit of the Magi at his baptism in the Jordan, and at his first miracle of turning water into wine at the wedding feast of Cana. This mixed theme made sense to these early people in the East because Jesus was not revealed to the people until his baptism.

This feast of the Epiphany was introduced into Gaul in the mid-4th century because the churches in that part of Europe had close ties to the East. In Gaul the Epiphany themes of the Magi, the baptism of Jesus, his transfiguration, and the miracle at Cana were developed.

By the end of the 4th century, Eastern and Western churches took over each other's Nativity feasts. Since then, Christmas and the Epiphany have been celebrated in both churches. This duplication led to the evolution of a separate theme for each. The Eastern church continued to emphasize the theme of Jesus' epiphanies with the gospel stories of Jesus' baptism and his miracle at Cana. In the Western church, the Epiphany evolved into a celebration of the gospel story of the visit of the Magi (Matthew 2:1–12) on the occasion of Jesus' birth: his epiphany to the gentiles.

The Christmas season officially ends the Sunday after Epiphany with the commemoration of Christ's baptism.

Magi

The gospel story of the Magi, so closely associated with Epiphany, is not meant to be read as an historical event. Rather, it is a reflection on an important aspect of the mystery of Incarnation: The Messiah has come to all people and not just to the Jews, a theme highlighted by

Matthew's gospel. The word "magi" is Greek and refers to a learned caste in Babylonia, probably astrologers and interpreters of dreams. It fits into the symbolism of supernatural circumstances that led representatives of the gentile nations to the Messiah. References to prophecies of the Hebrew Scriptures (for example, Isaiah 60:1–6) are used by the gospel author to emphasize the universal purpose of Jesus' birth. In Psalm 72:10ff, the King of Judah, one of the Messiah's titles, is promised gifts. Gold, frankincense, and myrrh, the three gifts mentioned in the gospel, were traditional symbols of homage in the East. Traditionally they have come to symbolize the destiny of Jesus: gold for his royalty, frankincense for his divinity, myrrh for his suffering and death.

This gospel reflection on the birth of the Messiah was embellished by popular details as the centuries passed. The magi were identified as kings by Tertullian (c. 160-225), and the number of Magi was set at three by Origen (d. 254) because of the three gifts mentioned. Their physical appearance comes from legends in the 9th century. They described the kings as representing the three major races and gave them names: Melchior, an old white man with a long white beard, bearing the gift of gold; Caspar, young and of darker hue, carrying incense; and Balthasar, a black man, offering myrrh.

Blessing of Homes
One popular religious tradition since the Middle Ages has been associated with the feast of the Epiphany: the blessing of homes with holy water and incense. The ritual calls for a priest or parent to mark, with blessed chalk, the inside of the main door with the initials of the Magi and a code of the current year connected with crosses: 20+C+M+B+01. Another explanation of the initials (C-M-B) is that they are the first letters of the blessing: *Christus mansionem benedicat* (Latin, "May Christ bless the house").

Candlemas
Two other feasts have a Christmas theme but fall outside of the traditional Christmas season. The first is Candlemas on February 2, forty days after Christmas Day. It could be considered the closing of the season of lights so evident during Christmastime. The gospel for this feast proclaims the words of Simeon that the infant Jesus will be "a revealing light to the Gentiles, the glory of your people Israel" (Luke 2:32).

This feast was celebrated in Jerusalem as early as the fourth century. Though originally called "Day of St. Simeon," it became a commemoration of the purification of Mary, in accordance with Jewish law, forty days after Jesus' birth: "When the day came to purify them according to the law of Moses, the couple brought him up to Jerusalem so that he could be presented to the Lord, for it is written in the law of the Lord, 'Every first-born male shall be consecrated to the Lord.' They came to offer in sacrifice 'a pair of turtledoves or two young pigeons,' in accord with the dictate in the law of the Lord" (Luke 2:22–24; see Leviticus 12:6–7).

By the end of the 7th century, this feast was celebrated in Rome on February 2 with the addition of a candlelight procession. This procession seems to have originated as a substitute for a similar pagan torch procession of expiation around the city walls. A hint of this penitential and expiation theme continued until recent times with the wearing of purple vestments. The day eventually received the popular title of Candlemas ("Candle Mass") because candles were blessed before the Mass and procession. Today this feast is called the Presentation of the Lord. Candles are still blessed and some form of procession may be held.

Annunciation

Another feast associated with the mystery of the Incarnation and, therefore, with Christmas, is the Feast of the Annunciation of the Lord. It has been celebrated on March 25 in the Western church since before the middle of the 7th century. The theme of the feast remembers God's decision, communicated to Mary through the angel messenger Gabriel that she would be the mother of an unusual child: "Great will be his dignity and he will be called Son of the Most High" (Luke 1:32).

The choice of a March 25 date from early centuries is tied up with the choice of December 25 for Christmas. A strong possibility is that March 25, the date of Jesus' death and last Passover, was considered by early Christians as the date of creation and the first moment of Jesus' Incarnation or conception. Once Christ's birthday was remembered annually with a feast on December 25, another feast remembering the beginning of Jesus' life in Mary's womb nine months earlier, on March 25, fell into place.

9

LENT

Led by a cross, the servers and priest moved slowly down the aisle, stopping at each station. The priest read a graphic account of the painful sufferings of Jesus along with a confession of guilt on our part in causing this shameful journey of the Lord. Fourteen times the full pews responded with genuflection: "We adore thee, O Christ, and we bless thee...because by thy holy cross thou hast redeemed the world." And reflected in song: "At the cross her station keeping, stood the mournful mother weeping, close to Jesus crucified...."

At home mothers were careful that breakfast and lunch combined did not exceed the main meal on Wednesday and Friday. And there was lots of fish and cheese. Children and adults gave up sweets, desserts, dances, and movies. The road to church was traveled many times during the week. A mood of sadness and severity settled over families and parishes. It seemed to match the dull time of the year as winter held fast and spring was reluctant to claim its due.

It was Lent in the pre-Vatican II years.

The whole church goes on retreat for six weeks about a month and a half after the Christmas season. This annual spiritual renewal prepares for the celebration of Christianity's most fundamental belief: Jesus was raised from the dead and is Christ, the Lord. Lent, therefore, has no meaning in itself. It prepares for Easter and new life. This has given rise to a great variety of religious traditions from the earliest centuries of Christianity. Three themes hold the six weeks together: (1) the mystery of Jesus' death and resurrection, (2) the implications of this mystery for those preparing for baptism, and (3) a spiritual renewal of faith and conversion on the part of those already baptized. These themes have not always received equal emphasis over the centuries. Preparation for baptism, the original heart of Lent, had almost disappeared until Vatican II reforms.

Origin
Lent is closely associated with the transition from winter to spring.

The word "lent," for example, comes from the Anglo-Saxon word for springtime, *lencten*. It describes the gradual *lengthening* of daylight after the winter solstice.

Already during the 2nd century, Christians prepared for the annual Pascha, or Easter, by fasting for two days. This was a natural thing to do in preparation for the holiest of times when, during the first generations, the Lord's final return was expected. In the 3rd century, this fast was extended to all of Holy Week. A distinct and lengthy season of preparation did not exist until the early 4th century.

Lent and Baptism

Lent evolved around the theme of baptism which, from at least the 3rd century, had been associated with the vigil of the anniversary of the Lord's resurrection: the Easter Vigil. During the first centuries preparation for baptism could last for several years. Adults seeking church membership could not just "sign up." They were tested for up to three years. During this time they were instructed, supported in their withdrawal from pagan practices and loyalties, and taught to live a new way. Only then were they admitted to candidacy for baptism. Finally, during what would become Lent, they received intense instruction, submitted to exorcisms, participated in special rituals, fasted on Good Friday and Holy Saturday, and were baptized during the Easter Vigil.

When the Roman persecution of Christians ended in 313, the church began a public and more concise process, catechumenate (Greek *katechein*, "to proclaim," "to teach"), of accepting new adult believers, catechumens, into membership. The catechumens' final phase of preparation for baptism always included a period of fasting to support changes in lifestyle.

This ritual preparation for Easter was a special time at first only for catechumens. Gradually it became popular for those already baptized to participate in this tradition of fasting. When the catechumenate was discontinued in the early Middle Ages, due to the widespread custom of infant baptism, Christians continued the tradition of fasting for forty days in preparation for Easter.

Penitential Theme

In the 4th century, preparation for baptism was joined by fasting and other penitential practices before Easter in preparation for absolution from public sins and crimes. This practice spread among other parishioners and not just public sinners. During the Middle Ages, it became universally popular with emphasis on personal sin. This penitential and more somber theme of Lent gave rise to the liturgical penitential color purple and to the dropping of the joyful acclamations of Alleluia and Glory to God during this season. In some places an elaborate "funeral" was held to "bury" the Alleluia. This penitential atmosphere of Lent was supported by other church disciplines such as the prohibition of weddings during these six weeks. To this day weddings are still discouraged because of the penitential atmosphere of the season.

Forty Days
Early in Christianity the discipline of fasting became associated with the number forty. This gradually determined the length of Lent. Fasting by catechumens, and then by other Christians, was done in imitation of Jesus' forty-day fast in the desert (Matthew 4:2), Moses' forty days on Mount Sinai (Exodus 34:28), Elijah's forty-day fast on his journey to Mount Horeb (1 Kings 19:8), and the forty years the Israelites spent in the desert. To this day the church's official title for Lent, *Quadragesima*, is Latin for "forty."

These forty days of fasting were originally counted from the beginning of the Easter Triduum (Latin, "three days") that began on Holy Thursday evening. This determined the date of the First Sunday of Lent. Fasting, however, was never done on Sundays, which were always considered weekly memorials of Jesus' resurrection, and therefore as "little Easters." By the 7th century, the six-week season of Lent was anticipated on Ash Wednesday and included Good Friday and Holy Saturday to keep the days of fasting at forty. The Eastern church excluded both Saturdays and Sundays from fasting, and its Lent begins a week earlier.

Sunday liturgies during Lent have always preserved a reference to the ancient process of the adult catechumenate with an emphasis on the journey to baptism. In 1972, the church revived the adult catechumenate with its publication of *The Rite of Christian Initiation of Adults* (RCIA). Now once again ceremonies highlight for both catechumens and parishioners the journey to baptism: the rite of election, the presentation of the gospel, the creed, the Our Father, the public scrutinies that replaced exorcisms on the third, fourth, and fifth Sundays, and the dismissal of catechumens after the homily to another part of the building for special instruction on the day's Scripture reading, popularly called "breaking open the word."

The church's liturgies are not preoccupied with the suffering and death of Jesus, as are most popular lenten devotions, until Holy Week.

Mardi Gras

Lent is immediately preceded by a celebration that has no mention on the calendar of the church year. The tradition of Mardi Gras (French, "fat Tuesday") began as a pre-lenten day of feasting and carnival (Latin *carnelevarium*, "removal of meat"). It was a "last fling" in preparation for the severe fasting and abstinence which began the next day on Ash Wednesday. This popular tradition probably had a practical purpose. Foods forbidden by the church's severe lenten discipline were the ones needing refrigeration. Since controlled refrigeration was unheard of until the 19th century, it made sense to eat what would otherwise spoil during the six weeks of Lent and to help other families to do the same with a party atmosphere.

Familiar features associated with carnivals were already popular by the 14th century. They reflected pre-Christian revelry and masquerading associated with ancient pagan observance of spring and New Year festivals celebrated at the spring or vernal equinox. Because church discipline forbade this kind of revelry during Lent, it was natural that it be substituted by a pre-lenten party-time.

Paczki

In ethnic Polish areas the baking, selling, and eating of *paczki* (pronounced poneski) is popular the day before Ash Wednesday. These are heavy deep-fried pastries, sometimes filled with fruit.

Shrove Tuesday

The day before Ash Wednesday is also called Shrove Tuesday. This name (Middle English *shriven*, "confession,") comes from an old custom of going to confession in preparation for the holy season of Lent.

Ash Wednesday

Ash Wednesday officially begins Lent and the Easter cycle on any date from February 4 to March 10, depending on the date of Easter. Ashes from burned palms saved from the previous year are placed on the forehead of parishioners. This custom of placing ashes on the heads of people and, originally, the wearing of sackcloth is an ancient penitential practice common among the Hebrew people (Jonah 3:5–9; Jeremiah 6:26, 25:34; Matthew 11:21). At first this ritual of ashes, along with its original scriptural meaning, was not directly connected with the beginning of Lent. As early as the 300s, it was adopted by local churches as part of their practice of temporarily excommunicating or expelling public sinners from the community. These people were guilty of public sins and scandals such as apostasy, heresy, murder, and adultery ("capital" sins).

By the 7th century, this custom had expanded in some churches into a public Ash Wednesday ritual. Sinners first confessed their sins privately. Then they were presented to the bishop and publicly enrolled in the ranks of penitents in preparation for absolution on Holy Thursday. After a laying on of hands and imposition of ashes, they were expelled from the congregation in imitation of the expulsion of Adam and Eve from paradise, with the reminder that death is the punishment for sin. "Remember, you are dust and to dust you shall return" (Genesis 3:19). They lived apart from their families and from the rest of the parish for the forty days of Lent (thus our word "quarantine"). Dressed in sackcloth and ashes, they were identified as penitents in the congregation and sometimes on the steps of the church. Common penances required that these penitents abstain from meat, alcohol, bathing, haircuts, shaves, marriage relations, and business transactions. Depending on the diocese, some penances lasted for years and even a lifetime.

During the Middle Ages, emphasis was placed on personal rather than public sin. As a result, traditions of Ash Wednesday in a mitigated form were adopted by all adult members of the parish. Traditions similar to those in today's parishes were observed throughout the church by the 11th century. In recent years an alternate formula for the imposition of ashes emphasizes a more positive aspect of Lent: "Turn away from sin and be faithful to the gospel" (see Mark 1:15).

Another form of penitential practice evolved under the influence of monks in the Celtic church in Britain and Ireland during the 6th to the 8th centuries. This was a private and individual form of penance for less serious sins. This new practice would influence the evolution of the sacrament of reconciliation more than the Ash Wednesday ritual.

Three kinds of traditions have given Lent its particular character: (1) those that support a somber atmosphere; (2) penitential practices, especially fasting and abstinence; and (3) devotions centered around the suffering Jesus. During the past twenty years these traditions have been joined by newer ones, adding a more positive dimension to Lent.

Lenten Atmosphere

The atmosphere of Lent takes on a somber mood. In parish liturgies the joyous Alleluia and Glory to God are dropped. The penitential color of purple is prominent in vestments and church decorations. The sanctuary is stripped of its usual festive decorations. Musical instruments were at one time discouraged

Until recent times it was customary to veil prominent statues and crucifixes in church with a purple cloth as a sign of sadness and mourning. In some churches, beginning around 900, one large cloth was hung between the people and the altar from the beginning of Lent. This was done to hide the heavenly glory depicted by statues of saints and crosses with the figure of the triumphant Christ. This custom came to symbolize the exclusion of all sinners from the altar just as public sinners were excluded. Since the 1600s, this veiling was limited to Passiontide, beginning on the fifth Sunday of Lent, originally called "Passion Sunday." On that Sunday (today only in Cycle B) the final words of the gospel are: "At that they picked up rocks to throw at Jesus, but he hid himself and slipped out of the temple precincts" (John 8:59).

Fasting and Abstinence

Fasting and abstinence are often linked together but are two different disciplines. Fasting has to do with the quantity of food eaten on particular days (little or none). Abstinence refers to the kind of food denied oneself, for example, meat. Fasting has always been a popular religious practice. Denying oneself a basic human need such as food for a period of time may be done for different reasons. It prepares for a feast. It promotes self-discipline. It supports one's prayers. It cleanses oneself of previous abuses and sin. All of these have been motives for the lenten tradition of fasting. Another motive has always been part of lenten fasting and abstinence: almsgiving, giving to the needy from what is saved through the discipline of fasting and abstinence, or from one's surplus.

Fasting and abstinence began as voluntary practices. Gradually they became very strict and were enforced by church law. From the 400s to the 800s, only one meal a day—usually in the evening according to local custom—was permitted. Flesh meat, fish, alcohol, and in some places even eggs and milk products were forbidden. Beginning in the 10th century, it became customary to eat this meal at noon. By the 14th, a light meal was permitted in the evening. In the Middle Ages the prohibition against fish and dairy products during Lent was lifted.

A rather severe lenten discipline of fasting and abstinence remained in force until 1966. Only one main meal was permitted on all days of Lent except Sunday for parishioners between the ages of

21 and 59. Two other meatless meals were permitted, sufficient to maintain strength, but together not equaling another full meal. This was coupled with abstinence from flesh meat, gravies, and condiments on Ash Wednesday and all Fridays for those seven years of age and older. On weekdays of Lent, meat was permitted only at the main meal except on days of abstinence.

Popular Penances

Other forms of penance not obligated by church laws have been popular throughout the centuries. Most of these occurred in the privacy of families and are still popular today: giving up desserts, candies, gum, soft drinks, alcohol, and "junk food" eaten between meals. Besides saving monies to be given to the needy, these popular forms of fasting and abstinence promote personal discipline and self-control. So, too, do other forms of contemporary lenten practices, such as limiting family television viewing.

Stations of the Cross

Traditionally, lenten devotions in parish churches have drawn attention to the suffering and death of Jesus. The most popular one is known as the Stations of the Cross. During the time of the crusades (1095-1270), it became popular for pilgrims to the Holy Land to walk in the footsteps of Jesus to Calvary. In the next two centuries, after the Moslems recaptured the Holy Land, pilgrimages were too dangerous. A substitute pilgrimage, the Stations of the Cross, became a popular outdoor devotion throughout Europe during the Middle Ages. They represented critical events from Scripture or tradition of Jesus' journey to Calvary and varied in number from five to 20 until the 18th century when Pope Clement XII fixed the number at 14. In the mid-18th century, Stations were allowed inside churches. The Stations became a familiar feature in Catholic churches. In the 1960s, it became popular to add a fifteenth Station representing the end of the journey: the resurrection. Some replace questionable stations with events of Christ's suffering mentioned in Scripture but not in the traditional 14.

Pretzels

Pretzels, a popular snack, had their origin in early Christian lenten practices. Because fat, eggs, and milk were forbidden during Lent, a special bread was made with dough consisting of only flour, salt, and water. These little breads were shaped in the form of arms crossed in prayer and were called *bracellae* (Latin, "little arms"). Among the

Germans the Latin word became "bretzel." These pretzels were a common lenten food throughout the Middle Ages in Europe and became an all year round snack, in its original shape, only in the 19th century.

Hot Cross Buns

Hot cross buns also became a popular food eaten during Lent. The custom began in England to bake buns, place icing on them in the form of a cross, and eat them on Good Friday. Eventually, they were baked and eaten throughout Lent and even during the Easter season.

Recent Trends

A trend began in the 1960s to emphasize the more positive aspects of discipline and good works. This trend received official sanction in 1966 in Pope Paul VI's apostolic constitution, *Poenitemini*, which limited obligatory abstinence to Ash Wednesday and all Fridays of Lent and the discipline of fasting to Ash Wednesday and Good Friday. While the emphasis today is on voluntary lenten practices, direction still comes from the historical evolution of Lent with its emphasis on baptism, personal conversion, penance, and the suffering and death of Jesus.

10

HOLY WEEK

It is obvious in parishes that something important is about to happen. Six weeks of penance, prayer, and special devotions come to a climax. Bold signs and symbols are everywhere. Rituals seem to be more exciting at this time than during the rest of the year. They tell a religious story that is powerful and unambiguous. Emotions are a mixture of relief and anticipation. It is Holy Week.

The spiritual journey of Holy Week closely follows ancient historical events. Parishioners move quickly from Jesus' triumph in Jerusalem on Palm Sunday to his passion and death. Holy Thursday rituals consecrating holy oils in cathedral churches, along with Last Supper liturgies in parish churches, are like a refreshing pause. They are a few hours of rejoicing before the reality of Jesus' suffering and death continues on Good Friday. Then there is a quiet waiting until the burst of the new light of resurrection conquers the dark of death at the Easter Vigil on Holy Saturday night.

The title that the Eastern Catholic church gives to this week says it all: the Week of Salvation. No one day or one religious tradition would be sufficient to celebrate such an immense happening.

The Pascha, or Passover
Originally the early church celebrated the Pascha as a single mystery. It included the mystery of Christ's death and resurrection. There were no separate holy days devoted to the separate events which make up this mystery.

The words "Pascha," "Pasch," and "paschal" come from the Hebrew *pesach*, a "passing by" or a "passing through." This became the popular word "Passover." The greatest of all Christian feasts is most profoundly associated with the greatest of all Jewish feasts. The Israelites were saved from slavery when the angel of death struck the firstborn of the Egyptians but "passed over" the chosen people. The remembering of this saving act of God became the heart of the Hebrew religious experience.

The Jewish Passover is a mixture of two ancient Hebrew festivals. There was the Passover itself, a spring festival during which nomadic shepherds sacrificed spring lambs. At the same time there was a festival of Unleavened Bread, a Canaanite agricultural festival adopted by the Hebrews after settling in Palestine. These two became the one public festival in the 7th century B.C.E. when Jerusalem became the sole sanctuary of the Jewish people. Celebrated on the 14th of Nisan, it combined the sacrificing of lambs in the temple and the eating of a sacred meal in the homes.

It was during the annual Jewish Passover that Jesus "passed through" suffering and death into new life, a divine act that saved all of humanity and creation from final death.

Holy Week

Holy Week is the heart of the church year. The word "holy" in the descriptive title "Holy Week" highlights this week as unique and most holy in the annual cycle of time for Christians. Official church rituals and other traditions observed during this week remember and make present the passing of Jesus from life to death to new life and all of creation along with him.

A distinct framework of Holy Week seems to have developed first of all in Jerusalem. There the actual sites were located where the historical events of Jesus' suffering, death, and resurrection occurred. When the Christian religion was legalized in 313, the baptized who lived in or near Jerusalem gathered publicly on the anniversary of the events at the places identified by tradition as "the holy places." They relived the events with songs, readings from the story (the gospel passion narrative), procession, and vigils. Much of what is known about the ancient religious traditions surrounding Holy Week and Easter come from vivid accounts written in diaries by Egeria. She was a pilgrim from northwestern Spain who visited the Holy Land in 381-384. These Jerusalem practices were brought to Europe by pilgrims to the Holy Land such as Egeria. In time, the universal church incorporated features of them into the official liturgies of what had become a "holy week."

Sacred Triduum

Originally, therefore, there was no Holy Week. The Pascha was celebrated in the context of a single day: the Easter Vigil. It began with sunset on the Sabbath evening and continued until dawn on the first day of the week or Sunday. By the 5th century, this Paschal Mystery had been broken down into its historical pieces, partly under the influence of borrowing from Jerusalem. The nucleus was called the Sacred Triduum (Latin, "three days"): Friday until Easter morning. It remembered the death, burial, and resurrection. Later, Holy Thursday was included because all days were reckoned from sunset of the previous evening.

With the end of the persecution of Christians, Christian emperors forbade work and all forms of amusements during this week. It was also a tradition that those in prison be pardoned. Holy Thursday, Good Friday, and Holy Saturday were enforced as holy days.

Palm Sunday

Holy Week begins with Palm Sunday—called Passion Sunday today—because the theme of Jesus' suffering and death begins with the reading of the passion. Parish liturgies begin with the blessing of palms somewhere outside of the usual assembly area, in imitation of the triumphant "parade" of Jesus from "Bethany" to "Jerusalem" (Matthew 21:1–11). The gospel of Jesus' triumphant entry into Jerusalem is read, followed by a procession into church, with people holding blessed palms and singing festive songs. Soon afterward, however, the theme of triumph changes radically with the reading of the passion narrative from the gospel of Matthew, Mark, or Luke (depending on what year of the liturgical cycle is being celebrated). Palm Sunday liturgy is devoted, therefore, more to the suffering of Jesus than to his triumphant reception by the people. By telescoping these events, the church emphasizes the meaning of Holy Week rather than presents an accurate historical progression of saving events. On Palm Sunday the church celebrates the beginning of Jesus' passage from life to death to new life: the Paschal Mystery.

Palms

Originally, people paraded or processed in the original footsteps of Jesus from the little village of Bethany into the city of Jerusalem. As part of the festivities they carried real palm fronds or olive branches, the two most common trees in Palestine (see Matthew 21:18). These were replaced with local versions of "palms" as the celebration of Palm Sunday spread throughout Europe and then the entire world: willow branches, cedar branches, pussy willows, and flowers. The "palm branches" commonly used in the United States are "ground palms" from Texas.

Ponce de Leon, the Spanish explorer, arrived at the territory known today as the state of Florida on Palm Sunday in 1513. He named the territory Florida because of the abundance of flowers evident, and because flowers were substitutes for palms in his native country, Spain.

Blessed palms have always been respected as holy objects or sacramentals. Some families place one or more on the wall behind a crucifix or holy picture until the next Palm Sunday, or they might braid them into crosses for wall decorations. Others save them and burn a little when some crisis, such as a storm, threatens. This custom may have originated in Austria, Bavaria, and Slavic countries where it was common to scatter bits of blessed palms around on the farm to protect fields and animals against bad weather and diseases. Some of these traditions may very well be superstitious practices, presuming that there is special power in the plants themselves. Already in ancient times Greeks and Romans believed that certain plants possessed mystical powers. Such was the case of mistletoe among the Druids in Celtic lands.

Before the beginning of Lent the following year, blessed palms are burned at the local church and the ashes used in the Ash Wednesday ritual.

Preparation Days

Monday, Tuesday, and Wednesday of Holy Week are preparation days, both spiritually and physically, for the holy days to come later in the week. Traditions of receiving the sacrament of reconciliation ("confession") during these days are reminiscent of ancient practices. During early centuries repentant sinners were absolved from their sins on Holy Thursday after six weeks or more of public penance. This day was chosen so that all could participate in the solemnities of the Holy Triduum and Easter. Older parishioners still remember when confession lines were long all week. Since the renewal of the sacrament of reconciliation after Vatican II, these crowds are spread out over several weeks. Most take part in popular sacramental communal penance services, often a joint celebration of neighboring parishes. Private confessions are still popular this time of the year.

Easter Duty

Reception of the Eucharist on the part of the laity became rare starting early in the Middle Ages. Feelings of personal unworthiness to receive Christ in communion resulted from an exaggerated emphasis on Christ's divinity in relation to his humanness and sacramental presence. It became more popular to look at and adore the Blessed Sacrament rather than to "take and eat." Communion eventually become so rare that the church began to mandate that it be received at least once a year on Easter Sunday (Council of the Lateran, 1215). This become known as the "Easter duty." Time for one's Easter duty was eventually extended to the period between the First Sunday of Lent and Trinity Sunday (first Sunday after Pentecost). This paschal precept remains in the Code of Canon Law (Canon 920): "Once admitted to the blessed Eucharist, each of the faithful is obliged to receive holy Communion at least once a year...during Paschal Time."

The presumption was that confession must be part of the Easter duty. The confession of grave sins remains the current law of the church (Canon 989): "All the faithful who have reached the age of discretion are bound to confess their grave sins at least once a year." Evidence in the 8th century of an annual private confession at the beginning of Lent comes from the Frankish kingdom. Absolution was then given on Holy Thursday as part of the absolution of public penitents.

Spring Cleaning

Other preparation activities were associated at one time with the first days of Holy Week. One, perhaps a matter of trivia, is the custom of spring cleaning. This practical activity was associated early in history with preparation for the celebration of Easter. Its parallel is the custom in Jewish families to rid the home of "the old" in preparation for Passover.

Holy Thursday

Holy Thursday begins the Triduum, which from the 4th century celebrated the Paschal Mystery. Originally these three days began on Good Friday. It was natural, however, to include Holy Thursday because Good Friday was reckoned from sunset on the previous evening. The oldest and still official name of this day is Thursday of the Lord's Supper. It commemorates the historical gospel events surrounding the Last Supper and the institution of the Holy Eucharist. Maundy Thursday, another popular title in English-speaking countries, comes from the solemn ritual of washing of feet in imitation of Jesus at his Last Supper. The title is a corruption of *mandatum* (Latin, "commandment") from the words of Jesus sung as the washing begins: "A new commandment I give you..."(John 13:34).

Originally Holy Thursday was a practical preparation for the three-day celebration of the Paschal Mystery rather than a part of it. On this day repentant sinners were absolved and re-incorporated into the parish community so that they could participate in the paschal festivities. New oils needed to be consecrated for use at baptisms and confirmations at the Easter Vigil.

The observance of the Lord's Supper in Jerusalem at the traditional place and approximate hour eventually influenced the universal church to imitate the tradition. Remembering the institution of the Holy Eucharist is the heart of Holy Thursday observance. Parish liturgies, once again since 1955, take place in the evening with joyful overtones. Bells ring and festive colors are used for vestments and decorations. The Glory to God, not sung since Ash Wednesday, returns for this brief moment. The tabernacle is empty so that all might receive communion from bread consecrated at this Mass.

The tradition of avoiding the joyful sound of bells during the rest of the Triduum began in the 9th century in the Carolingian kingdom. It symbolized the humiliation and suffering of Jesus. In place of bells, wooden noisemakers called clappers were used.

Washing of Feet
The Holy Thursday ritual has included a ceremonial washing of feet by the presiding celebrant since the 5th century in some local churches, since the late 7th century in Spain and Gaul, and the 12th in Rome. This ritual imitates Jesus' Last Supper action of humility and service. Appropriate songs are sung during this symbolic washing. Twelve participants are chosen from the parish at large or from those in parish leadership positions. Some parishes deliberately choose these "twelve apostles" from the very poor or "rejected" citizens to emphasize the theme of service. In the early church this ritual was common during the year as an act of charity and was even considered a sacrament.

Chapel of Adoration
At the end of the Holy Thursday liturgy, consecrated communion bread is carried in procession with incense and song to a chapel of adoration. It will be received the next day in communion. After placing the consecrated bread in the tabernacle, an atmosphere of quiet waiting with the Lord begins. It is popular that parishioners spend a holy hour sometime before midnight in the adoration chapel.

Stripping the Altar
The first hints of a new theme quickly become obvious: an anticipa-

tion of suffering and death. The altar table, symbolic of Christ, is stripped in silence. At times in the past, this action was considered symbolic of the stripping of Jesus before his crucifixion. In early centuries, however, as is again the practice today, the altar table was stripped without ceremony after every Mass. This is an example of the many ancient liturgical customs preserved over the centuries during Holy Week and reinstated in the post-Vatican II liturgical reform.

People begin leaving quietly for their homes. An atmosphere of sadness and reflection begins. Until recent times popular thinking considered these hours as a "wake" before the tomb, anticipating Good Friday. More properly, they are hours of "waiting" with Jesus as the saving events begin to unfold.

Forty Hours Devotion

A kind of Forty Hours Devotion was observed in these ancient Holy Thursday traditions surrounding the reservation of the Eucharist to be used on Good Friday. In the 10th century, the practice began in some churches of wrapping the crucifix venerated on Good Friday, or the corpus alone, in a cloth. It was laid in a symbolic tomb. In some areas consecrated hosts were added. This began forty hours of prayer, lasting until the Easter Vigil. Then on Holy Saturday afternoon or Easter morning the resurrection was celebrated by bringing the Blessed Sacrament from the "tomb" and enthroning it on the main altar where it was venerated. When the Easter Vigil was moved to Holy Saturday morning, these forty hours of prayer had to begin on Holy Thursday. The more popular form of Forty Hours Devotion began in the 16th century.

Chrism Mass

Earlier in the day of Holy Thursday (now in many dioceses anticipated for practical reasons on Tuesday of Holy Week) the bishop, clergy, and parish delegations of the laity gather at the cathedral church. There, in solemn ritual, the holy oils used during the year in parishes throughout the diocese are consecrated. These are the oil of catechumens (pure olive oil used to anoint those preparing for baptism), oil of chrism (pure olive oil mixed with fragrant balm, used in baptism, confirmation, and ordination), oil of the sick (pure olive oil used in the sacrament of the anointing of the sick). Parish representatives carry these oils back home where they will be part of their parish's celebration of sacraments for the coming year, beginning with the Easter Vigil.

Holy Thursday has not attracted many popular traditions. The main one is the waiting with the Lord in the parish chapel of adoration until midnight.

Seder

Another popular tradition today, observed in some parishes, is the eating of the Seder meal (Hebrew, "order" of the four cups of blessing). This is the sacred meal eaten by the Jews during the Passover and the meal from which ritual elements of the Mass were taken. The ritual is conducted by the father of the group. It features telling the original story of the Passover and the eating of these symbolic foods: matzoh (or unleavened bread), morar (bitter herbs representing the bitterness of slavery in Egypt), haroset (representing the brick mortar used by the enslaved Hebrews in building the Pharaoh's cities), parsley and boiled eggs (symbolic of springtime and new life), dipped into salt water (symbolic of the tears of the Israelites). At the heart of the ritual is the blessing of unleavened bread and cups of wine and a repeated eating and drinking of these symbolic foods.

Used in a Christian context, the eating of the Seder often includes references to the actions of Jesus at the Last Supper. Today many liturgists question this Christian celebration of the Seder meal. It is a very precious Jewish tradition and a Christian use of it might seem disrespectful. Christians, however, might benefit from participating in a real Seder meal with Jewish friends. Some parishes have begun a tradition of a brief memorial ritual and a parish supper preceding the liturgy of the Lord's Supper.

One of the ancient names of Holy Thursday was Pure, or Clean, Thursday. This title remembers two ancient liturgical rituals: absolving repentant sinners, and cleaning and washing the stripped altar on this day. It also reflects the popularity in ancient times—when frequent bathing was unheard of—of actual physical cleansing in preparation for Easter: washing, bathing, and shaving. This was a "spring cleaning" of the body!

Good Friday

Good Friday is the anniversary of the death of Jesus on the cross just outside the walls of Jerusalem. This moment will be completed the following day as the Saturday night hours change into Sunday and death turns into resurrection. The origin of the term "Good" in the title of this day is unknown, but probably emphasizes the saving value of the historical event of the crucifixion of Jesus. Another theory is that it is a corruption of "God's" Friday. The theme of this day throughout history has been one of quiet sadness and mourning for the crucified and dead Jesus.

On this one day of the year the Eucharist is not celebrated in its usual form of the Mass. During the first centuries no Eucharist was celebrated on weekdays. This customary absence of weekday Eucharist took on special meaning for Good Friday when the sacrificial dimension of the Mass began to be emphasized. The absence of Mass respects the historical sacrificial action of Jesus on the cross. Consequently, the church emphasized a liturgy of the word with a reading of the passion narrative and psalms prophesying the suffering of Jesus.

The church's Good Friday liturgy takes place in the afternoon or evening hours. It is the finest example of the prayer services held regularly in parish churches in ancient times before daily Mass became popular. The emphasis is on Scripture reading and prayers. The readings from both the Hebrew and Christian Scriptures develop the theme of Jesus' suffering and death. The prayers continue the ancient practice of general intercessions, now a part of all Masses, the Prayer of the Faithful.

Veneration of the Cross

Late in the 4th century, the veneration of the cross was introduced into Good Friday traditions in Jerusalem. Generations before, according to legends, Helen, the mother of the first Christian emperor, Constantine, discovered in the Jerusalem area the cross on which Jesus was crucified. It became an annual tradition at Jerusalem to offer the cross for the faithful to kiss and venerate. Later this custom, and fragments of the cross, relics, spread throughout the Roman Empire. It was incorporated into the Roman liturgy by the 8th century. The slow procession of people to kiss a cross held by ministers remains a dramatic feature of today's Good Friday services. Until recent times the celebrant and servers, without shoes, approached the cross with a series of genuflections before kissing it.

Mass of the Pre-Sanctified

During the Middle Ages the simple communion service of the Good Friday liturgy evolved into the Mass of the Pre-Sanctified ("Mass" with bread consecrated the day before). The ritual began to imitate a regular Mass without the Eucharistic Prayer. Early in its history the laity stopped receiving communion just as they had at any Mass. The priest alone, therefore, received communion on Good Friday. In 1955, the traditional ritual was restored: the Liturgy of the Word, the veneration of the cross, and communion by the people.

Fasting
Good Friday fasting expressed personal penance and sadness over the death of Jesus. As early as the 2nd century, this tradition of fasting, sometimes from all food and drink, was observed for forty hours. It prepares for the Easter festivities and has always been a characteristic of Good Friday. In many places in the church this custom of fasting was very severe, more severe than official church discipline asked for. Remnants of this tradition are still evident. On this day, some families abstain not only from from meat (the church discipline) but also from such ordinary foods as dairy products. Some—strange to the casual observer—customs still prevail on this day, for example, toast deliberately burned.

An atmosphere of quiet and even silence prevails in many families, with a curtailing of radio, television, and secular music. Until recent times almost all of secular culture respected the spirit of Good Friday. Most businesses and places of employment were closed from noon until 3 P.M. Today this custom is observed only in scattered places.

Tre Ore
Many parishioners still remember the Tre Ore (Italian, "three hours") Good Friday services in their parish churches. This tradition incorporated the official Good Friday liturgy and expanded it to three hours, the amount of time Jesus spent on the cross. There were popular prayers and devotions such as the Stations of the Cross, rosary, and sermons on the last words of Jesus. These devotions remain popular in some parishes. This Tre Ore tradition began in Lima, Peru, in 1732. It spread to the other Latin American countries, and then to England, Italy, and the United States. It never became popular in other countries.

The Tre Ore tradition is very mild compared to customs elsewhere. It was popular in some countries, especially in Latin America, to hold elaborate funeral processions on Good Friday, carrying a statue of the dead Jesus. These ended at "tombs," often with the Blessed Sacrament present, where people came to visit as at a wake.

Hot Cross Buns
In England, as mentioned previously, it was a popular custom to bake sweet buns, ice them with a cross, and eat them on Good Friday.

These hot cross buns eventually became a popular food eaten all during Lent. In early Christianity these buns were flat, unleavened imitations of the Passover bread. There is a possibility that this tradition originated in pre-Christian times. Egyptians used small loaves, stamped with horns, in the worship of the Mother Goddess, Isis. Greeks used cakes stamped with a cross in their devotions to goddess Diana.

11

THE EASTER VIGIL

In the midst of the early dark of night a fire begins to flicker outside the church. An Easter Candle, boldly marked with the symbols of the current year and of Christ's divinity and glorious suffering, is lit from the new fire. It is carried prominently into the midst of the people. There it is heralded with joyful song: "Light of Christ...Come, let us adore him." From this one light, the candles of hundreds of assembled believers are lit until the church is ablaze with new light. A cantor sings an ancient and beautiful song (*Exultet*, "Rejoice") before the Easter Candle. Powerful Scripture readings about water and new creation are proclaimed. An Easter water is blessed with the singing of the Litany of Saints and with sacred oils consecrated just days before. Catechumens step forward, speak their baptismal vows with the supportive voices of the congregation around them, and are baptized. Bells ring out. Flowers, especially Easter lilies, and joyful banners decorate the sanctuary. Alleluias are sung for the first time in six weeks. Jesus Christ is risen from the dead!

No other moment of the church year is as rich in powerful and early symbolism as the Easter Vigil. It is *the* night of all nights. It is the heart of Christianity. It is Easter!

The daytime hours of Holy Saturday, continuing the atmosphere of Good Friday, have been observed as a time of quiet and fasting from the earliest centuries. The day had no liturgy or religious traditions of its own. There was an atmosphere of anticipation for the coming of night and for the celebration of the resurrection.

Easter Vigil
An annual celebration of the Lord's resurrection goes back to the first generation of Christianity. For the first three centuries this was the only feast observed throughout the church. This original celebration of what would become Easter was done by way of a vigil (Latin *vigilia*, "a watch," or "waiting"). It was natural that Christians chose the night hours to celebrate their religious experience of a Christ victorious over

death and sin and their victory along with his. It was during those dark hours, turning into the first day of the week (Sunday), that this mystery had occurred (Matthew 28:11; Mark 16:1; Luke 24:1; John 20:1).

It was a common belief in early Christianity that the risen Lord would return during these night hours of the Easter Vigil. It was natural, therefore, that all be present and waiting. This would be his final and glorious coming, and the end of time still proclaimed today with faith during each Mass: "Christ has died, Christ is risen, Christ will come again!"

With some modifications, especially in length, today's renewed ritual echoes that of early centuries. As soon as the evening star became visible, the night-long ritual began. The first hours were spent in Scripture readings and prayers. The readings from Scripture, usually twelve in all, emphasized a prophetic theme of a new creation and salvation through water, such as the story of creation, the fall, the flood, the sacrifice of Isaac, the Passover, the crossing of the "Reed Sea," and the entry into the Promised Land.

As the hours of the night unfolded, this theme was ritualized in a new creation through the waters of baptism, especially the baptism of adults. This ritual, which gave a distinct theme to the Easter Vigil, began with the solemn blessing of the Easter water, with a chanting of the Litany of Saints, by plunging the lit Easter Candle into the water, and by mixing it with holy oils. Then the catechumens who had been in preparation, sometimes for years, renounced Satan's influence on their former lives, confessed their faith, and were baptized, anointed, and dressed in white robes. By the 5th century, in the Roman church, a second anointing, or chrismation, was done by the bishop. This would evolve into the sacrament of confirmation.

During the first centuries it was a tradition to give blessed milk and honey to those newly baptized. This gesture symbolized that the newly baptized were infants in the faith, called neophytes. It also symbolized their having just crossed over into the new Promised Land flowing with milk and honey. This practice, marking an important moment in life, was borrowed from pagan mystery cults.

Finally, as the hours of vigil approached dawn, the newly baptized shared the Eucharist for the first time with the community of believers.

Easter Fire
The impressive blessing and lighting of the Easter fire, which still

begins the vigil today, was not part of the ritual in ancient times. Among the Germanic people in pre-Christian times, bonfires in honor of pagan deities were popular to announce the beginning of spring and to assure good crops. After Christianity spread among these people, the church forbade these spring bonfires as a pagan practice. During the 6th and 7th centuries, however, Irish missionaries brought to the continent a tradition of blessing a bonfire outside of the church on Holy Saturday night. This tradition had been started by St. Patrick to counter the influence of spring bonfires among the Celtic Druids. The tradition became popular in the Carolingian empire, spread to Rome, and eventually was incorporated into the liturgy of the Easter Vigil.

The lighting of a new Easter fire also had a practical purpose. The lamps in church used to be extinguished Holy Thursday night. Consequently, a new fire had to be lit for the celebrant and readers to see by.

Easter Candle

The lighting of the Easter Candle seems to have originated in the ancient daily ritual of *Lucernare* ("lighting of the lamps"), as darkness fell. The tradition of lighting candles held by people present began in Rome in the early centuries. There the dark of night at the Easter Vigil was filled with candles symbolic of the resurrected Christ.

In the Frankish kingdom, further symbolism was added to the Easter Candle and continues today at the discretion of the pastor. A cross is cut or traced into it with the proclamation: "Christ yesterday and today, the beginning and the end," adding the first and last letters of the Greek alphabet, "Alpha and Omega." The numbers of the current year are added in the four angles of the crossbars with the proclamation: "All time belongs to him and all the ages; to him be glory and power through every age forever. Amen." Four grains of incense, sealed with wax red nails, are inserted at the ends of the crossbars, and one is inserted where the crossbars meet with the words: "By his holy...and glorious wounds...may Christ our Lord ...guard us...and keep us. Amen."

Holy Saturday Morning Liturgy

In the early 400s, the number of adults baptized became fewer and infant baptism was the usual situation. Since the Easter Vigil no longer needed so many hours, the concluding Eucharist began to be celebrated before midnight by the 6th century and during the early hours of Saturday evening by the middle of the 8th. During the 6th century, an Easter Sunday morning Mass had become popular. Over the years, the vigil was celebrated earlier and earlier. In the Missal of Pius V (1570) it became fixed by church law as an early Holy Saturday morning liturgy, preserving its original form except for baptisms. The entire symbolism of the original night vigil was kept, but now had no meaning. Because of its length, often several hours, and because it had lost its original meaning as *the* celebration of the resurrection, the Easter Vigil was poorly attended by parishioners. It was not uncommon for parishioners, carrying containers, to arrive toward the conclusion to get some new Easter water to use at home as a sacramental. Most parishioners considered Easter Sunday morning Mass as the normal celebration of the Lord's resurrection.

Renewal of Easter Vigil

Today the Easter Vigil has regained its rightful place as the most important ritual of the year and as the primary celebration of Easter. This happened first in 1951 by way of experiment and was finalized in 1955. In its renewed form, the Easter Vigil is almost the same as that in early centuries, except that the ritual takes about two hours rather than all night. It has four clearly defined parts: the service of light, the liturgy of the word, the celebration of baptism, and the Eucharist.

The renewal of the Easter Vigil has resulted in what seems like two Easters in the typical parish. Each year, however, the Easter Vigil is becoming for more and more parishioners what it had been in its origin: the night of all nights and the primary celebration of resurrection, or Easter. The renewal of the adult catechumenate in parishes has added an important feature to the Easter Vigil that had been lost for centuries: the baptism of adults. For other parishioners, Easter Sunday morning Mass, officially the second Easter Mass, is still the Easter experience.

The elaborate and beautiful ritual of the Easter Vigil calls for extensive preparation by the parish team and many other parishioners. The church is decorated, sacramentals of oil, incense, water, and fire are readied, and the liturgy is rehearsed. Adult catechumens begin their final hours of preparation.

Until recent decades Holy Saturday was a day of fasting and partial abstinence (meat was permitted only at the principal meal) in preparation for the greatest feast of the year. This discipline of fasting continued even when the solemnities of the Easter Vigil were celebrated during the early morning hours of Holy Saturday, concluding with all the joyful overtones of Easter. It was a reminder that the mystery of Easter was still associated with the night hours and early Sunday morning.

In recent years this tradition of fasting has returned with the renewal of the adult catechumenate. Adults preparing for baptism at the Easter Vigil usually spend some time in a mini-retreat with fasting and prayer as the hours of the Easter Vigil approach.

Blessing of Easter Baskets

Popular traditions on Holy Saturday are associated in some way with preparations for the festivities of Easter. On this day or during the days preceding, eggs are boiled and dyed, Easter clothes are purchased, and foods prepared. The blessing of special foods for Easter is still a popular tradition, especially among people of Polish ancestry. Baskets of food are brought to church where they are blessed by the pastor.

12

EASTER

Spring is in the air. Something new seems to be brewing. The past few months have not been very exciting. In fact, there have been depressing moments. Every once in a while the weather hinted of spring. But the hints did not last long. Families suffered from cabin fever. A quarter of the year has passed since the cheerfulness of Christmas. But now there seems to be promise of something new and good.

The past six weeks in the parish have been intense. The call to conversion has echoed repeatedly. It has been a season of penance: not much excitement there! Decorations have been subdued. The ritual journey during the past week, Holy Week, has been full of symbolism. The waving of palms gave way to a passion story. A supper banquet gave way to a cross. And last night the cross gave way to a new fire, new oils, new water—and new life.

It is obvious that something wonderful has happened as people walk into church. They are greeted by a church decorated with signs of new life: bright colors and Easter lilies. Alleluias ring out. It is Easter morning!

For many, if not most, parishioners, this is the celebration of Easter. In every parish, however, the main celebration occurred the night before with the Easter Vigil. Sunday morning Easter Mass evolved in history when the Easter Vigil was anticipated during the early morning hours of Holy Saturday.

The theme of Easter morning echoes that of the Easter Vigil. It remembers and celebrates the very foundation of Christianity: Jesus is raised from the dead and is Lord. Those who believe and are baptized share in this resurrection to new life. This theme will continue for the next fifty days of the Easter season.

It was natural that the very first followers of Jesus would hold this moment sacred. It was the anniversary of that wonderful time when they experienced him risen and still among them. His death had occurred on the most important of all Jewish feasts: the Passover. His resurrection fulfilled all that the Passover had meant to them as Jews.

It was an exodus, or passage, from the old times and the oppression of slavery to spiritual freedom. Jesus was the Paschal Lamb, slain to achieve this freedom.

Christ's resurrection was the sign of new beginnings: a springtime. This theme was part of the evolution of the Passover long before the Exodus from Egypt. The ancestors of the Jews had celebrated a springtime festival of the first fruits of their planting with a sacrifice of grains and breads, and the first fruits of their flocks with a sacrifice of lambs. Eventually these feasts were combined as an annual memorial of the mystery of their escape from Egypt, and the passing over them by the angel of death. For 3000 years, and still today, Jews celebrate this drama of miraculous salvation by repeating the ancient story with song, readings, and symbolic foods: the Seder meal. Now, as throughout history, the ritual is observed in the evening of the fourteenth day of the month of Nisan on the Jewish lunar calendar.

It was the Seder meal of this Passover that Jesus celebrated with his friends the night before his crucifixion, with the request that it be celebrated in a new way in his memory. This they did on the weekly anniversary of his resurrection, the first day of the week, Sunday. It was only natural that the annual anniversary be highlighted with special solemnity.

Date of Easter

Early in Christianity a controversy arose over setting the date of the annual Pascha. Some, called the *Quartodecimans* (Latin, "fourteenth"), claimed that it should be celebrated annually on the precise date of Jesus' historical Passover: the 14th of Nisan (first day of the full moon that followed the spring equinox), usually a weekday. Others insisted that it always be a Sunday, because Christ was raised from the dead on the first day of the week. This controversy was a high priority on the agenda at the Council of Nicaea called by Emperor Constantine in 325. The decision was that it be observed on the Sunday following the first full moon after the spring equinox. In the West, only the Celtic church in Britain and Ireland refused to accept the date until 664 because of their own Celtic calendar. Easter can occur on any Sunday from March 23 to April 25.

Fertility Theme

From very early times the baptism of new Christians took place during this annual ritual. This practice evolved because of the intimate bond between the resurrection of Jesus to new life and the new birth of the baptized. This Easter theme of new life has overtones of *fertility*. Another religious movement was popular in the Roman Empire during the generations when Christianity was becoming popular. These were the pagan fertility cults. There is little evidence that Christianity deliberately borrowed beliefs and practices from these cults. It is natural, however, that it be influenced by these cults just as it is always influenced by the real world in which it thrives.

One example of a fertility theme occurs during the Easter Vigil: the emphasis on fire and water. This may have been influenced by a contemporary Roman spring festival of fire and water which had fertility overtones: fire being a male symbol and water the female. During the pagan ritual a flaming torch was plunged into water. Until recent times the blessing of the church's Easter water included a threefold plunging of the lit Easter Candle into it. This fertile water is then used for the rebirth of the baptized. This action of plunging the candle is now optional.

Name of Easter

In almost every language except English, the name for this annual memorial of the resurrection is some form of the word "Passover" (for example, Pasch, from the Hebrew *Pesach*, "Passover"). When Christianity arrived in the north countries, its springtime celebration of the resurrection received a new name from the Teutonic people, a name used today by English-speaking people: Easter. At one time it was thought that this name came from an Anglo-Saxon spring goddess, Eostre. This is how Venerable Bede (d. 735) explained it. However, there is doubt that such a goddess ever existed. A better explanation lies in people's misunderstanding of a Latin phrase for Easter Week, week "in white vestments" or garments of the newly baptized (in *albis*), thinking it was the plural of *alba* in the Latin idiom for "dawn," the birth of the new spring sun in the *east*. This was translated in Old High German as *eostarun*. Regardless of the exact origin of the term, the symbolism remains: Christ is the sun that rises at dawn—in the east.

Easter Sunday Mass

Easter Sunday did not exist in the early church. What is celebrated today as Easter occurred during the night hours preceding dawn on Sunday, the Easter Vigil. This primary celebration of Easter is emphasized once again today (see previous chapter). The Easter Sunday Mass was introduced when the Easter Vigil was anticipated early on Holy Saturday morning. No special rituals accompany Easter Sunday Mass except those that were re-introduced with great solemnity the night before at the Easter Vigil: joyful resurrection songs (especially the Alleluia), baptisms, renewal of baptismal vows, a sprinkling of the congregation with the new Easter water, and the joyful decorations of Easter lilies and banners.

Religious traditions associated with Easter are not all Christian in origin, but most have received a Christian interpretation over the centuries. A different mood is evident during this season than that of Christmas. Yet it is just as exciting and joyful partly because of the evidence of spring in parts of the world thawing out from cold winter months, partly because personal resurrections were achieved through lenten efforts, and partly because the lengthy penitential season of Lent is finally over.

Easter Duty

The church still teaches that "once admitted to the blessed Eucharist, each of the faithful is obliged to receive holy communion at least once a year. This precept must be fulfilled during paschal time, unless for a good reason it is fulfilled at another time during the year" (Canon 920). The need for this law evolved in the Middle Ages when people began staying away from communion out of a sense of unworthiness. The Lateran Council (1215) made it a universal law. The Paschal season extends from the first Sunday of Lent until Trinity Sunday, actually one-fourth of the year.

Sunrise Services

The Easter tradition of sunrise services was already popular in the Middle Ages. In churches these were usually in the form of early morning Mass. In many areas of Europe, however, there was dancing and singing at the first sign of the Easter dawn. These rituals were very possibly a continuation of New Year celebrations that coincided with the spring equinox among many peoples of Europe. They welcomed the new power of the sun and new life in creation.

Sunrise services are popular throughout the United States among Protestant and ecumenical groups. They began in the mid-1700s among members of the Moravian church in Pennsylvania. The famous sunrise service at the Hollywood Bowl began in 1921.

New Easter Clothes

Wearing new Easter clothes may be traced to the new white robes in which the newly baptized at Easter were clothed. They are also symbolic of the newness of resurrection. This symbolism has been lost for most. The practice, still evident today, is probably associated more with the change of seasons along with a desire to look one's best at Easter church services—especially if it is a rare appearance! There is also a possibility that this wearing of new clothes may have originated in ancient times as part of New Year festivities originally held at the spring equinox.

Easter Parade
During the Middle Ages in Europe, people in their new Easter clothes would take a long walk after Easter Mass. This was a kind of procession preceded by a crucifix or the Easter Candle. This tradition was condemned by Protestant reformers. Even though its original meaning was lost, the tradition evolved into the Easter parade. It is still popular in many cities in the United States today, especially on Fifth Avenue in New York.

Easter Lamb
The sacrificed lamb was the key symbol of the Passover Seder. It continued as a symbol of Jesus, the Lamb of God, slain and raised from the dead to gain freedom for all from the slavery of sin and spiritual ignorance. The Easter Lamb became an important symbol in Christian art. It also became popular to include the symbol among Easter decorations and to bake Easter breads and cakes in the shape of a lamb.

Easter Ham
From ancient times in Europe, cooked ham was as popular as lamb for festive occasions. It is natural that it grace the table on this, the greatest of all feasts.

Easter Eggs
The egg has become a popular Easter symbol. Creation myths of many ancient peoples center in a cosmogenic egg from which the universe is born. The egg, therefore, is a natural symbol, not only of creation, but also of re-creation and resurrection. In ancient Egypt and Persia friends exchanged decorated eggs at the spring equinox, the beginning of their new year. These eggs were a symbol of fertility for them because the coming forth of a live creature from an egg was so surprising to people of ancient times. Christians of the Near East

adopted this tradition, and the Easter egg became a religious symbol. It represented the tomb from which Jesus came forth to new life. Because eggs were at one time forbidden by the church's lenten discipline of fasting and abstinence, they were a precious Easter food.

Easter eggs are usually given to children, either in Easter baskets or hidden for the children to find. They are first boiled and then dyed with bright colors. Among some ethnic groups these eggs, usually with the contents removed, are painted with elaborate designs. Among the Slavic people these are called *pysanki* ("to design"). The custom of decorating trees outdoors with decorated, hollow Easter eggs originated in Germany.

Easter egg hunts, and even the egg-rolling on the White House lawn, are contemporary versions of egg games played on Easter for centuries in European countries.

Easter Bunnies

Little children are usually told that the Easter eggs are brought by the Easter Bunny. Rabbits are part of pre-Christian fertility symbolism because of their reputation to reproduce rapidly. Their association with Easter eggs goes back several hundred years to vague legends in Germany. There the custom of making candy rabbits also originated. The Easter Bunny has never had a religious meaning.

Easter Lilies

Easter lilies did not exist in the North America until about 100 years ago. The white trumpet lily, which blooms naturally in springtime, was introduced here from Bermuda by Mrs. Thomas P. Sargent. The popular name "Easter lilies" comes from the fact that they bloom around Eastertime. They have become associated with Easter as much as poinsettias are with Christmas. In early Christian art the lily is a symbol of purity because of its delicacy of form and its whiteness. For the same reason it serves well as a symbol of resurrection.

Mystagogia

Easter does not end abruptly. It begins a season. Like all major feasts in the church year, it is celebrated with an octave, a weeklong festival. During the early centuries, those who were baptized at the Easter Vigil would gather daily during Easter Week for further "instructions in the Christian mysteries." called "mystagogia." This mystagogia has been revived today in parishes. Once again, it is an important feature of the newly baptized adults' journey of new faith continuing for the fifty days of Eastertime.

Pentecost

The Easter season lasts for fifty days, ending with *Pentecost* (Greek *pentekoste*, "fiftieth"). Ranking second only to Easter, the feast of Pentecost must be understood in the context of the Jewish feast by the same name. Its other name in Jewish tradition is Feast of Weeks, a full season of seven weeks of thanksgiving beginning with Passover Sabbath (see Tobit 2:1; 2 Maccabees 12:32). This prolonged festival celebrated the theme of harvest and thanksgiving. It evolved before the time of Christ into a memorial of the covenant and, by 300 C.E., a memorial of the giving of the Law.

By the end of the 2nd century, Christians were observing a similar fifty-day festival of rejoicing after the annual Pascha. People prayed standing, and fasting was prohibited. It seems that originally the followers of Jesus continued to observe the Jewish festival, a time of "first fruits" (see 1 Corinthians 16:8, 15:20, 23) rather than a distinctly new theme. During these weeks, fasting and kneeling were forbidden because of the joyful experience of resurrection.

By the late 4th century, the feast of the Ascension was celebrated in some parts of the church on the fortieth day after Easter (see Acts 1:3, 9–11). Originally, this mystery of the ending of Jesus' visible presence among his followers seems to have been observed as part of the outpouring of the Spirit on the 50th day, or Pentecost. For the first time, the original 50-day festival was broken. In many dioceses in the U.S., the Ascension has been moved to Sunday and replaces the seventh Sunday of Easter.

The weekdays between the Ascension and Pentecost are a preparation period for the outpouring of the Spirit. It is popularly called the Pentecost Novena (see Acts 1:14).

Pentecost itself closes out the Easter season. It celebrates the overwhelming experience of God pouring out the Spirit upon the first community of those who believed Jesus was the Lord and Christ (see Acts 2:1–4). Pentecost is called, therefore, the birth of the church or the birth of the church's mission.

The color of vestments and decorations for Pentecost is red. It symbolizes the intense love and fire of the Holy Spirit. Other symbols of the Pentecost event are the dove (see Luke 3:21–22), the tongues of flame (see Acts 2:1–4), and wind (see Acts 2:2).

13

ORDINARY TIME

The Easter cycle and Christmas cycle are so rich with religious traditions that the remainder of the year often seems ordinary at first glance. The remaining 33 or 34 weeks are in fact called Ordinary Time. This title, however, does not mean that these weeks, and the Sundays around which they revolve, are unimportant. On the contrary, it is during these weeks that the special character of Sunday is experienced. Except for four special devotional feasts of Christ after Pentecost, no special theme "distracts" from the wonder of the original meaning of Sunday as the Lord's Day.

Very few religious traditions are directly connected with the weeks of Ordinary Time. The traditional color used for liturgical vestments and church decoration is green, the color of hope and life. Other popular religious traditions occur briefly, but they are connected with other special days that are independent of the liturgical season, such as Halloween and Thanksgiving.

Trinity Sunday
Four solemnities during Ordinary Time are celebrated as devotional feasts of our Lord, officially called Solemnities of the Lord during the Season of the Year. The first of these is Trinity Sunday or the Solemnity of the Trinity. Emphasis on the doctrine of the Trinity evolved in the 4th and 5th centuries when the Arian heresy swept through the church. This heresy denied that Jesus was equal to God. Before the year 1000, a special feast devoted to the Trinity was celebrated in the Frankish kingdom on the Sunday following Pentecost. It was promulgated in the universal church by Pope John XXII in 1334.

Two religious traditions are associated with the Trinity. The Sign of the Cross made on the body in several forms has been popular since early centuries. It is popular to add the trinitarian formula: "In the name of the Father, and of the Son, and of the Holy Spirit. Amen." The *doxology* is another ancient trinitarian prayer that was first used in the Eastern Church: "Glory be to the Father, and to the Son, and to the Holy Spirit." In the early 4th century, the concluding words were added: "As it was in the beginning is now and ever shall be, world without end. Amen." This doxology was introduced in the Western church in the 5th. It is traditional that psalms and hymns end with these prayerful words.

There are several popular symbols used for the Trinity. Since the 6th century, the Trinity has been represented by an older man (the Father), a younger man (the Son), and a dove (the Holy Spirit). Another symbol of the Trinity is a triangle surrounded by light rays with an eye inside. A version of this symbol is on the Great Seal of the United States and is reproduced on the one-dollar bill. Still another symbol is what tradition says was used by St. Patrick, the shamrock.

Corpus Christi

The Solemnity of the Body and Blood of Christ, popularly called by its Latin title, *Corpus Christi* ("Body of Christ"), is celebrated on the second Sunday after Pentecost. Its origin in the 12th century is connected with an exaggerated emphasis on the real presence of Christ in the consecrated bread to be adored to the exclusion of a fuller meaning of Eucharist as celebration, a meal to be eaten. People in the Middle Ages, feeling unworthy to receive Christ in communion, preferred to look at the Blessed Sacrament. This led to the introduction of an elevation of the bread and cup during Mass and ultimately to public displays such as the popular Benediction ritual. The special feast devoted to the Body and Blood of Christ was introduced to the universal church in 1264. A tradition says that St. Thomas Aquinas wrote the prayers and hymns for the feast. Today the former Feast of the Precious Blood on July 1 is incorporated in this solemnity.

Corpus Christi Procession

The most obvious religious tradition associated with this feast is the Corpus Christi procession. It was becoming common already in the late 13th century, and in a hundred years was adopted in most countries. This popular procession included carrying the Blessed Sacrament, visible in a vessel called a monstrance (Latin *monstrare*, "to show"). In Germany the procession even wound its way into the fields, similar to Rogation Day processions. In most places the procession included features of a pageant with lavish decorations and flowers. It was popular to stop at outdoor altars, called stations, where there were prayers, songs, and blessing with the Sacrament.

The motive for the procession was to publicly display a personal faith in the Real Presence.

The Corpus Christi procession is an exercise of devotion and not a liturgical ritual. Its celebration falls, therefore, under the jurisdiction of local bishops. Since Vatican II this tradition has not been observed as in previous centuries. In some places it has been replaced with an outdoor Mass. One of the reasons for its curtailment is the reform and renewal of the liturgy in the post-Vatican II era. The meaning of the Eucharist has been recaptured in the context of a meal and the church's public worship, with most parishioners receiving communion when they participate in the Mass. The original motives for the procession, especially the need to look at the Blessed Sacrament and be blessed by it, instead of "take and eat," no longer apply.

Benediction
Benediction has been a popular tradition since the Middle Ages when people no longer received communion frequently. A consecrated host is put in the monstrance, incensed while hymns are sung, usually the English versions of *O Salutaris* and *Tantum Ergo*. Then the people are blessed with the Blessed Sacrament. This ritually should conclude some kind of prayer service.

Feast of the Sacred Heart
On the Friday following the Solemnity of Corpus Christi is the Solemnity of the Sacred Heart. The theme of this day honors Jesus for the love symbolized by his heart. Devotion to the Sacred Heart became popular with mystics in the 13th and 14th centuries, with special promotion by the Jesuits in the 17th. The tradition became widespread as a result of a series of visions of the Sacred Heart to St. Margaret Mary Alacoque, a French Visitation nun, in 1673-1675. Almost 200 years later, in 1856, a special feast was mandated for the universal church. In 1899, Pope Leo XIII ordered that the world be consecrated to the Most Sacred Heart of Jesus. Pope Pius XI elevated the feast to the same rank as Christmas. There are many religious traditions associated with devotion to the Sacred Heart apart from the feast itself.

Christ the King
Another devotional feast dedicated to Christ during the Ordinary Time of the year is that of Christ the King. It was established by Pope Pius XI in 1925 as a spiritual weapon against what were considered

destructive forces of the age: increasing atheism and secularization. The year 1925 was also the 16th centenary of the First Council of Nicaea, which taught the unity of Christ with the Father and, therefore, with the Father's rule.

The Feast of Our Lord Jesus Christ, Universal King, was originally celebrated on the last Sunday of October. More recently it has been moved to the final Sunday of the church year. This is its proper context because the church year ends with Sunday Scripture readings emphasizing the endtimes and the fulfillment of the pilgrimage of the church and of its Lord. This special Sunday becomes a sort of "final Lord's Day." Other than the liturgical celebrations in churches, the feast of Christ the King has attracted no particular popular religious traditions.

PART FOUR

THE SANCTORAL CYCLE

COMMUNION OF SAINTS

MARY

PURGATORY

POPULAR SAINTS AND LEGENDS

14

COMMUNION OF SAINTS

We name our children after them at baptism. We name our churches after them, too. We look to them as models for our own struggling faith. When we need a special favor we tend to go to them. We venerate their relics and images. We remember some of them with festivals. Some of their names, coming from ancient times and peoples, sound strange to our contemporary ears. Until recently, many of their names were kept alive only by nuns who took their names at profession of vows.

Devotion to saints, with Mary having the highest priority, is a distinguishing feature of Catholicism. This tradition goes back to the early generations of Christianity. It was modified in emphasis, but not cancelled, by reform efforts following the Second Vatican Council.

Throughout the centuries the church community honored saints by reading their names during the Eucharistic Prayer and by celebrating their feast days on its annual church calendar. This latter practice gave rise to the sanctoral cycle in the church year, sometimes seeming to rival the more important temporal cycle that remembers the basic events and mysteries of Christianity.

Religious traditions associated with saints were not planned by the church. Like the liturgical seasons of the church year and traditions associated with them, devotion to saints and the sanctoral cycle just happened among the people. As the church reflected on these practices, it began to understand itself as a communion of saints.

Martyrs and Persecution
The first traditions began by honoring martyrs. These were Christians who testified to their faith with death. Some of the earliest martyrs died as a result of struggles within the Jewish synagogue system. As followers of Jesus began to express a religious identity centered in Christ as Lord, they clashed with religious authorities who sometimes called for their deaths. This happened to St. Stephen (Acts 6:8–15, 7:1–60). Years later, the apostle Paul was turned over to the

Roman officials by synagogue leaders and eventually put to death. Before his conversion to Christianity, Paul had cooperated with the death of Stephen and had actively persecuted Christians (Acts 8:1–3, 22:4).

Intermittent persecutions by the civil government of the Roman Empire produced tens of thousands of martyrs. These persecutions occurred from the time of Emperor Nero in 67 until Emperor Constantine's decree of freedom in 313. People who live in a nation with a strong commitment to freedom of worship, as in the United States, might find it difficult to appreciate a time when the public practice of faith could lead to execution.

The Roman Empire was co-extensive with those geographical areas where Christianity was becoming popular. A clash between the two was inevitable. The church refused to recognize the legitimacy of the empire's deities, including the divinity claimed by the emperors themselves. Civil law, enforced by branches of government equivalent to our state, country, township, and city, forbade the active practice of the Christian faith and assemblies for this purpose. The enforcement of this law was haphazard, often depending upon the bias or political advantage of those in power.

During times of active persecution, Christians assembled secretly, possibly using secret codes to identify each other. When arrested, many bravely and publicly chose death rather than deny their faith. Some early controversies within the church were related to these persecutions; for example, did those who weakened and denied their faith have to be rebaptized?

Friends and co-believers gathered at the burial places of martyrs on their death anniversaries, which were called birthdays because the saints had been born to eternal glory on that day. Martyrs ("witnesses") were honored because they had imitated Jesus' own paschal mystery of bloody suffering and death. The Second Vatican Council underscores this truth: "By celebrating the passage of these saints from earth to heaven, the church proclaims the paschal mystery as achieved in the saints who have suffered and been glorified with Christ" (Constitution on the Sacred Liturgy, 104).

It was common for pagans, too, to remember dead relatives and friends at their graves on the annual anniversaries of death, with meals and sometimes with sacrifices. Christians, however, remembered martyrs with a joyous sense of victory. At the actual places of burial, they would read accounts of their deaths and celebrate the Eucharist. These tombs of martyrs were clearly identified and cared for because civil authority, even during times of persecution, usually allowed respectful and even public burial. Altars and chapels—and eventually large basilicas—were built over these tombs.

Fundamental to the veneration of saints is Christianity's religious conviction that there is life after death and eternal victory for the saved. The newly formed Scriptures spoke of this conviction already at the turn of the first century. In Revelation 14:13, the Spirit calls out: "Happy now are the dead who die in the Lord! ...they shall find rest from their labors, for their good works accompany them." This same Scripture describes these victorious saints as being specially sealed (14:1–5), and classifies them as "...saints, apostles, and prophets" (18:20).

Special honor was given to martyrs: "When the Lamb broke open the fifth seal, I saw under the altar the spirits of those who had been martyred because of the witness they bore to the word of God" (6:9). Tradition indicates that most, if not all, of the original apostles were put to death. The apostles Peter and Paul became martyrs when the early community in Rome suffered its first persecution under Emperor Nero in 67 C.E.

Polycarp, bishop of Smyrna (c. 155), was probably the first martyr to be given cultic veneration. This practice was not invented by Christians. Cultic veneration of the dead is rooted in Jewish traditions surrounding the veneration of the tombs of patriarchs, prophets, martyrs, and, later, rabbis of special reputation and influence.

Confessors
During the first centuries, some Christians publicly testified to their faith before civil tribunals but were not put to death. These were called confessors. They suffered exile, torture, and prison. After their death, they received the same honor that martyrs did. St. Nicholas, bishop of Myra, was such a confessor (d. 350). Devotion to this saint would contribute to modern Christmas customs and his name would be taken over by the Santa Claus myth.

Other Saints
A third kind of saint was honored beginning in the late 4th century. These were virgins and ascetics. Among the ascetics were monks who fled to deserts in Egypt after the end of persecutions. They wanted to find holiness and attachment to Christ by rejecting what they considered a corrupt world. Their lifestyle and sometimes extreme asceticism were likened to martyrdom.

Spread of Devotion to Saints

Until the 5th century, saints were honored only in the city or village where they lived and died. Each locality kept a list of its own saints and a record of the death of martyrs, confessors, bishops (who often were martyrs or confessors), and other holy men and women. Their names were read during the Eucharistic Prayer. In large cities where the Christian population was large and persecution was severe, for example in Rome and Antioch, notaries were appointed to keep these records. During some persecutions the numbers were so great that only the records of the better known were kept. The others were honored with one Feast of All Martyrs already in the 5th century. This evolved later into our Feast of All Saints.

In the 5th century, local churches began to borrow lists from each other, especially names of saints who had universal appeal. This practice was often accompanied by the sharing of relics (a venerated portion of a saint's body; see page 113). These relics were considered a pledge of special protection for the community. An annual celebration evolved around these patrons.

Some local churches borrowed saints from others simply because they had none of their own. For example, the Germanic tribes, after their conversion, borrowed lists from Rome because they did not have a Christian past to remember. To this list they added their own holy men and women.

During the Middle Ages, lists of those saints who had a universal meaning or appeal for all church communities became systematized. These were saints whose lives and ministries had benefited the church in an extraordinary way. During the 9th century, there was consensus on the apostles and evangelists (Matthew, Mark, Luke, John), and martyred popes were added to the universal list in the 11th century. Eventually, the Roman list included saints from other localities, and the list became representative of the universal church. When it became popular for local churches to adopt the Roman liturgical books, the list of saints, too, was adopted.

At the end of the 12th century, "modern" saints were added to the universal list for the first time. The first was St. Thomas à Becket, Archbishop of Canterbury, martyred in 1170. Others were members of new religious orders such as the Franciscans and Dominicans. Unfortunately, the veneration of so many saints from the clergy and religious life implied that heroic holiness could be achieved only by church leaders, isolated from the cares and turmoil of family life and secular employment. This tendency to canonize saints from religious communities has continued into recent times. It is becoming a priority today, however, to balance this with saints of both genders from among the laity.

Abuses

In the Middle Ages, abuses in the veneration of saints were widespread. Invocation of their assistance replaced imitation and veneration. As people became obsessed with miracles, possession of relics became almost pledges of miracles. Shrines, filled with these relics, often replaced local churches and the Eucharist in importance.

Reformers attacked the veneration of saints because of the abuses surrounding it, including the practice of seeking indulgences attached to relics and pilgrimages to shrines.

Abuses have continued into contemporary times. Superstitious practices, such as burying a statue of St. Joseph to sell property, continue in some places.

Communion of Saints

The practical faith of Christians regarding saints is a living out of the church's understanding of itself as a communion of saints. This belief, found already in the Apostles Creed by the late 5th century, goes back much further in popular practice. It describes the church as a community or fellowship of all the faithful, living and dead, called together by God and transformed in Christ and the Spirit. This whole community is present and is most effectively expressed and celebrated whenever people gather for the Eucharist.

In the traditional language, this fellowship of the faithful includes the church triumphant (saints in heaven), the church militant (pilgrim church on earth), and the church suffering (those in purgatory). This doctrine was reaffirmed by the Second Vatican Council: "For all who belong to Christ, having his Spirit, form one church and cleave together in him (see Ephesians 4:16). Therefore, the union of the wayfarers with the brethren who have gone to sleep in the peace of Christ is not in the least interrupted. On the contrary, according to the perennial faith of the church, it is strengthened through the exchanging of spiritual goods" (Dogmatic Constitution on the Church, 49).

Remembering the Saints

An ancient tradition is to remember saints by reading their names during the Eucharistic Prayer. This practice continues in the liturgy today. Eucharistic Prayer I preserves the ancient Roman list but gives the presider the option to shorten it: "In union with the whole Church we honor Mary, the ever-virgin mother of Jesus Christ our Lord and God. We honor Joseph, her husband, the apostles and martyrs Peter and Paul, Andrew, (James, John, Thomas, James, Philip, Bartholomew, Matthew, Simon and Jude; we honor Linus, Cletus, Clement, Sixtus, Cornelius, Cyprian, Lawrence, Chrysogonus, John, and Paul, Cosmas and Damian), and all the saints. May their merits and prayers gain us your constant help and protection."

Later the presider prays: "For ourselves, too, we ask some share in the fellowship of your apostles and martyrs, with John the Baptist, Stephen, Matthias, Barnabas (Ignatius, Alexander, Marcellinus, Peter, Felicity, Perpetua, Agatha, Lucy, Agnes, Cecilia, Anastasia), and all the saints."

Patron Saints
The tradition of taking a saint's name in baptism began in Germany and France in the Middle Ages. This custom soon spread throughout the church. The exception was Ireland until after the Norman invasion (1066), in the 11th century. There it was considered at first an irreverence. A baptismal saint becomes a special and personal patron, protecting the person who bears her or his name. It was expected that the baptized eventually learn the story of their patron saints, model themselves after them, and pray to them for guidance and protection. In Catholic countries today, it is still a custom to emphasize the annual feast day of the patron saint more than a person's birthday.

Taking a particular saint as a patron and model of one's own personal faith might seem somewhat out of character for contemporary believers. These saints lived in such different times. Their lives, however, continue to testify to how a baptized person can walk with the mystery of God and thrive in faith. Their lives tell how the Good News of the gospel can be lived in a practical way. This does not mean that people of today should copy saints in some external way. They can be, however, a stimulus to one's own personal efforts to follow the way of Jesus in our own time, situation, and culture.

Today this tradition of giving a particular saint's name at baptism is often ignored. The church still recommends that a saint's name be chosen, and by law (Canon 855) counsels the parents, sponsors, and the pastor to see that a name foreign to a Christian mentality is not chosen.

A variation of giving a saint's name in baptism is the sanctifying of geographical locations. Centuries ago, it was the practice of Catholic explorers and founders of future cities to name sites after an attribute of Jesus or a name of Mary or a particular saint. Hundreds of geographical locations in the United States were named in this way by the Spanish and French; for example: San Diego (St. James), San Francisco, Los Angeles, St. Louis, and Corpus Christi. Thousands of towns and cities today are named after some saint.

Holy Days

It was common in the Middle Ages to honor saints with holy days of obligation. In the early 10th century, all of the apostles were honored in this way. So, too, were St. Michael, St. Stephen, St. John the Baptist, and other saints from the early centuries. In the United States only the general feast of All Saints on November 1, along with Christmas, January 1, Ascension Thursday (when not moved to the following Sunday), Assumption of the Blessed Virgin Mary on August 15, and Feast of the Immaculate Conception on December 8 are holy days of obligation.

Feast Days

At one time almost every day of the calendar honored one saint or another, many of them unknown to parishioners. These were called feast days. The first reform of the calendar of saints' feasts was done by Pope Pius V (1570) after the Council of Trent. This reformed calendar had 158 feasts. A multiplication of saints' feasts occurred again, especially early in this century. Soon there were 300 feasts, and counting, with many more on the local calendars followed by dioceses and religious communities. This left very few days each year for the more basic unfolding of the liturgical seasons. Even if the day were dedicated to a more significant event, mystery, or saint, a second (or even third) official prayer of the day remembered another saint.

The Second Vatican Council in its Constitution on the Sacred Liturgy called for a reform of this calendar "so that the entire cycle of the mysteries of salvation may be suitably recalled" (108) "lest the feasts of saints should take precedence over the feasts which commemorate the very mysteries of salvation" (111). The new official calendar (1969) retained for the universal church only those feasts that remembered saints who have a meaning for the entire church. The others, in a process of decentralization, have been reduced to local celebrations in countries, regions, dioceses, and religious communities.

Every parish, diocese, religious community, and religious institution has a patron saint. So, too, do most nations, states, cities, and towns with a Catholic population. At one time these saints were honored with local holy days and public festivities that included pageants, parades, carnivals, banquets, and dancing. This still happens in some Catholic nations. Usually, however, the observance is limited to a liturgical celebration within the church community.

Relics

The religious tradition of venerating the relics of saints began with the custom of solemnly burying the bodies of martyrs and caring for their graves. This popular practice of veneration was eventually extended to their exhumed clothes, to the dust of their graves, and to objects touched by these holy relics. By the 5th century, there were warnings from church authorities against abuses and superstitious practices associated with the veneration of relics.

In the Middle Ages, preoccupation with holy relics increased with great enthusiasm as the more important official Latin worship of the church became foreign to the laity. Relics, sometimes inauthentic and at most only legendary, were moved from places of martyrdom and burial to other countries, cities, and villages. These relics, often encased in elaborate reliquaries made from precious metals, were displayed so that the people could venerate them. It also became a tradition to include relics of saints in the construction of the church's altar and eventually in the altar stone. This latter practice has been changed in the Rite for Dedication of an Altar. It allows relics only if great care has been taken to certify the relics as authentic. They must be large enough to be recognized as parts of the saint's body. The Code of Canon Law also limits the presence of major relics to permanently fixed altars (c. 1237).

Individuals acquired real or "pseudo" relics and used them for private purposes of devotion and intercession before God. This led to questionable or superstitious practices. The church continued to issue warnings and corrections and today carefully regulates this religious practice (canon 1190).

Images

As with other traditions honoring the saints, the veneration of their images originated with the martyrs. It became popular, for devotional purposes, to substitute images or icons for their actual relics. Images could be even more practical because relics, due to disintegration, had no form. The intercessory power attributed to saints was transferred from devotion to their relics to their images in mosaics, paintings, and eventually statues.

Making images of saints gradually evolved into a complicated system. They were constructed in such a way, accompanied by symbols, that they spoke clearly of the person and attributes of the saint. The image of St. Peter, for example, is bald and holds a set of keys that symbolize his authority in the church. Evangelists hold a book. St. Joseph, the husband of Mary, is usually represented as an old man with a lily, a symbol of purity. The image of the later St. Catherine of Siena also holds a lily. Arrows always accompany St. Sebastian, who was put to death by piercing; St. Isidore, bees; St. Cecilia, an organ.

In modern times, as the number of saints grew by way of the church's process of canonization, it became popular to wear the image of a particular saint in the form of a blessed medal. This is done to seek the saint's protection or intercessory power.

Praying to Saints
Probably the most popular tradition associated with the veneration of saints is the practice of praying to them, asking them to intercede with God for a special favor. This practice is partly the result of an overemphasis on the divinity of Christ to the exclusion of his humanness. Christians began to feel more at home with intercessors who were like themselves. This practice, however, does not deny the mediation role of Jesus Christ.

Vatican II both endorses and clarifies this tradition: "For after they have been received into their heavenly home and are present to the Lord (2 Corinthians 5:8), through him and with him and in him, they do not cease to intercede with the Father for us. Rather, they show forth the merits which they have won on earth through the one Mediator between God and [humans], Christ Jesus (see 1 Timothy 2:5). There they served God in all things and filled up in their flesh whatever was lacking of the sufferings of Christ on behalf of His body which is the Church (see Colossians 1:24). Thus, by their interest our weakness is very greatly strengthened" (Dogmatic Constitution on the Church, 49).

In modern times, people began praying to particular saints who had gained a popular reputation of interceding for precise causes. St. Anne, for example, became the patron of pregnant women, and St. Anthony the patron for the recovery of lost articles. A popular tradition, a mixture of devotion, desperation, and superstition, is to bury a statue of St. Joseph in a piece of real estate to promote chances for a sale. This is an example of popular lore not encouraged by the church.

Litanies

Litanies were a form of praying in pagan religions and among the Hebrews (see Psalm 136). During the Middle Ages, they became a popular way of praying to the saints. The Litany of the Saints is the oldest. Its form is very simple: addressing saints by name followed by the petition of "We beseech thee to hear us" or "Pray for us." In the later Middle Ages, local versions, with endless lists, were popular. Even though there is one version for the universal church, local churches and national conferences may and often do have their own versions. The Litany of Saints is used at ordinations, at the Easter Vigil for the blessing of baptismal water, and at Forty Hours Devotion.

Feast of All Saints

The Feast of All Saints, still a holy day on November 1, began in early centuries as a "catchall," remembering martyrs whose names were not known and who therefore did not have their own festivities. It was introduced in Rome on May 13, 610, as the "Feast of All Holy Martyrs" by Pope Boniface IV. The occasion was a gift of the ancient pagan temple of the Pantheon to the church by the Roman Emperor, Phocas. First celebrated on May 13, it was transferred to November 1 for the universal church during the pontificate of Pope Gregory VII (d. 1085). By then it included all the saints. The reason for the new date may have been a practical one. It seems that so many pilgrims came to Rome for the feast that it was moved to the fall when more food would be available after the harvest. More probably it was the adoption of the date popular in the Irish and English church. The new date spread throughout the church. Its eve, All Hallows Eve or Halloween, gave its name to a pagan Celtic Druid custom still popularly observed on October 31.

Canonization

Through a juridical process called canonization, the church declares a person to be a saint in heaven and to be venerated throughout the church. The word itself simply means "to be officially put on the list." During the early centuries the spontaneous acclamation of local devotees was sufficient for future veneration. During the 6th and 7th centuries, the number of saints receiving veneration after their deaths and having feasts in their honor increased rapidly. The spontaneous process, however, was open to abuses, since it did not take into account unbiased knowledge of the life of the "saint." A need was felt for some kind of regulating process which included an investigation of the life of reputed saints.

At first, only the local church authority, usually the bishop, conducted this investigation. It gathered evidence of a reputation of holiness, a sustained practice of visiting the saint's tomb and seeking the saint's intercession, and evidence of miraculous favors.

As the authority of the church became more centralized in Rome, it was natural that this process eventually be done by papal offices. Another motive was the matter of prestige. The first papal canonization was that of Bishop Ulrich of Augsburg (d. 973). At first, papal involvement was confined to giving consent for the transfer of relics and public veneration. In 1234, Pope Gregory IX initiated norms for the only legitimate process of investigation. This responsibility was assigned to the Sacred Congregation of Rites in the Roman Curia in 1588 and, with modifications, the process remains in effect today through the Congregation of the Causes of Saints.

The process of canonization, which usually takes generations to be finalized, is familiar to anyone acquainted with court procedure. It begins in the local diocese where the "saint" lived or worked. If there is a reputation of holiness, a "postulator" (similar to a defense attorney) presents the evidence to a panel of judges appointed by the local bishop. A "promoter of the faith" (similar to a prosecuting attorney), once popularly called "the devil's advocate," challenges the evidence with objections. The case is then written up and given to officials in Rome. The pope decides if the cause is to be introduced. In 1969, Pope Paul decreed that local bishops must consult the Holy See before initiating this first process.

This investigative process covers the person's orthodoxy (in writings), heroic exercise of virtue, and evidence of miracles (unless a martyr).

The same process which took place in the local diocese is eventually repeated more in depth in Rome. Evidence is presented of heroic practice of virtue or martyrdom and, in a separate investigation, miracles worked through the "saint's" intercession are confirmed. Again, this evidence is challenged by the promoter. If the cause or case holds up, the person is solemnly and publicly beatified by the pope, with veneration restricted to the city, diocese, region, or religious community from which the saint came.

After evidence of more miracles, the whole process is repeated, often generations later. Finally, there is a solemn liturgy during which the saint is canonized and recommended for universal veneration.

Halo

The halo surrounding the head of a saint's image has a pre-Christian history. It was used among the Greeks and Romans as a symbol of divinity for their gods and goddesses and in particular Apollo, the sun god. It was also used to distinguish Roman emperors on their coins. The halo was adopted by Christians in the 4th century as a sign of sanctity in images and mosaics. To distinguish Christ from saints, the halo around Jesus' head included a cross.

MARY

Little children built May altars. They crowned a statue of the Blessed Virgin Mary sometime in May. Women, men, and children carried rosaries and many prayed the rosary daily with meditation on mysteries that were thoroughly familiar. A grotto with flickering vigil lights was a familiar feature on parish grounds. An altar dedicated to Mary was an obvious fixture in every church. When the congregation sang in the vernacular, chances were that the song told of the praises of Mary. Public prayer services featured communal recitation of the rosary and litanies. Devotees followed exciting news of apparitions. They obeyed and promoted the messages of the Lady in blue. Legion of Mary members became important lay ministers in parishes.

Devotion to Mary, one of the most obvious features of Catholicism, originated in early Christianity. It was closely associated with the mystery of her son, Jesus Christ, and did not have the multiplicity of forms so evident in modern times.

It took centuries for the early church to clarify its faith in Jesus and his human and divine natures. This happened by way of theological discussions, controversies, and council decisions. As the church began to appreciate the depth of mystery surrounding their Lord, it also identified its relationship to Mary. The church discovered her as Mother of God, model of what the church is called to be, and the most powerful intercessor with God.

Hyperdulia
Mary is given a veneration above that of all other saints. This is because of her unique relationship to Jesus, to the God from whom he comes, and to the church which continues his presence. This veneration, called hyperdulia, is expressed in official dogmas, feast days, and in multiple forms of private devotions on the part of Catholics. Her role as a woman in relation to the mystery of church and salvation is of great importance today.

Early Cult

There is little historical evidence concerning Mary. She seemed to have lived out her life as a respected member of the Christian community at Ephesus. The new Scriptures of Christianity give little indication of the esteem she would eventually receive from the universal church. The gospel of Matthew draws attention only to her virginal conception of Jesus (Matthew 1:18–25). The gospel according to Luke gives her more attention as the one chosen by God because of her faithfulness and humility (Luke 1:46–55). In this gospel she is described also as trying to understand the mystery surrounding her son and herself (Luke 2:19, 23–24, 51). In John's gospel and the book of Revelation, written at the turn of the 1st century, there is a beginning of a Marian typology and theology. This is especially true of the relationship between Mary and a church that was rapidly developing its identity in confrontation with the Roman Empire (John 19:26–27; Revelation 12:12ff).

There seems to have been no particular cult surrounding the person of Mary among early Christians. They were preoccupied more with martyrs during the centuries of persecution. In the early 3rd century, attention to Mary's virginal conception of Jesus became popular. This belief rests on the gospels according to Matthew and Luke. It was emphasized further by an apocryphal gospel, the Protovangelium of James, written about 150 but not included in the New Testament. This theme, along with the theme of Mary as the New Eve, was promoted also by the writings and teaching of the defenders of Christianity, Justin (d. 165) and Irenaeus (d. 200).

Other Marian themes evolved alongside theological controversies about the nature of her son, Jesus. In 431, the Council of Ephesus officially defined that the human and divine natures of Jesus are united in one divine person. This meant that Mary, the mother of Jesus, is the mother of God (Greek, *theotokos*).

The Council of Ephesus increased devotion to Mary. Churches were dedicated to her. Her feasts began to multiply on the church calendar. By the beginning of the 6th century, local churches were celebrating Mary's falling asleep ("Dormition"), later described as her bodily assumption into heaven. It was considered fitting that the body which gave birth to Jesus be spared any bodily corruption. By the mid-600s, the church of Rome was observing five Marian feasts: Mother of God (January 1), the Nativity of Mary (September 8), the Annunciation (March 25), the Presentation (February 2), and the Assumption (August 15).

Intercessory Role

A preoccupation with Mary and her powerful intercessory role with God began to mushroom as spirituality and theology began to take a road separate from Scripture. By the beginning of the 8th century, her spiritual motherhood of all Christians and her maternal influence with God, along with her importance for salvation, were popular beliefs in the church. During the Middle Ages this theme was distorted as people began to believe, under the influence of popular preachers, that Mary appeases the wrath of God who is a stern judge. New titles highlighted this popular conviction: Redemptrix of Captives, Refuge of Sinners, Mediatrix between God and Humankind, and Mother of Mercy. It seemed as if Mary had taken control of heaven!

Bernard of Clairvaux (d. 1153), an influential medieval theologian and spiritual writer, taught that Mary had an intimate role in redemption, that God willed people to have everything through her, who is the mediatrix with the mediator, Jesus.

The Protestant Reformation challenged and even attacked popular beliefs about Mary. It emphasized the one mediatory role of Jesus. Some reform leaders, such as Martin Luther, maintained a personal devotion to her. Catholic Counter-Reformation efforts defended Mary, her role as intercessor, and the doctrines officially taught by the church. Differences in attitudes toward Mary and her role remain a cause of division today between Catholics and other Christians.

Modern Devotion

In the 17th century, there was a flowering of Marian devotion in Spain and France. In France, St. Louis de Montfort (d. 1716) promoted a devotion that came to be known as "true devotion to Mary" or slavery to Mary. This was a total dedication and submission to Mary, as mystics had surrendered themselves to God. A French school of spirituality, led by Jean-Jacques Olier (d. 1716), promoted the role of Mary in the interior spiritual life of Catholics, especially seminarians. This emphasis on Marian spirituality for celibate priests would naturally influence the promotion of devotion to Mary in parishes.

A time of rationalism and skepticism regarding Mary occurred in the 18th century, especially among Catholic theologians in Europe. Exaggerated Marian piety was attacked. Several generations later, under the influence of the Enlightenment, there continued to be strong opposition among theologians and spiritual writers toward exaggerated Marian spirituality. This opposition was especially strong in Europe, except in Spain and Italy. In Italy, popular attitudes and legends were supported by the influential spiritual writer St. Alphonsus Liguori (d. 1787).

Two major doctrines about Mary, with related holy days, were defined by the church in modern times: the Immaculate Conception and the bodily Assumption of Mary into heaven. The doctrine of the Immaculate Conception professes that Mary was conceived without original sin by her parents, traditionally known as St. Anne and St. Joachim. Some medieval theologians, St. Thomas Aquinas among them, argued against this teaching because it seemed to remove Mary from the common lot of her sisters and brothers. A feast with this theme was first approved by Pope Sixtus IV in 1476.

About 400 years later, on November 27, 1830, St. Catherine Labouré (d. 1876) claimed to have had a vision of Mary as the Immaculate Conception. Mary commanded that a medal be made of the vision of herself surrounded by an oval frame made up of the words: "O Mary, conceived without sin, pray for us who have recourse to thee." This is the origin of the Miraculous Medal, called this because of the miracles received through a faith-filled wearing of it. This stimulated interest in the doctrine, but it was still opposed by liberal Catholics in Europe. Pope Pius IX (d. 1878) conducted a consultation with the world's bishops. On December 8, 1854, he solemnly decreed the teaching as dogma (*Ineffabilis Deus*).

Devotion to Mary and mariology (theology of Mary) was very popular during the generations preceding Vatican II. About 100 years ago, Leo XIII wrote several encyclicals promoting the praying of the rosary. Early in this century, St. Pius X promoted the spiritual motherhood of Mary, and Benedict XV promoted Mary as Queen of Peace. The Legion of Mary, founded by Frank Duff in 1921 in Dublin, Ireland, became a popular and effective apostolic organization in Catholic parishes throughout the world. By 1964, it had more than a million active members.

Theologians continued to develop the foundations of Marian themes, to which Pope Pius XII (d. 1958) gave support. He also encouraged a correct balance in devotion to Mary. In 1942, he consecrated the world to the Immaculate Heart of Mary. On August 15, 1950, after consultation with the bishops of the world, he officially defined the dogma of the bodily Assumption of Mary into heaven (*Munificentissimus Deus*). Three years later he announced a Marian Year and established the feast of the Queenship of Mary on May 31.

Local, national, and international Marian congresses became popular in the mid-1900s. Biblical and patristic studies promoted a mature devotion to Mary and focused attention to the Mary-Church analogy.

Cautions

The Second Vatican Council turned attention to other theological themes. In doing so, it put the Marian momentum into perspective. The council devoted Chapter VIII of its important Dogmatic Constitution on the Church to "The Role of the Blessed Virgin Mary, Mother of God, in the Mystery of Christ and the Church." It endorsed traditional veneration of Mary, especially by way of liturgy. It urged that devotion to Mary be kept within limits of sound orthodox doctrine and that it avoid the two extremes of exaggeration and minimizing: "Let the faithful remember...that true devotion consists neither in fruitless and passing emotion, nor in a certain vain credulity. Rather, it proceeds from true faith, by which we are led to know the excellence of the Mother of God, and are moved to a filial love toward our mother and to the imitation of her virtues" (67).

On February 2, 1974, Pope Paul VI issued his "Guidelines for Devotion to the Blessed Virgin" (*Marialis Cultus*). He emphasized (24-38) that devotions to Mary should be trinitarian and christological in their focus; give due place to the Holy Spirit; show a clear awareness of the church; and take careful account of the contributions from Scripture, liturgy, ecumenism, and anthropology. "The ultimate purpose of devotion to the Blessed Virgin is to glorify God and lead Christians to commit themselves to a life which conforms absolutely to his will" (39). In this document Pope Paul VI also encourages two popular devotions: the praying of the Angelus (41) and the rosary (42-54). He warns, however, that the rosary should not be promoted too exclusively: "The rosary is an excellent prayer, but the faithful should feel serenely free toward it. Its intrinsic appeal should draw them to calm recitation" (57-58).

Today, devotion to Mary continues to be reassessed in light of Scripture, pastoral concerns, and ecumenism. Some traditional practices, such as the wearing of the scapular, are no longer as popular as in previous generations. More emphasis is being placed on scriptural prayer services and public liturgy. "We are returning to Mary because in our theology, devotions and art, Mary is returning to us. She is a sister who walks with us, a human being who struggled to understand the meaning of her life, a widow who experienced loneliness. She, one of us, is the mother of Jesus, in whom God and the human race historically met" (Bishop Kenneth Untener, Saginaw, Michigan).

Little Office of Our Lady
The earliest religious traditions that honored Mary were public festivals celebrating with liturgy her unique relationship to God. In the Middle Ages a more private kind of tradition evolved. For the laity who could read, The Little Office of Our Lady became popular and continues into modern times, revised in 1988. This devotion is a series of psalms and readings from Scripture with analogies to Mary. It imitates in an abbreviated form the Divine Office prayed or sung by monks and clergy.

Hail Mary
The Little Office of Our Lady used an original form of the Hail Mary as an antiphon already in the early Middle Ages. In the 12th century, the Hail Mary became a basic prayer to be learned and recited frequently by all. It is a combination of the angel Gabriel's greeting at the Annunciation: "Rejoice, O highly favored daughter! The Lord is with you. Blessed are you among women" (Luke 1:26–28), and Elizabeth's recognition of Mary's unique motherhood when the two pregnant women met: "Blessed are you among women and blessed is the fruit of your womb" (Luke 1:42). Later, the devotional words seeking Mary's intercession were added: "Holy Mary, Mother of God, pray for us sinners now and at the hour of our death. Amen." This addition happened when popular prayers began to change in their nature from praise to petition.

Rosary
The rosary takes its name from a popular title for Mary: "Mystical Rose." As a form of private prayer, it originally consisted of 150 Our Fathers prayed daily in substitution for the 150 psalms by those who could not read. It was also a common penance given after confession to sinners who had to use beads to count the prayers. By the early 12th century, Hail Marys were substituted for the Our Fathers, divided into three groups of 50 (called rosaries), and each of these divided into five groups of 10 (called decades). Three sets of themes, or mysteries, concerning Jesus and Mary (Joyful, Sorrowful, and Glorious) established the themes for the praying of the rosary. Some of these were borrowed from ancient prayer services associated with the hours of the day. St. Dominic (d. 1221) popularized the rosary through his preaching.

Antiphons
Marian antiphons were composed between the 11th and 12th cen-

turies and sung in Gregorian chant. They are known better by their Latin titles: *Alma Redemptoris Mater* ("Sweet Mother of the Redeemer"), *Ave Regina Caelorum* ("Hail, Queen of Heaven"), and *Salve Regina* ("Hail, Holy Queen").

Saturday

Just as Sunday had always been devoted to Jesus Christ, Saturday eventually became Mary's day. This tradition was promoted in Carolingian times by Alcuin (d. 804). A votive Mass in Mary's honor has commonly been offered on Saturday throughout modern times.

May and Mother's Day

The springtime month of May is popularly devoted to Mary. Statues dedicated to her are showered with bouquets and crowns of flowers. The second Sunday of May, Mother's Day (celebrated in Spain on the Feast of the Immaculate Conception, December 8), often takes on Marian nuances. There was an annual Mothering Sunday celebrated in England on the fourth Sunday of Lent at least from the 17th century until the early 19th. Our Mother's Day, however, has become a secular observance, although it did not begin that way. The tradition began through the efforts of Anna M. Jarvis (1864-1948) with church services in Grafton, West Virginia, and Philadelphia, Pennsylvania, in honor of Anna Jarvis's own mother. In 1910, the governor of Oklahoma issued the first Mother's Day proclamation. The following year all the states did so. Congress and the Executive Office cooperated in 1913 in a national resolution establishing the second Sunday of May as Mother's Day. Anna Jarvis died, disillusioned that her religious efforts had become almost entirely secular and commercial. Incidentally, a Father's Day observance seems to have begun in Spokane, Washington, by Sonora Smart Dodd in 1910.

Month of the Rosary

The month of October is dedicated to Mary under the theme of the rosary because of the feast of Our Lady of the Rosary on October 7. In the 15th and 16th centuries, there was an extensive promotion of devotion to the rosary. On October 7, 1571, Christians won an important naval battle against the Moslem Turks at Lepanto Strait (near western Greece). The credit for the victory was thought to be the rosary. Pius V ordered that the annual anniversary of this victory be celebrated with a Marian feast of Our Lady of Victory. In 1573, Gregory XIII permitted churches with a rosary altar to celebrate a feast of the Holy Rosary. After another victory against the Moslem Turks in 1716, Clement XI extended the feast to the universal church.

Marian Litanies

Late in the Middle Ages, litanies seeking Mary's intercession became common. This simple and popular form of praying addresses Mary by a series of titles with the petition: "Pray for us." The Litany of Loreto, familiar to Catholics, was approved by Sixtus V in 1587. It received this title because it was popular at the shrine of Loreto in Italy. This litany was made popular by St. Peter Canisius. It has about fifty titles for Mary; the most recent, "Queen assumed into heaven," was added by Pius XII in 1950.

Angelus

By the 14th century, it became customary to ring church bells to remind the faithful to pray in honor of Mary and to remember the mystery of the Incarnation. This tradition of the Angelus (Latin *angelus,* "angel," the first word of the Angelus prayer) imitates the ancient monastic call to prayer by ringing the church bells. It is still popular today in many parishes. A series of Hail Marys, spaced with invocations to Mary and a concluding prayer, is prayed as the church bells ring at 6 A.M., noon, and 6 P.M.

Apparitions

Visions, revelations, and pilgrimages have always been associated with devotion to Mary. Places where visionaries claimed that Mary appeared have become places of pilgrimage. Soon after the Spaniards arrived in what would become Mexico, Mary appeared in 1531 to an Indian, Juan Diego, at Guadalupe, leaving her image on his cloak made of cactus fibers. In 1846, a young boy and girl claimed to have seen her in the French Alps at La Salette. She sat weeping over the dishonoring of Sunday and the sin of blasphemy. At Lourdes, France, she appeared in 1858 to Bernadette Soubirous and identified herself as the "Immaculate Conception." A miraculous spring appeared at the site and is still a center of international pilgrimages and healing. In 1917, at Fatima in Portugal, she was reported to have appeared to three small children and identified herself as "the Lady of the Rosary." The theme of Fatima—peace, and the conversion of Russia through the praying of the rosary—has been popular among many Catholics. Other apparitions have received church approval and have popular shrines and pilgrimages associated with them: Guadalupe in

Mexico, Knock in Ireland, Czestochowa in Poland, and Montserrat in Spain, Banneux, Belgium, and Beauring, Belgium.

Church approval of apparitions, shrines, and public veneration surrounding them does not make them official doctrine. Nor are their messages public revelation for church membership. Approval or disapproval begins on the local level by the bishop of the diocese. Most claims are rejected after study by church authority. Despite church disapproval, devotees often continue to believe in them and make pilgrimages. This was the case in recent times at Necedah, Wisconsin, and Bayside, New York. More recently, visions of Mary at Medjugorje, Yugoslavia, have been in the news. Bosnia-Herzegovina bishops, after several years of investigation, have said there is no proof of these apparitions at Medjugorje. At the same time they encourage liturgical and pastoral care of pilgrims. Vatican officials have not endorsed the validity of the apparitions.

The Vatican Congregation for the Doctrine of Faith stresses that the local bishop is the first and the main authority in apparition cases. In the most difficult cases, the Congregation becomes involved as well. The church's final judgment is whether the events are of a supernatural nature or not; there is no mention of Mary. The following guidelines help bishops weigh the evidence:

1. The facts in the case are free of error.
2. The person(s) receiving the messages is/are psychologically balanced, honest, moral, sincere and respectful of church authority.
3. Doctrinal errors are not attributed to God, Our Lady, or a saint.
4. Theological and spiritual doctrines presented are free of error.
5. Moneymaking is not a motive somehow involved in the events.
6. Healthy religious devotion and spiritual fruits result, with no evidence of collective hysteria.

Images

A statue or picture of Mary is found in every Catholic church and many homes. This tradition of honoring Mary by venerating images of her goes back to 3rd-century images found in catacombs. These images spread, usually showing Mary as a Madonna (Mary as mother holding the infant Jesus) often crowned as a queen. After the early 4th century, images of Mary as a queenly mother or as an empress were influenced by court ceremonies adopted from the Roman culture. Pictures and statues of Mary today often show some relationship to Jesus (for example, Madonnas), or one of her special features (for example, the Immaculate Heart), or a description from apparitions (for example, Our Lady of Guadalupe, Lourdes, and Fatima).

Scapular

The tradition of wearing the scapular began with St. Peter Damian's (d. 1072) promotion of Mary's role in helping the souls in purgatory. The Carmelite scapular, or "brown scapular," is the most common. There is a legend that Mary appeared to St. Simon Stock in 1251 and showed him the brown scapular. The apparition promised that whoever wore it until death would be preserved from hell, and on the first Saturday after death would be taken by Mary from purgatory into heaven. The church has always been careful to point out that no religious article is miraculous in itself and that salvation always depends upon the life and faith of the wearer. Altogether, there are eighteen different scapulars approved by the church for private devotion.

Dozens of feast days and several holy days on the church's calendar pay honor to Mary's uniqueness as a person and her relationship to her son, Jesus Christ, and to members of the church. Two of these, the feasts of the Assumption (August 15) and the Immaculate Conception (December 8) are holy days in the United States.

Blessing of Flowers and Herbs

Still popular among Polish Americans is the blessing of flowers and herbs on the feast of the Assumption. This continues a tradition still popular in Poland. August 15 is a day of thanks with first fruits offered to God. Bouquets of flowers and herbs are adorned with blue ribbons and then taken to church for a special blessing.

16

PURGATORY

"Dies irae, dies illa..." (That day of wrath...) sang the children's choir or lonely organist in parish churches several days a week. This mournful, lengthy, Latin poem was used for funerals and also for daily Masses for the dead. It described a popular attitude toward death in pre-Vatican II generations. Black vestments told of the same. At the end of these daily Masses an interesting ritual was customarily performed. The priest blessed and incensed a catafalque (resembling a coffin, when no body was present), which was surrounded by unbleached beeswax candles.

Stipend books in the parish office were full of Mass intentions for grandma and grandpa. If parishes had too many of these, and they usually did, the intentions were sent to missionaries and religious communities—wherever there were priests who needed the income.

On All Souls Day, November 2, individual parishioners faithfully visited church, prayed six Our Fathers, Hail Marys, and Glorys for the intention of the Holy Father. In doing so, they received a plenary indulgence for a soul in purgatory, thus freeing a soul for heaven. Then these parishioners left church for a moment, returning to repeat the ritual for the benefit of another soul.

The story told by these traditions was clear. Those who have died are in a mournful place, purgatory.

Integral to the church's understanding of itself as the Communion of Saints is its attention to those in purgatory. This has taken the form of remembering the dead during Mass and, more than this, actually offering the fruits of the Mass for particular persons who have died. Concern for the dead, along with concern for one's own fate after death, has motivated the evolution of the Catholic tradition of indulgences. A feast day remembering the souls in purgatory began to be celebrated on November 2, with the whole month of November eventually being dedicated to remembering the dead.

It was common thinking, among both pagans and Christians, that the soul gradually leaves the body after death. Pagans left offerings periodically at gravesites as an expression of this belief. On these days of remembrance, according to ancient Roman custom, a meal called *refrigerium* was eaten with an empty place signifying the dead person. Pagans also celebrated an annual festival from February 13-22 to remember their dead relatives.

Purgatory
The popular belief that the soul gradually leaves the body gives a hint of a journey after death, a journey that involves some kind of purification. This was a conviction of pagans and apparently of Christians, too. Interestingly, contemporary experience and research regarding near-death experiences indicate that such a journey is not so far-fetched.

The foundation of the church's teaching regarding those in purgatory lies in the constant belief and practices of believers. Already in early times, the Christian practice was to remember their dead on the 3rd, 7th, and 30th day and on the annual anniversary. It soon became common to celebrate the Eucharist on these anniversaries.

In 211, Tertullian spoke of the Christian observation of the anniversary days of their departed as an established tradition. Hippolytus (d. 235) mentions prayers for the dead in the context of the Eucharist. This practice became universal by the end of the 4th century. The Ecumenical Council of Lyons II taught that undergoing purification after death could be assisted by the prayers and good works of the living and by Masses offered for them.

In the Middle Ages, Masses for the dead came to be called Requiem Masses after the first word of the entrance antiphon (Latin *requies*, "rest").

There is no undisputed scriptural foundation for the church's constant tradition that the eternal destiny of the dead can be influenced by the prayers of the living. The popular biblical argument comes from the Scriptures, 2 Maccabees 12:38–46: "Turning to supplication, they prayed that the sinful deed might be fully blotted out...for if he were not expecting the fallen to rise again, it would have been useless and foolish to pray for them in death." There is one reference to prayer for the dead in the New Testament: "May the Lord have mercy on the family of Onesiphorus...when he stands before the Lord on the great day, may the Lord grant him mercy!" (2 Timothy 1:16–18).

The New Testament does not provide final answers to the question of what happens after death. Its approach is that the endtimes have already begun with Christ and will be fulfilled in the immediate future with his second and final coming.

1 Corinthians 3:12–15 speaks of a fire associated with the endtimes: "That day will make its appearance with fire, and fire will test the quality of each one's work" (3:13). Well-known Christian teachers in the 2nd and 3rd centuries, for example, Justin (d. 165) and Tertullian (d. 225), indicated that the dead wait in their graves for this final coming and judgment. Origen (d. 254) taught that everyone will experience some kind of purification as part of a final judgment. He also insisted that everyone will be saved after a purifying fire, a teaching eventually condemned by the church. St. Augustine (d. 430) taught that martyrs and the just enter heaven immediately at death, a teaching always held by the church.

In the 6th century, the notion of fire in the Christian Scriptures ceased to be a symbol of purification and became associated with actual punishment after death. This gave rise to the description of "suffering souls in purgatory." In the Middle Ages, belief in a purifying-punishing fire became common in the Western church. With the help of art and popular preaching, purgatory became a minor version of hell, the only difference being that purgatory has an end. This exaggeration produced a hyper-attention to the needs of those suffering there and a feast day provided for their benefit.

Prayer for the Dead
The practice of offering the fruits of a Mass for a particular person who has died became popular almost at the same time as the tradition of daily Mass in the 7th century. This tradition became so widespread that it led eventually to abuses involving multiple Masses each day and abuses related to the offerings of money or stipends.

In the 16th century, Protestant reformers challenged the efficacy of prayer for the dead. They preached against practices associated with this tradition, especially the tradition of indulgences and Masses for the dead. The Council of Trent defended the church's teaching and practices but condemned abuses. During modern times a preoccupation with the needs of those in purgatory continued. Parishioners were accustomed to daily Masses for the deceased, celebrated in black vestments, with absolution prayers for the dead person prayed at a catafalque, placed where a coffin is at funerals. Although not forbidden, the use of the catafalque has become obsolete. Absolution prayers are to be used only when the body of the deceased is present.

Vatican II repeated the traditional teaching on the value of praying for the dead in its Dogmatic Constitution on the Church (51-52). It cautioned, however, against abuses and excesses. Today the dead are remembered at Mass but usually without special Masses formulas and a funeral atmosphere.

Belief in a process of purification after death has continued to mature. Emphasis is no longer on a physical agent (for example, fire) of purgation or punishment, or on a particular physical place and time. Theological reflection today considers purgatory as a positive process after death by which persons come to a perfect understanding of self and relinquish all self-centeredness. To remember the dead and to pray for them is still an important tradition.

The most popular religious tradition associated with souls in purgatory is to pray for the dead. These prayers remember them as still related to oneself in the mystery of the Communion of Saints. These prayers also hope to influence their condition if they are still undergoing purification. The form of these prayers may be a spontaneous thought or prayer, reaching out to loved ones, a more formal praying, or a remembrance during Mass.

November 2

In the 7th century, monks began offering Mass on the day after Pentecost for their departed community members. In 998, the Benedictine monastery of Cluny began celebrating a feast to remember all of their dead on November 2. This practice spread to other monasteries and eventually to parishes served by secular clergy. In the 13th century, Rome placed the feast day on the annual calendar for the universal church. The same date was kept so that all of the departed members of the church as part of the Communion of Saints might be remembered on successive days, the triumphant saints in heaven on November 1, and those in purgatory on November 2.

At the end of the 15th century, Spanish Dominican priests began the custom of celebrating three Masses on November 2. Benedict XIV gave this privilege to priests of Portugal, Spain, and Latin America, and Benedict XV extended it to all priests in 1915. The tradition continued until recent times.

Indulgences

It is still a wholesome religious tradition to pray for those in purgatory and to gain indulgences for them and for oneself. The tradition of indulgences, however, was not connected at the beginning with helping the "souls" in purgatory.

Originally indulgences had to do with sinners still living. From the beginning, the church seemed to have exacted some kind of penalty or penance to satisfy the harm done by sin, especially murder, adultery, apostasy, and heresy. Even though guilt itself was erased through forgiveness, some form of satisfaction seemed in order. Eventually, a system was worked out detailing the kind and length of public penance, often very severe. This was considered "the temporal punishment due to sin." The sacrament of penance continued to evolve, and examples of serious ("mortal") personal sin greatly expanded. By the 11th century, the church, in the person of the local bishop, began drawing upon its jurisdictional power and treasury of spiritual merits to reduce (partial indulgence) the length of penance (for example, by 500 days) or to cancel it altogether (plenary indulgence). Plenary indulgences became popular in the eleventh century as rewards for taking part in the crusade to free the Holy Land from the Moslems.

By the mid-13th century, indulgences became separated from the sacrament of penance and became part of the pope's authority. The number and kind of indulgences multiplied and any particular penitential effort was often eliminated.

In 1476, Pope Sixtus IV granted the first plenary indulgence applicable to those in purgatory. These indulgences became popular because of a growing preoccupation with these "suffering souls" and with one's own eternal destiny. It was common to publish the exact number of days or years of "temporal time" to be erased. In the beginning these indulgences were associated with some form of almsgiving. Eventually, they became an important source of income for the church, "sold" by preachers. This situation became a direct cause of the Protestant Reformation. The Council of Trent condemned abuses but supported the value and practice of indulgences.

The unfortunate practice of associating money with indulgences very probably was a spin-off of the church's attempt to introduce more humane practices among converted barbarians. Among these tribes it was customary to exact a bloody death penalty for crimes. The church persuaded them to substitute money or indulgence.

The practice of gaining indulgences continued to be popular until the present time. In 1967, Pope Paul VI clarified the church's teaching on the practice of indulgences (*Indulgentiarum Doctrina*). The practice must always be seen in light of the church as the Communion of Saints with a real bond between the triumphant souls in heaven, the souls in process of purification (purgatory), and the pilgrim church on earth. There can be and should be an influence on one another within this communion. The spiritual treasury that the church draws on in granting an indulgence is the infinite merits of Christ's redeeming actions in the sight of God. The number of days of temporary punishment is no longer to be stated as part of an indulgence. Nor are indulgences automatic in the sense that the effect occurs regardless of a person's spiritual condition and intentions.

Stipends

Closely associated with remembering the dead is the practice of offering "the fruits" of the Mass for them, accompanied by some form of offering, or stipend, for the priest. This custom originated in early centuries when the gift procession at Mass included, besides the bread and wine for the Eucharist, food and money gifts both for the poor and for the ordinary support of the priest. These gifts were essential because clergy could not engage in secular employment due to demands of ministry on their time. When these "offertory processions" ceased in the 12th century, the Mass stipend took the place of all the voluntary contributions. At times abuses were widespread. The connection in the popular mind of money with the mystery of the Eucharist was unfortunate, as if one were "buying" a Mass.

In modern times, Mass stipends, along with stole fees connected with baptism, weddings, and funerals, have been carefully regulated by church law. Today, the notion that one who makes an offering for a particular intention can claim a right to the fruits of the Mass is no longer accepted. It is contrary to post-Vatican II theology and understanding of the Eucharist. In fact, prayers during the Eucharist have always been offered for many individuals and groups beyond the stipend intention. The stipend intention, therefore, becomes only one of the many intentions.

The new Code of Canon Law (1983) uses the term "Mass offerings" rather than "stipends." This change suggests that the church considers the donation as a free-will offering rather than a contractual payment. As a free-will donation, it only expresses a desire that the church remember a particular intention while praying.

The main reason for continuing the practice of Mass offerings lies in the long tradition of providing financial support to the church's mission. There still might be a moral problem, however. Well-intentioned but poorly informed Catholics might think that they are getting something special for their money that is specifically theirs. The principal beneficiary of the Mass is always the entire church as the Communion of Saints.

Priests individually or as a group may refuse offerings. Today in many dioceses, stipends and stole fees associated with the administration of sacraments become part of parish income. The clergy's allowance or salary is adjusted accordingly.

A growing popular practice is to have an offering box available along with a special book for parishioners to write their intentions. This book is brought forward in the gift procession at Mass to symbolize the offering of prayers of the whole worshipping community.

Visiting Graves

One of the most ancient customs related to respect for the dead is to visit and care for graves, place flowers at them, and to pray there in memory of loved ones. This has continued throughout the centuries. Sometimes these visits are paid on special days of the year, such as Mother's Day, Father's Day, and Memorial Day. November 2, the Feast of All Souls, along with the whole month of November, is a popular time to visit the graves of loved ones. In some parts of North America, grave blankets of evergreens are placed over the graves of loved ones at Christmastime.

Because the population is so mobile in contemporary society, not all family members can visit the graves of loved ones regularly. It is not uncommon that children—and parents—do not even know where their immediate ancestors are buried. In this case, pictures of loved ones become especially important, along with stories told about them.

November

During pre-Christian times, it was common for pagans to celebrate rituals related to their dead at the end of harvest in late fall. These customs very possibly influenced Christians to do the same. The month of November has traditionally been dedicated to the theme of death and to those who have died. The month begins with the feast of All Saints on November 1, and the next day with the feast of All Souls.

The theme of death for November fits the natural atmosphere of the month in the northern hemisphere. The harvest is completed, a dying becomes evident throughout nature, cold weather and a hint of winter become more prevalent, and the dark of night becomes more pervasive.

Black as Liturgical Color
Black was already considered one of five liturgical colors (with white, red, green, purple) in the 13th century. It is associated in the Western world with the theme and atmosphere of death and mourning. As such, it was used until recent times for funerals and Masses for the dead. It is seldom used today, however. Emphasis today is on the positive and joyful theme of resurrection for funerals. The color white is symbolic for this theme and is now used almost universally for funerals.

17

POPULAR SAINTS AND LEGENDS

Until recent times the dashboards of cars owned by many Catholics, and some Protestants, featured a little statue or medal of St. Christopher. This sacramental seemed to guarantee safety in an age of vehicle mania. On March 17, tens of thousands of people, and a good number of politicians, march in a St. Patrick's Day Parade in major cities, with public festivities in countless other cities and towns. They wear green and even drink green. On February 14 many people exchange valentines and gifts of love and affection.

People of all faiths or no faith enjoy these public festivities, with obvious secular overtones. Many forget that these days are indirectly associated with Catholicism's preservation of the veneration of saints. Paradoxically, these particular festivities honor three saints whose existence is at most a shadow in the church's long list of saints. Except for St. Patrick, they were not known to have made an extraordinary contribution to the universal church. One of them, St. Christopher, probably did not exist as any particular person. St. Patrick contributed greatly to the conversion of a particular people: the Irish. St. Nicholas is known more for legends that hide the real person, and for his name, stolen by Santa Claus, than for his actual ministry and veneration as a confessor during a time of persecution. St. Valentine, one of possibly many Valentines who suffered during a persecution, somehow had his name associated with love notes. Yet these saints became especially popular, so much so that legends evolved around them.

Thousands of saints are honored by the church, and individual Catholics have their favorites. So do countries and ethnic groups. Sometimes devotion to these saints follows people as they emigrate, becoming patron saints of parishes in distant lands. For example, in the Diocese of Saginaw, Michigan, at a rural crossroads, popularly called Sheridan's Corner, sits a church dedicated to St. Columbkille, or St. Colum Cille as he is known in his native Ireland. He, with St. Patrick and St. Brigit, is a patron saint of Ireland.

Born of princely family in 521, he was baptized Criomhthann ("fox") and later given the name Colum Cille ("dove of the church"). He studied under Finnian, the master teacher of Irish monks, and was ordained a priest. He was a poet and was associated with *filid*, the professional Irish poets or chroniclers of lore and legend in story and verse. Later in life he would promote the legitimacy of these bards within Christian Ireland. Eventually fifty monasteries in Ireland and Scotland would be associated with St. Colum Cille.

He spent the last 34 years of his life as an exile for Christ on the island of Iona off the west coast of Scotland, 135 miles from Londonderry, Northern Ireland. He promoted an integration of the Christian church into Celtic society. Although St. Colum Cille immersed himself deeply in the affairs of his times, including political ones, he was also known for his outstanding holiness. He died in 597, and his feast is on June 9. Later, from Iona, Irish monks would continue his missionary spirit, taking the gospel to the continent of Europe.

Many saints have been popular since the beginning of Christianity, especially the apostles, martyrs, and confessors. Others became popular through the process of local churches borrowing from each other's lists of holy men and women. And still others became saints through the church's juridicial process of canonization and are known only in the localities or religious communities where they lived and served God and people. In June 1988, for example, Pope John Paul II canonized 117 people martyred in Vietnam during the 18th and 19th centuries.

St. Christopher

In the late 1960s, in the process of reforming its calendar of the church year, the church dropped St. Christopher. This was a shock to Catholics who would not get into a car without a little statue or medal of him on the dashboard. He was the popular patron of travelers.

What happened? The church could find no proof, other than legends, that an individual by this name had ever lived. The name, or word, Christopher (Greek, "one who bears Christ") apparently had been found scratched on a tomb in early centuries. It was presumed that the tomb contained the remains of a person by the name "Christopher," but it probably referred to the kind of person he was who was buried, just as we would use the description, "a Christian."

The legend of St. Christopher is familiar. He was a giant of a man who served in the Roman army. Once he used his height to carry a child across a river in flood stage. As he did so, the weight on his shoulders became heavier and heavier. The child, who was really the Christ Child, informed Christopher that he was carrying not only the weight of the world but also that of the creator of this world. The Christ Child baptized his bearer in the river, giving him the name "Christ Bearer." Christopher died a martyr's death for his new Christian faith.

St. Christopher became the patron against sudden death during times of epidemics. It was popular to put his image on the outside walls of houses and along roads so that his power could be invoked frequently during dangerous times. Because of the legend of ferrying the Christ Child, he also became the patron of travelers, with wayside chapels devoted to him. When the automobile became popular, it was natural for many Catholics to keep his protecting image in the car.

The church did not prohibit seeking St. Christopher's protection— whoever he was—when it removed his feast from the annual calendar. The church, however, reminds its people that no thing has miraculous power in itself. Safe driving is still safe driving. Seeking protection against someone else's unsafe driving is still a good and wholesome religious tradition.

St. Nicholas

Not much more is known about St. Nicholas than about St. Christopher. Records show that he was a bishop of Myra Demre (in present-day Turkey). He was imprisoned for his faith during the persecution promoted by Emperor Diocletian in the early 4th century, and freed by Christianity's friend, Emperor Constantine. He died in 350 and was soon honored with an annual feast day on December 6. He became the most venerated saint in the Byzantine Catholic Church. His relics were transferred to Bari, Italy, in 1087 by Italian business people and are still venerated there in the church of San Nicola. He became the patron saint of Sicily, Russia, Greece, and many cities in Austria and Germany. He was also known as the patron saint of children, mariners, bakers, and merchants. His popularity spread throughout Europe in the Middle Ages.

Legends tell us the following story. Nicholas was born of rich parents but became an orphan. When he grew up he gave his possessions to the poor and dedicated himself to doing good for others secretly. He would sneak money at night through the windows of poor people's houses. One popular legend has him coming to the aid of a nobleman who had lost his family's wealth and was about to sell his daughters to regain it. St. Nicholas secretly tossed purses of money into the man's home to prevent this tragedy.

Nicholas was chosen by local bishops to be bishop of Myra and he continued to devote himself to the religious education of children, treating them with presents. After spending time in prison for professing the faith, he continued his service to the poor and children in Myra. According to legends, St. Nicholas continued to help the poor and children even after his death.

These legends gave rise to an annual "visit" from the saint, dressed in white beard and bishop's robes, to children on the eve of his feast day on December 6. "St. Nicholas" would encourage children to prepare well for Christmas, test them on their prayers, and give them little presents of candy and fruit. (To see how this tradition and St. Nicholas's name turned into our popular tradition of Santa Claus, see chapter 7).

St. Valentine

History tells us only that several Christians by the name of Valentine were martyred for their faith. One, very probably a priest, was martyred on February 14, 270, during a persecution promoted by Emperor Claudius II. A basilica was dedicated in his honor in 350 in Rome. His annual feast day on February 14 soon became associated with a tradition of boys and girls exchanging a promise of love. This was done in different ways over the centuries and evolved into our present tradition of exchanging Valentines on February 14 along with gifts and other special signs of love and affection.

How did St. Valentine become associated with these customs? An early legend says that Valentine, while in prison awaiting death for his Christian faith, sneaked a note to the daughter of his jailor, signing it with the words, "from your Valentine." Another tells of his curing the jailor's daughter of blindness. Another legend describes Valentine as a friend of little children, who tossed notes of affection into his cell when he was imprisoned for his faith.

A more likely explanation lies in the fact that on about the same day as the annual feast of St. Valentine, there was a pagan Roman festival, *Lupercalia* (Latin *lupus*, "wolf"). It celebrated the pastoral god, Lupercus (Roman equivalent to the Greek god Pan), to gain protection from wolves. This festival came under the patronage of Juno, the goddess of marriage. As part of the festivities, young boys and girls chose partners, proposed marriage, and became engaged, or at least picked a partner for the following year. The festival also had fertility overtones. When the Roman Empire became Christian, the traditions of this festival continued, but St. Valentine replaced the pagan goddess Juno as a patron of love.

There are two other explanations of the tradition of exchanging love notes, or "valentines," on February 14. There is an old English belief that on this date birds choose their mate. This was noted by Chaucer in the 14th century, who also mentions the exchange of notes. There is also the possibility that the tradition was accidentally associated with the feast day of St. Valentine because it falls at the time of the transition to springtime, the season of lovers.

Homemade valentines became a tradition on February 14, especially in England. Commercial valentines became popular in the early 19th century.

St. Patrick

The feast day of St. Patrick, March 17, has taken on many secular features with parties and parades. This is due to the influence and political power of the Irish Americans after their immigration during the 19th century. St. Patrick is their patron.

Much of our information about St. Patrick comes from his own writing, especially from his *Confession*. He was born a Roman citizen of wealthy parents in the British Isles about 385. When he was sixteen years old he was kidnapped by pirates and sold as a slave in Ireland. He worked there as a shepherd for six years, experiencing a spiritual awakening and divinely inspired dreams. Then he escaped to France, as promised in a dream, and eventually was reunited with his family. Years later he dedicated himself to the study of religion under St. Germanus at Auxerre, France, and was ordained a deacon. He desperately wanted to return to Ireland, the place and people of his enslavement, but was rejected at first by superiors. He was finally ordained bishop by Pope Celestine I and returned to Ireland in 432. There he ministered effectively for thirty years, baptizing thousands, including whole tribes, and establishing parishes and religious communities.

The efforts of St. Patrick were resisted in an organized way by the Druids, pagan religious leaders and sorcerers among the Celts. Legends tell of St. Patrick's miracles as he gradually undermined the power of the Druids among the people. Not long after his death in about 461, Patrick's disciples completed the conversion of the Irish nation.

Legends about St. Patrick became so popular after his death that it is now hard to separate fact from fiction. The best known of these is that he charmed all the snakes in Ireland into the sea where they drowned. Another, which is possibly authentic, led to the custom of the "wearing of the green" on March 17. Patrick used the three-leaf green shamrock to explain the mystery of the Trinity: Each of the three leaves represented the Father, Son, and the Holy Spirit. The stem represented the Godhead from which the three proceed. The shamrock had been used at the time of St. Patrick in Celtic fertility rituals. It was symbolic of three goddesses. Its leaves were ritually burned and the ashes sprinkled over fields to provide good crops.

Secular observance of St. Patrick's Day began in Boston in 1737 by Protestants to benefit the needy of Irish blood. This tradition continued after the Revolutionary War under joint Catholic-Presbyterian coordination. The most famous celebration is the St. Patrick's Day Parade along New York's Fifth Avenue.

PART FIVE

SACRAMENTS AND SACRAMENTALS

THE NATURE OF SACRAMENTS

BAPTISM

CONFIRMATION

EUCHARIST

RECONCILIATION

ANOINTING OF THE SICK

MARRIAGE

ORDERS

THE NATURE OF SACRAMENTALS

SIGNS

SYMBOLS

DEVOTIONS

18

SACRAMENTS

Principle of Sacramentality

Catholics are "sacrament people." We have always depended on the use of things, places, and persons to touch divine presence and to be touched by it. Catholics subscribe wholeheartedly to the truth that "there is more to life than meets the eye." We believe that we come in contact with this "more" by way of sacraments and sacramentals. By celebrating them we preserve our fundamental religious beliefs and pass them on to another generation.

The familiar pattern of sacramental rituals holds the assembly together. The effectiveness of the rituals depends on faith. A believer's openness to mystery is very important for anyone participating in the church's rich symbolic life. Without faith, words are words, water is water, bread is bread, and wine is wine. But with faith we step beyond the senses into a mystery dimension. Words of Scripture become a divine communication. Waters of baptism become a mystery-filled moment of new birth. Bread and wine become Communion and Presence.

Catholics share this principle of sacramentality with peoples throughout history, both Christian and non-Christian. From the most ancient of times, we humans have just naturally acted out important transitions in life by way of some kind of community or group ritual that makes use of sacred places, things, and persons. We do the same to remember important group experiences, face cyclic needs, or celebrate answers to the big questions of life and death. Like people of ancient times, we believe our social or community life has a God-dimension to it. By way of community rituals we come to grips with guilt and purification, initiate new members, celebrate communion with each other and with our God through a sacred meal, dramatize dependence or gratitude with ritual sacrifices, restore health, dramatize the meaning of death and farewell of loved ones, make sexuality and family life holy, and anoint chosen leaders to serve us.

Origin of Catholic Sacraments

It was natural that followers of Jesus depended upon sacred symbolism. They were not alone in this. When Christianity was beginning to spread throughout the Roman Empire, popular mystery cults were present almost everywhere. While there is no proof that the early followers of Jesus borrowed directly from these popular and usually secret groups, there are similarities in the sacramental rituals of both traditions.

The earliest of Christians naturally depended upon the symbolism and rituals that were part of their Jewish roots. Along with Jesus they had lived within the Hebrew tradition that celebrated their relationship with God in springtime rituals, the Passover, and other cyclic feasts, sacred places, burnt offerings, pouring of oil, rising incense, ritual meals, and scapegoats. Even before they knew themselves as a separate religious group or "church," they were already reliving Jesus' life-death-victory drama by telling the story and ritualizing it annually under the new spring moon like the clans of ancient times. In doing so they experienced the mystery of their own drama of life, death, and new life.

Christians, therefore, did not reinvent the sacramental wheel; nor did they dream up new religious forms. They borrowed the ones they were used to—simple, down to earth, now pregnant with new meaning—and went on from there. They learned about conversion, death, and resurrection, by going down into water, being anointed with sweet smelling oil, and by dressing in new white robes. Excitement and enthusiasm continued through the touch of the community's outstretched hands. They remembered Jesus and grew in relationship with the risen Lord by sitting weekly with him at table as they shared a holy bread and cup. Their own persecution-death-victory dramas were understood in light of his.

Greek-speaking Christians in those early times called these, and other, ritual religious experiences *mysteria*, or "mysteries." Latin writers began using the term *sacramentum*, or "sign," to describe the same thing. The fundamental truth expressed by these terms is the coming together of God and people, the divine and human, in a saving experience.

There was no intention during early centuries to limit the number of sacraments to seven. Any ritual that celebrated a divine saving action was considered a mystery or sacrament: feasts days such as Easter and Pentecost, actions such as the ritual washing of feet and imposition of blessed ashes, along with the more major ones we would come to know as "the seven." Some lists of sacraments were very short, others had as many as thirty. In the mid-13th century the number was finally set at seven. Other holy things and rituals came to be called sacramentals (see Chapter 19).

As separate European languages evolved out of Latin and "barbarian" tongues, the western Catholic church chose to continue Latin as its language of worship. This had a drastic influence on sacraments. They still formed the center of religious activity and community life, but they had become unintelligible to all but the clergy. And poorly educated clergy did not always understand the sacred rites they performed. Details got out of focus. The power of ritual frequently got confused with magic and superstition. Abuses were prevalent.

The Reformation of the 1500s challenged much of Catholic sacramentality. Most Protestants kept only the rituals of baptism and Eucharist as sacraments because they were clearly mentioned in Scripture. The Catholic church continued to defend its sacramental traditions, with almost no change between the 1500s and the mid-1900s. Catholics "received" the sacraments faithfully, but sometimes with little insight into their rich and living symbolism. Instead of the community rituals that they had been, sacraments tended to become private affairs: confession in a dark "closet"; baptism on a Sunday afternoon with few persons (and usually not the mother) present; anointing of the sick as last rites in the shadows of death in a private bedroom or hospital room.

The Second Vatican Council mandated the renewal of the sacraments. Since then the principle of sacramentality has again become the living center of Catholic spiritual life.

BAPTISM

Baptism: An Initiation Process
Early Christians moved easily from the baptism made popular by John along the River Jordan to their own water ceremony. They required it for commitment to the new Way preached by Jesus and for membership in their community of faith. We have this description from as early as the turn of the first century: "...baptize in running water, in the name of the Father and of the Son and of the Holy Spirit. If you do not have running water, baptize in some other water, and if you cannot do it in cold water, do it in warm. If you are without either, then pour water on the head three times in the name of the

Father and of the Son and of the Holy Spirit. Let the baptizer, the one to be baptized, and others who can, fast before the baptism, but order the candidate to fast one or two days beforehand" (*Didache* 7:1-4).

At first it seems that new Christians were accepted into the community through this water ceremony without much formal preparation. Soon, however, persecution made it important to test candidates for their sincerity, both to protect the community and to meet the challenges that lay ahead. Candidates usually witnessed the Eucharistic liturgy only after baptism.

At a fairly early date, baptism became associated with the annual Easter Vigil. Surviving written records from this period are not plentiful, but it seems that in many places adults were tested for up to three years while they were instructed, supported in their withdrawal from pagan practices and loyalties, and taught to live a new way. Only then were they admitted to candidacy for baptism. Finally, during what would become Lent, they received intense instruction, submitted to exorcisms and other special rituals, fasted on Good Friday and Holy Saturday, and were baptized during the night of the Easter Vigil. This period of preparation leading to initiation at the Easter Vigil was the beginnings of the *catechumenate,* which would reach its golden age in the 4th and 5th centuries.

Baptistries

Baptistries became prominent features of churches, basilicas, and cathedrals. Some of these were elaborate separate buildings. Others were built into the entryway or vestibules of the place of worship, and some were close to the sanctuary. Different forms of baptism were popular. In some baptistries, the elect were fully immersed, usually three times, in a pool. In other baptistries, the elect stood in shallow water, with the waters of baptism poured over them.

Immediately after the water ritual the newly baptized were anointed with a sweet smelling oil, chrism. Sometimes the anointing was lavish, covering most of the body, with men and women separated, deaconesses performing the ritual for women. Then the newly baptized were dressed in new white robes that they sometimes wore all Easter week. Holding a burning candle, they were led to the altar table for Eucharist.

Private Baptism

In the early 4th century the Roman persecution of Christians ended and the church gained religious freedom. Becoming a Christian became the popular thing to do as church and state began to blend together. There were mass conversions to Christianity that often overwhelmed the catechumenate and contributed to its decline. Eventually, most of the unbaptized left in Europe were newborn infants. The catechumenate process gradually fell into disuse, and other practices developed, some of which continued right into our own century.

By the 11th century it was considered a grave responsibility to baptize babies as soon as possible after birth. This was a consequence of a high infant mortality rate and the conviction that the unbaptized could not be saved. In the 14th century this became church law and remained the usual practice until recent years. Eventually baptism was no longer closely associated with the annual Easter experience. Adults were baptized in a private ceremony following a period of private instruction. The ordinary celebration of baptism became associated with infants, a rather simple ceremony, usually on a Sunday afternoon, with godparents and a few others present. Seldom was the mother present for two reasons. First, baptism usually closely followed birth; second, the mother was considered "unclean" until a ritual of purification was performed. Baptistries no longer were a prominent feature of the place of worship. A baptismal font, often in an out-of-the-way corner, became common. Just a little bit of water was poured onto the forehead of the infant.

Renewal of Baptism

Today, however, we have returned to more ancient practices. The baptism of infants frequently takes place in the midst of the worshipping community after the Sunday homily or at least in a more celebrative manner at another time. The adult catechumenate has been restored since 1972. Once again adults journey toward full faith with the whole parish community involved in some way as catechists, sponsors, godparents, and hospitality hosts. As in ancient times, public rituals once again grace the process: Rite of Acceptance, Rite of Election, Scrutinies, Presentation of the Creed, Presentation of the Our Father, dismissal after the Service of the Word for further breaking open the Word, baptism, confirmation and First Eucharist at the Easter Vigil, and a period of follow-up, or mystagogy. Baptismal pools, for immersion or for standing in, once again are designed as a prominent feature in the remodeling or building of churches.

Important sacramentals are still associated with baptism of infants: recitation of promises by those present, marking of the infant with the sign of the cross, pouring of water or immersion, anointing with holy chrism, clothing with a white garment, giving of a lighted candle, touching of the ears and mouth (optional).

For the close association of baptism with the season of Lent and Easter, see pages 71 and 90. For the customs associated with baptismal names and patrons, see page 111.

CONFIRMATION

Confirmation is a kind of accident in the development of Catholic sacramental rituals. During the first four centuries there was no uniformity in the initiation ritual as a person was led from the waters of baptism to the table of Eucharist in the same night or early dawn. Generally, the newly baptized were welcomed from the waters by the bishop, the official representative and leader of the local community. He, often with others, would lay hands on them. Or the bishop would extend his hands over them. If they had already been anointed, the bishop would often add still another anointing, called chrismation. The forehead was anointed with perfumed oil, often in the form of a cross. A ritual kiss of peace followed. Then the newly baptized were led to the Eucharistic table for the final stage of initiation into the church. This was the ordinary ritual in Rome in the year 215.

Eventually this second anointing was seen as distinct from the baptism ritual. It became associated with the coming of the Holy Spirit, a reliving of the Pentecost experience originally associated with baptism itself. During the first generations of Christianity baptism had often been accompanied by signs of the Spirit's presence: speaking in tongues, prophesying, and healing. By the time the church had gained her religious freedom in the early 4th century, these gifts had all but disappeared.

When it became the usual practice in local churches to baptize infants as soon as possible after birth, the bishop could not always be present for the special anointing and welcoming ritual. Also, in barbarian lands of Europe there were no bishops at first, only missionary monks and priests who baptized adults and children. Where the Western Catholic church was well established, this special anointing was postponed until the bishop was able to visit the parish. This ritual of welcoming by the bishop was, consequently, no longer experienced as a natural progression in the initiation ritual from the waters of baptism to the table of Eucharist. In this separated condition, the anointing took on its own character. The laying on of hands was replaced by the bishop's special anointing of the forehead in the form of a cross, sealing the person's baptism. This anointing has been called "confirmation" in the Western church since the mid-5th century.

Outside of the city of Rome, this separate anointing by the bishop was slow to catch on in many areas. Often, the baptized either did not receive the second anointing or the ritual was done by the local priest. Finally, between the 9th and 13th centuries the Roman tradition spread throughout Europe with the understanding that the purpose of confirmation was to strengthen the faith of the baptized person. The bishop's caress of the cheek, a sign of welcome and peace, was replaced with a slap to symbolize the spiritual battles facing the believer.

Until the 13th century it was expected, and even mandated by local church authorities, that infants and children be confirmed early in life, usually before the age of two. Then the ideal age began creeping upward because children did not need to defend their faith. Soon it was seven, then twelve, fourteen.... After the Council of Trent, young people between the ages of seven and twelve were to be confirmed.

Until modern times confirmation still occurred before first Eucharist, which was normally received during the early teens. The original order of initiation sacraments was preserved. At the beginning of the 20th century, however, it became popular to receive communion at an earlier age. This practice was encouraged by Pius X in 1910. After that, pastoral practice saw confirmation slipping out of the original sequence of initiation sacraments, coming sometime after the receiving of first Eucharist, when the bishop could visit the parish, often in cycles of up to five years.

In 1972 the American bishops settled on early adolescence, between the ages of ten and twelve, as the proper age for confirmation. In more recent times, however, confirmation tended to become the sacrament of Christian maturity, received in the mid to late teens, at a time when persons could freely and maturely make a commitment to their baptism.

Order of Initiation Restored

Today, however, the age of confirmation in the U.S. varies greatly from diocese to diocese. Following the popularity and importance of the restored initiation process, begun with the publication of the *Rite of Christian Initiation of Adults* in 1972, some dioceses have restored the original order of the initiation sacraments: baptism, confirmation, and Eucharist, with confirmation celebrated at the age of reason (about 7) and before first Eucharist, often at the same Mass. This is in keeping with the preference expressed in the church's official rites. Other dioceses have decided on ages varying from nine or ten to the late teens. When adults and children of catechetical age come for baptism, all three sacraments are always celebrated in the original order as part of one ritual.

EUCHARIST

It was the smell of Catholicism—a sweet smelling odor of incense that permeated all Catholic churches until recent times. The smell was a leftover from lavish incensing of the Blessed Sacrament during Benediction. A large consecrated host was always kept in the tabernacle. Every week, sometimes more often, this host was placed in a special container, called a monstrance, and exhibited for all to see and adore. To the tunes of *O Salutaris hostia* and *Tantum ergo sacramentum...* this sacred host was devoutly incensed. Then the congregation was blessed with it.

Many Catholics tend to think of the Eucharist as separate or a combination of separate sacred objects: consecrated bread received in communion, consecrated bread exhibited to be adored and be blessed by in Benediction, and consecrated bread to be visited and kept vigil with in the tabernacle. This attitude evolved in the Middle Ages and prevailed until recent times.

In reality, however, from the time of the apostles, Eucharist (Greek *eucharistein*, "to give thanks"), has referred to the entire combination of rituals that hold the assembly of believers together for worship. It includes, therefore, the sharing of the Word of Scripture, offering of prayers, and keeping alive the memory of Jesus by remembering the Last Supper. This concludes naturally in the sharing the bread that is his body broken for us and the cup that is his blood poured out for us. The Eucharist is the whole ritual that has come to be known as the Mass. The word "Mass" comes from the Latin *missa* or "dismissal" of those assembled, first the catechumens after the Service of the Word and the whole congregation at the end.

The Eucharist, therefore, is not only a holy bread and a holy cup, it is a holy moment—a saving action. It has been the faith of Catholics from earliest times that Jesus Christ is present during this Eucharistic ritual. Those who share the bread and cup with each other become one with Christ and one with each other, because it is the one Christ whom they share.

The sacrament of Eucharist is first of all associated with the evolution of the Lord's Day, Sunday (see pages 19-25), and was celebrated only on Sunday for the first centuries. The Eucharist evolved rather quickly from a fellowship meal to a ritual meal accompanied by other religious activities: a Scripture service, an offering of gifts of bread and wine, a thanksgiving prayer over these gifts, a praying of the memorial words of Jesus from the Last Supper, a breaking of bread, and finally the sharing of this holy bread and cup by those present. From early times a portion was always saved to send to the absent and the sick.

Eucharistic Sacrifice

The Letter to the Hebrews in the Christian Scriptures interpreted this Eucharistic experience as a holy sacrifice. It proclaimed Jesus as priest, offering himself as the perfect victim to the heavenly Father. This belief quickly became popular. Prior to this, sacrifice had been closely identified with animal sacrifice in both pagan religions and Judaism—and Christians at this time did not want to be closely associated with either tradition. In fact pagans sometimes accused Christians of being atheists because they did not offer sacrifices to gods. When the notion of sacrifice became legitimate, however, it quickly caught on. Communion came to be experienced as a sacrificial meal. Later on the Eucharistic bread came to be called a host (Latin *hostia*), a term originally referring to an animal sacrifice.

Distancing from Laity

When Christianity gained its religious freedom in the early 4th century, the Eucharist, or Mass, gradually evolved into a more complicated and more standardized ritual, and became even more lengthy when Sunday became a day of rest in 321. Soon, in many cities, Mass was celebrated by ranks of clergy in the presence of the laity, whose level of participation was gradually diminishing. The adoption of Latin as the official language of worship, while peoples' languages were rapidly evolving into new tongues, further separated the Eucharist from the living experience of the people.

Eucharistic attitudes and practices continued to change during the Middle Ages. More and more people withdrew into their own private devotions, being physically present at Mass but not participating in it. It was a ceremony to attend and watch, a drama that unfolded with pomp, incense, and glitter of priestly robes. All this added to the mystery of what the laity no longer understood. Their spirituality no longer depended upon participating in the Mass.

Deterioration of Meaning and Practice

As centuries passed, churches became larger. Cathedrals and basilicas and churches replaced the house churches of early Christianity. A simple wooden altar was replaced by stone and marble. By the 6th century the altar was moved to the far end of the church building. The priest, offering the sacrifice, presided with his back to the people. The mysterious Eucharistic prayers, especially the words of consecration, were whispered softly. Emphasis was placed on adoration. Eventually the consecrated elements of bread and wine were elevated above the priest's head so that the people could see and adore. Bells were rung by assisting ministers to inform the people that important things were happening in the ritual (such as the consecration), with little bells in the sanctuary to get the attention of the congregation and big bells in the tower to notify the neighborhood. To *see* the Eucharist became more important than to take and eat. In the 14th century it was common for people to rush from church to church to see elevations, believing that a glimpse would give good luck or protect them from a sudden death.

Emphasis on the holiness of the consecrated bread escalated. Priests were required to genuflect every time they touched it, and had to keep their fingers joined until rinsed after communion. Touching the sacred vessels was reserved to the ordained. A crucifix became a fixture on or above the altar to emphasize the sacrifice of Jesus; the altar backdrop was filled with statues to remember the saints. By the year 1000 the consecrated bread, considered too holy to be touched by the laity, was placed on the tongue. This emphasis on the divinity of Christ and the holiness of the consecrated bread prevented people from receiving communion. They felt unworthy to do so. Finally the church had to legislate that communion be received at least once a year, leading to the church law of the Easter Duty in 1215. These customs and attitudes continued until recent times. An exaggerated devotion to the real presence, along with a mixture of discipline and preparation, resulted in a Eucharistic fast. All who wished to receive communion in the morning had to abstain from all food and drink, including water, from midnight. This included the priest. Beginning in the early 1950s water was permitted. In the mid-1960s food was permitted up to one hour before communion, with special consideration for the sick.

In the 12th century, tabernacles with reserved consecrated bread were becoming elaborate locked safes, placed in the sanctuary area. (In the 16th century, it became popular to place the tabernacle on the altar itself.) The tabernacle, along with the monstrance, became a center for Eucharistic devotions. Side altars became popular so that private Masses could be celebrated, often simultaneously with Mass at the "high" altar. Stained glass windows and multiple statues attracted the attention of the people, ancient visual aids promoting religious devotion.

For many centuries, a great variety still existed in how the Mass was celebrated in the Western church. In Gaul (western Europe), a multiplication of private prayers recited by the priest was introduced in the late Middle Ages, along with multiple signs of the cross over the bread and wine. Later, Rome, in a state of deterioration, had to look north to the land of Charlemagne for hand-copied books detailing the celebration of sacraments. In this way these new additions became part of the Roman books and *the* way of doing things throughout the Western church.

In 1570 Pius V issued an official edition of the Roman missal, and made it mandatory for all of Western Catholicism. It included exact detailed rubrics. The invention of printing made it possible for every priest to have a copy. For the next 400 years the Mass would change little throughout the Western Latin Catholic church.

Renewal of Eucharist

From the Middle Ages into modern times Eucharistic piety had little connection with the original meaning of the Eucharist. People continued to do their own thing with devotional books and rosary while the clergy did theirs in front in Latin. Worship outside of Mass, associated with the tabernacle or Benediction, became more effective than the Mass itself for people's spirituality.

All this began to change with the liturgical movement that began in the last years of the 19th century. The Second Vatican Council (1962-1965) in its first decree, the Constitution on the Sacred Liturgy (1963), turned the entire church back toward the original meaning of Eucharist. Rapid changes followed: emphasis on the people's active participation, the ritual simplified, flexible, audible, and in the language of the people. The altar, looking more like a table once again, moved back among the people. The priest once again presides facing the people, inviting their response and participation. Preaching of homilies, communion of Word, is again as important as the communion of bread and cup. Lay leaders have become involved as ministers and members of liturgy commissions. Today most people who assemble take Jesus at his word: "Take and eat...Take and drink!"

RECONCILIATION

Sin: Human Experience
Humans have always found something lacking in their personal behavior. Moral conduct has always been guided by codes, taboos, and laws within families, clans, or tribes. Some moral codes were very elaborate, for example the Code of Hammurabi, king of Babylon in the 18th century B.C.E., and the moral legislation found in the books of Leviticus and Deuteronomy of the Hebrew Scriptures. Some process of making amends for violations, sins, has always been part of human experience, too. Since proper behavior was considered legislated by the gods, atonement for violations was a religious matter. This varied from temporary exclusion or excommunication from the clan, rituals of purification, special sacrifices as sin offerings, fasting, prayer, and, in extreme cases, death.

Gospel of Reconciliation
Jesus himself and the earliest of Christians were used to penitential rituals prescribed by the Hebrew Scriptures and Jewish traditions. The chief one was the Day of Atonement when the high priest ritually confessed his and the people's sins to God. He then transferred the sins of the nation to a goat, called Azazel, which was then driven into the wilderness. This is the origin of the term "scapegoat." The high priest then offered the required sacrifice in the Temple in Jerusalem as a sign that all would change their lives. Locally, rabbis recommended penitential acts, such as the wearing of sackcloth and ashes.

Jesus preached a gospel of God's love and forgiveness. He was comfortable in associating with sinners, showing them his sincere love and companionship. Sinners flocked to him. Later, however, his church would find it difficult to deal with the matter of sin and forgiveness. The earliest Christian communities continued their Jewish penitential practices. They expelled members in extreme cases until they repented. The apostle Paul urged this (see 1 Corinthians 5:1–13). Baptism was considered *the* means of repentance and response to Jesus' invitation to a new life—the Kingdom of God. Early Christians presumed that all would wait in baptismal innocence for a quick return of Jesus Christ in glory.

Beginnings of Ritual Penance

These early Christians were not blind to the reality of ordinary sins. So they confessed their sins to one another and prayed for healing (see James 5:16). When Christ's Second Coming did not happen as quickly as they had once thought, and church communities had to deal with members who had not lived up to their commitment, there evolved a need for some kind of absolution ritual. At a very early date, a penitential formula was included when Christians gathered for the Eucharist: "On the dominical day of the Lord (Sunday) come together to break bread and give thanks, *after having also confessed your sins so that your sacrifice may be pure*" (*Didache*, 4:14, end of 1st century, emphasis added).

Intermittent persecutions by Roman civil authorities accelerated the need for a ritual of penance and absolution. Some Christians weakened and denied their faith. Should they be allowed back into the community? And how about murderers, adulterers, and idolaters? Rigorists wanted to deny any absolution and readmittance. Others insisted that forgiveness be quick and complete, the kind modeled by Jesus.

Public Penance

By the 4th century a public ritual had evolved to deal with the most serious of sinners. This included a confession of sins to the local bishop and readmittance to the worshipping community after proof of conversion and extensive penance. The priestly authority to represent the church in absolving from sins was reserved first to the bishop and later to all priests. Sinners were publicly identified as penitents, a distinct group in the local parish. Centuries later, remnants of this public ritual identification would be preserved in our Ash Wednesday service. These penitents were often dismissed from the assembly after the liturgy of the Word, just as the catechumens were. Penances were harsh and often public, sometimes lasting for years or even a lifetime. Some common penances were: total abstinence from wine, meat, sexual relations with spouse, business dealings, bathing, shaving, or having one's hair cut. It was common to wear sackcloth, ashes, and even chains.

At Mass these penitents were prayed over by the presider and congregation. In some places penitents had to stand at the doors of the church, begging for the prayers of those who entered. Absolution and readmittance to the community occurred before the Easter Vigil, often on Holy Thursday. A common conviction was that there was only one opportunity for repentance after baptism. It was not unusual, therefore, for serious sinners to postpone entering the ranks of penitents until old age.

Private Penance
This public form of the sacrament of penance was not very popular because of the rigorism associated with it. It was common that serious sinners asked for absolution only at the time of death. A private form of confession and penance, repeated frequently, evolved in monasteries because of the conviction that all are sinners to some degree. When these monks evangelized Ireland in the 5th century, they carried this form of the sacrament with them, making it available to Catholics in the neighborhood of their monasteries. For the sake of uniformity, priest monks used small books listing common sins according to degree of seriousness and recommended penances for each. Effort was made to ensure that the punishment (penance) fit the crime (sin). Priest confessors had to become "judges" to do this. Ordinarily absolution was given when the penance was completed, except in the danger of death or the impossibility to return later. Priest confessor and penitent would prostrate themselves before the altar as part of the ritual.

Early in the 6th century, monks from these Irish centers carried this private form of the sacrament to the mainland of Europe. For a while there was tension between the old and harsh way of doing this sacrament and the more practical form developed by the monks. Momentum was on the side of the repeated private form, although it was still somewhat unofficial. By the end of the 10th century, absolution was commonly given before the penance was completed. In the 11th century the use of books of penances were discontinued, and penances become lighter.

Already in the 8th century, people were urged to confess at least three times each year. Later, confessing once a year, joined to the Easter duty of receiving communion, was mandated for all by the Fourth Lateran Council in 1215.

By the 13th century this unofficial private form of the sacrament of penance had become the official sacrament of repentance. A change in attitude also had evolved: forgiveness of sins occurred through the absolution by a priest rather than through the sorrow and penance of the penitents. A distinction between mortal and venial sins also occurred. Originally, mortal sins referred to the kind requiring public penance. Now they described the kind that, unforgiven, would merit eternal punishment. Venial sins, on the other hand, could be easily pardoned on both sides of death.

Purgatory and Indulgences

The conviction that something still had to be done after death became popular once penances became easier and absolution readily available. The penance received in the sacrament was meant to shorten one's time in purgatory (see pages 129-130) rather than cancel all effects of sin. Because some punishment due for sins always remained, even after death, some method of dealing with it had to be designed. The practice of indulgences (see pages 131-133) evolved as a consequence. According to this tradition, bishops and then priests had the authority to cancel part of the public penance required of penitents. This authority, associated with their power to bind and to loose (see John 20:22–23), allowed them to apply the infinite merits of Christ to a particular individual. During the 13th century it became popular to transfer these indulgences to souls in purgatory. Unfortunately, these indulgences often were attached to the offering of funds for the building and repair of churches. Eventually this practice was the catalyst for Martin Luther's challenge to the Catholic church and to the Protestant Reformation.

Most Protestants rejected this sacrament of penance. The Catholic church, on the other hand, reemphasized its importance as it had evolved in the Middle Ages, with its stress on private confession and its association with indulgences.

These private confessions usually took place before the altar. After the Council of Trent (1545-1563), however, St. Charles Borromeo designed a confessor's chair boxed in by screens, a design that lasted for hundreds of years. In 1614 the official ritual mandated this style for the sake of anonymity and to protect women from solicitation. This anonymity was also protected by the seal of confession, which forbade the revelation of any confessed serious sin under pain of excommunication. Until the 20th century, the sacrament of penance was ordinarily received once a year as a preparation to receive communion at Eastertime. When Pius X emphasized frequent communion, the conviction still continued that pious Catholics always confess first.

Contemporary Practice

By the middle of the 20th century, it became harder to justify the extreme legalism that had been associated with the sacrament of penance right into modern times. Shifts in moral thinking occurred. Sin in the truest sense came to be associated more with internal choices about fundamental options rather than with external actions. And the gospel message rather than traditional moral laws once again became *the* effective guideline for morality.

In 1973 the church responded to new insights and emphases. It issued a new ritual for the sacrament of penance, one that would highlight its communal dimension and call to conversion. It contained three rites.

The first rite is a private form that encourages priest and penitent to converse face to face, sharing prayer and Scripture together, and including spiritual counseling and meaningful penance. This has led to the designing of reconciliation rooms to replace the small traditional confessionals.

A second rite is a semi-private form, popularly called communal penance. It begins with an assembly devoted to song, prayer, Scripture reading, and preaching. Then penitents are invited to approach one of the priest confessors for a brief private confession and absolution.

A third rite, a public form, popularly called general absolution, is available in situations of emergency or when too many penitents are present for private confession. Sins absolved in this latter way are still to be confessed privately later.

Finally, there is a form of penitential celebration without absolution. Its purpose is to encourage a sense of conversion.

This sacrament is still in a pattern of transition. Communal penance services have become very popular, especially during the seasons of Lent and Advent, often with several parishes cooperating. Private confession is still available in all parishes, often in connection with spiritual direction. Some parishes provide communal services with general absolution, even though cautioned not to do so by church authorities.

People have not denied that they are sinners. There is no absolute consensus, however, on what to do about conversion and the consequences of sin.

ANOINTING OF THE SICK

Shamans and medicine men and women have struggled with sickness and pain since the dawn of history. Making use of such sacramentals as dances, chants, incense, and masks, they bore witness to the power of evil associated with people's physical and spiritual limitations. They believed that the gods controlled health and sickness.

The Jewish people were just as holistic in attitude. While using the best of known medicines and cures, they confessed that healing was controlled by God (see Psalms 32, 38, 88, 91). They looked to a messianic age when all physical and moral evil would be eliminated.

Christians believe that Jesus did everything the prophets foretold of the messianic age. He was lavish in his healing of every kind of sickness and disability, even bringing the dead to life. Often he would join to this healing a forgiveness of sin. This ministry of healing was practiced also by his disciples whom he sent out on a kind of internship (see Luke 9:1, 10:9; Mark 6:13). Later, after Jesus left them, the apostles continued this healing ministry (see Acts 3:1–10, 14:8–18). Charismatic healing flourished in some communities (see 1 Corinthians 12:9) and enjoys a revival today.

The Letter of James describes clearly the practice of physical and spiritual healing in early Christianity: "Are any of you sick? Then call for the elders of the church and have them pray over them, anointing them with oil in the name of the Lord. The prayer of faith will save the sick, and the Lord will raise them up; and anyone who has committed sins will be forgiven" (see James 5:14–15).

During early centuries Christians privately used oil blessed by the bishop or priests as an internal and external healing remedy. In this form it was used as a kind of medicine or ointment or salve. In some localities blessed oil was also used publicly to anoint penitents as part of an extensive reconciliation process. Only with the 5th century is there evidence that priests rather than the laity used oil to anoint the sick. Church authorities encouraged this official use of oil as a healing sacramental, probably to counteract the people's temptation to seek pagan remedies.

Transition to Anointing of the Dying

Until the Middle Ages people continued to use oil privately as a practical means for physical healing. If they were dying, however, they received absolution and communion, instead of anointing. This Eucharist was called Holy Viaticum, Latin *viaticus*, "way," "journey." When people started to postpone their request for absolution from sin to the time of dying, because of the harsh penitential demands by the church, a reconciliation ritual soon became associated with the deathbed. This ritual, always conducted by a priest, began with a confession. Then there was an anointing, not for healing but because an anointing often was part of the official public penitential practice. This ritual ended with prayer for forgiveness and absolution.

During the time of Charlemagne in the 9th century, this deathbed absolution ritual found its way into the official books in the section that included the ritual for the anointing of the sick. Later generations of bishops and priests presumed that this ritual had come from Rome and was, therefore, official. In this way the anointing of the sick for healing purposes was taken out of the hands of the laity. From then on the anointing was performed only for the seriously ill and was joined to the ritual for a final absolution from sin and Viaticum. The ritual still prayed for healing, however, and parts of the body most in pain were anointed in the form of a cross.

By the end of the 9th century the ritual had become the Last Rites and had become well established in Catholic customs and traditions. For a while the ritual was performed by many priests concelebrating, often in the local church, with multiple sprinklings with holy water, incensing, litanies, and laying on of hands. Because this elaborate ritual called for a large financial donation, common people had little access to the final anointing. Celebration by a single priest eventually became the norm.

Gradually, prayers for physical healing were dropped. The spirit of the ritual was one of preparation for death only. No longer was a hurting part of the body anointed—only the senses, feet, and hands with a prayer that sins committed by them be forgiven: "Through this holy anointing and his tender mercy, may the Lord forgive whatever sins you have committed by sight..." And the anointing followed absolution and communion. It had become the last anointing (Latin *extrema unctio*, Extreme Unction). In this form it was finally listed as one of the seven sacraments in the Middle Ages.

Because the ritual included absolution from sin, followed by the Eucharist, what purpose did the anointing have, since sins were already forgiven? Medieval theologians concluded that the anointing cleansed a dying person from the remnants of all her or his sins committed during life, a final preparation needed to enjoy the glory of heaven. Therefore, the sacrament should not be given to someone who might recover and thus prevent the very purpose of the sacrament! It had become the transition from this life to the next instead of from sickness to health.

Current Practices

The Council of Trent returned to more ancient understandings by teaching that this rite of anointing both forgives sins and also heals the sick. Unfortunately, however, this particular teaching of Trent had little effect on pastoral practice or popular understandings of the sacrament. In the 1950s a gradual change in thinking evolved because of research into the ancient practices related to the use of oil to anoint the sick for healing. The sacrament once again was offered to those who were seriously ill and not necessarily dying. The notion of applying the name "Last Rites" to this anointing was challenged. Communion or Viaticum, properly speaking, should be the last ritual. Contributing to this conviction was the practice in the Eastern church of anointing the sick publicly in churches.

The Second Vatican Council supported this direction in thinking. The renewal of the sacrament, now called the Anointing of the Sick, was completed in 1972. Several forms of this ritual are now available. If it probably is the final anointing, then it should be accompanied by Communion or Viaticum and, if desired, confession. Those with less serious illness may receive the sacrament alone or with others in a more public fashion, for example in the parish church. Once again the emphasis is on healing rather than absolution from sin. Only the forehead and hands are anointed with the prayer: "Through this holy anointing may the Lord in his love and mercy help you with the grace of the Holy Spirit. May the Lord who frees you from sin save you and raise you up."

MARRIAGE

There was no particular Catholic wedding ritual until after the 11th century. The civil government of the Roman Empire had always regulated marriages and divorce and continued to do so after the church gained religious freedom in 313. Only when the decaying empire lost its power to enforce its laws did bishops assume authority over marriage customs.

Early Christians married according to the popular ways of their culture. It was a civil, personal, and family matter. What was peculiarly Christian, however, was a new attitude toward the permanence of the marriage bond. Jewish tradition permitted many wives and permitted husbands to divorce spouses who were guilty of shameful behavior (and sometimes allowed divorce for even minor reasons). Jesus promoted a much higher norm to strive for: monogamy, no divorce (see Luke 16:18; Mark 10:1–12; Matthew 5:31–32, 19:3–9). Exceptions, however, were allowed already in the first generations of Christianity (1 Corinthians 7:12–16; 2 Corinthians 6:14–18).

Bishops continued to allow divorce but only on the grounds of adultery. A double standard often was evident; the wife, but not the husband, was usually prohibited from remarrying. Still, no consistent policy toward the absolute permanence of the marriage bond existed. Only with bishop St. Ambrose of Milan (d. 397) did the conviction of the absolute indissolubility of marriage begin to surface.

From the beginning, therefore, the church adopted as its own the current cultural attitude toward marriage, with the primacy of the husband evident. The apostle Paul, comfortable with this attitude, took pains to balance it with spiritual and symbolic insights into the mystery of marriage: it is a sign of Christ's union with and love for his body, the church (Ephesians 5:21–33). These spiritual insights did not enter into the ritual itself. Young men and women continued to marry according to local traditions. Generally in some symbolic fashion, the father "gave away" his daughter to the groom in her own home, usually placing her hand into that of her new husband. Many of the popular customs still associated with weddings came from the early Roman times and the Germanic tribes of Europe. Because fathers controlled the destiny of their children, the bride's father was compensated for the loss of a fertile member of his family by gifts of money or property. Later this became symbolic: in place of the "price for the bride" a precious ring was placed on the bride's finger. The marriage officially occurred when the woman's father brought her to her new home. There she was carried over the threshold by her new husband—possibly a ritual left over from ancient times when brides were "carried away" or abducted by raids on other clans. Once inside her new home the bride was fed a piece of sacred cake (originally done to introduce her to her new gods). Even the special bridal dress and garlands of flowers come from ancient Roman times.

In the East, a garland was draped over the couple to symbolize their union. In the West a veil frequently was placed over the couple. No formula or blessing by a representative of the church was necessary. Then there was a joyful procession to the husband's home for a big feast. When Christianity spread among the Germanic peoples, their traditions were adopted, too. It is interesting to note that their customs (for example, the popular custom of the engagement ring) were often very similar to those of other peoples.

Gradually it became a popular tradition to have a representative of the clergy, as guest of the families, give a special blessing to the newly married couple during the wedding feast. Sometimes the clergy would be invited to do what the father would do; for example, placing the bride's hand into the groom's. In some localities the priest would drape the couple with a veil just as, in the Eastern church a garland of flowers was used. Until the 5th century, however, the only Catholics who had to have a special blessing at their wedding were priests and deacons! The blessing of the "bridal chamber" or bedroom was also common.

A Problem with Sex

Very early in the history of the church, religious leaders began to look upon the sexual dimension of marriage as a necessary evil, always tainted with some sin. This attitude was made popular by Manichean heretics who claimed that material things and sexual matters were sinful by their nature. Marriage was discouraged and allowed only for the procreation of children. This heresy was contrary to the teaching of Christianity, but shades of this attitude crept into Catholic tradition, promoted even by St. Augustine (d. 430).

The conviction that procreation of children was the first and most important purpose of marriage never left Catholicism entirely. The second, and lesser, purpose was to promote fidelity among adults. In the Middle Ages marriage was considered good only as a solution to concupiscence or "desires of the flesh." Only in recent times have the notions of love, companionship, and bonding been emphasized as equal to procreation.

Marriage Becomes Sacrament

No particular ritual was demanded by the church until after 1000. Then bishops began to insist that the exchange of consent be done before witnesses (often to ensure the woman's free consent) and be solemnly blessed by a priest. At first weddings were held in church only to make it more convenient to get the required blessing. The exchange of consent would be done at the church door, followed by a nuptial Mass and blessing. By the 12th century all was done in the same ceremony with the priest assuming responsibilities once carried out by parents or guardians, for example, placing the bride's hand into that of the groom. Even the tradition of kissing the bride evolved within this Catholic ritual. The priest would give the kiss of peace to the groom who in turn passed it on to the bride.

Finally, at the Fourth Lateran Council in 1215 marriage was included in the official list of the church's seven sacraments. Difficulties continued, however. How could an activity that involves material concerns and sexuality be a sacrament? Once marriage was recognized as a sacrament, it had to be admitted that it is a source of special grace and therefore good in itself.

The heart of the sacrament was finally determined to be the exchange of consent, completed or sealed in intercourse. Its indissolubility continued to be presumed unless it could be proved that the original contract did not exist for some reason. In the 15th century, the church developed its process of annulment of certain marriages through its church courts.

The Council of Trent (1563) summarized the church's teaching about marriage. It declared that in the future no Christian marriage would be valid and sacramental unless it was contracted before a priest and two witnesses. Later this requirement was limited to Catholics. Also, marriages had to be announced publicly three weeks in advance. These announcements, popularly called "the wedding banns," are, today, an optional practice.

Only in the late 1700s in France did churches, Catholic and Protestant, lose legal control over marriage. The Napoleonic Code of 1792 ordered all marriages to be civil. After that all countries began allowing civil marriages.

Current Thinking and Practice

At mid-20th century many Catholic theologians began emphasizing that sex had a more fundamental purpose in life than procreation and education of children. Marriage and sex, like love itself, were important in themselves. In sum: The primary purpose of marriage was the personal fulfillment and emotional growth of the spouses.

While the official church resisted this new emphasis, Vatican Council II adopted a more personalist interpretation of marriage. It maintained, however, the church's traditional teaching (Church in the Modern World, 48). Since then the ritual has been revised. Couples may now choose from a variety of Scripture readings and formulas for exchange of consent. In some places they have even greater freedom in designing their wedding: writing their own vows, choosing other favorite readings to accompany Scripture. In the case of an interfaith marriage, they may even invite the non-Catholic's pastor to preside with the Catholic priest.

The church has continued to support efforts to strengthen marriage. Adequate preparation is required by all dioceses. Some require a waiting period up to six months. Enrichment efforts are popular, notably the Marriage Encounter movement.

ORDERS

Priesthood as we know it in the Catholic church was unheard of during the first generation of Christianity, because at that time priesthood was still associated with animal sacrifices in both the Jewish and pagan religions. The first Christians continued to recognize the legitimacy of the Jewish Temple and priesthood at Jerusalem. In their local communities they continued a style of community leadership common in Jewish communities, looking to elders to provide leadership and to preside over their Eucharistic assemblies. These were chosen in a ritual that included being prayed over and having hands laid on them. In the Greek Scriptures, these elders are called *presbyteroi*. Other ministers were chosen in a similar ritual. (See Acts 13:1–3; 1 Timothy 4:14; 5:22.)

In 70 C.E. Jerusalem and its temple and Jewish priesthood were destroyed by Roman armies. Jews were scattered. Christians began to look to Jesus as *the* priest, a development in their thinking reflected clearly in the letter to Hebrews. All the baptized shared this special priesthood because all had become one with Christ.

A clearly defined local leadership in the form of elders, or *presbyteroi*, became still more important when the original apostles and disciples of Jesus died. The chief elder in each community was often called the *episkopos* (Greek, "overseer"). In English this came to be translated as "bishop" (Latin *episcopus*). Ordinarily he presided over the community's Eucharistic assembly.

Someone had to be responsible to preserve and preach the true beliefs when heresies began to evolve. Consequently, local leaders began to consider themselves the successors of the apostles in the sense that they preserved the teaching of the apostles. By the end of the 2nd century the local bishop was considered *the* source of true teaching.

Origin of Catholic Priesthood

When the Eucharist came to be regarded as a sacrifice, the role of the bishop took on a priestly dimension. By the 3rd century bishops were considered priests. Presbyters or elders sometimes substituted for the bishop at the Eucharist. By the end of the third century people all over were using the title "priest" (*hiereus* in Greek and *sacerdos* in Latin) for whoever presided at the Eucharist.

Ordination Process

For the first 150 years presbyters were usually chosen by the people in the local community whom they would serve. They chose the bishop from among presbyters. Later only the presbyters or neighboring bishops had a vote in choosing the bishop. People still had some voice of approval. Deacons were usually appointed by the bishop. All these ministers were ritually selected, or ordained by a laying on of hands. The ordination was to specific ministries. The bishop was given the authority to offer the Eucharist, bind and loose from serious sin, and to assign other ministers. Presbyters were given the authority to counsel members of the community and to govern. Deacons were chosen as servants to the bishop.

Expanding Orders of Clergy

When the church obtained legal standing in 313, it already had an organized system of ministers and community leadership: presbyters or elders, bishops or chief elders, and deacons. In some communities, especially in the East, deaconesses were also part of the local ministry system. The Council of Nicaea (325), however, mandated that deaconesses no longer be considered clergy.

It did not take long before even more ranks or orders evolved. Subdeacons helped deacons. Exorcists helped at rituals for initiation and repentance. Lectors were trained to read the Scriptures. Porters were responsible for janitorial and guard duties, the latter especially important during times of persecution. Acolytes served as secretaries and messengers of bishops. These special ministries were counted among the clergy by the 5th century. Eventually they were considered stepping stones to priesthood, advancing through the ranks, so to speak.

In some communities other ministries were very active. Widows and virgins organized to pray and to serve the poor and sick. Specially selected catechists or teachers instructed catechumens.

Christian communities grew rapidly, creating further need for leadership. Bishops emerged as the head of this local leadership. They were a sort of a father of a family, shepherd, administrator, judge, teacher, PR person with the non-Christian and often antagonistic neighbors, and the priest at the Eucharistic sacrifice. Ordinarily, they still ministered closely with the local elders or presbyters.

Deacons continued to be practical ministers within the local community, pretty much assisting the bishop. They served the poor, took care of financial matters, assisted at the Eucharist, and prepared catechumens for baptism.

Presbyters Become Priests

When Christianity became the official religion of the Roman Empire, large numbers of converts and multiplication of communities or parishes called for more ordained personnel. This was especially true of outlying areas. Presbyters were already available. They made ideal substitutes for the bishop. In this way presbyters, originally councils of elders or advisors, began serving alone in local communities. Their authority was seen as coming directly from the bishop. At first their delegated ministry was limited to presiding over the Eucharist and baptizing.

Soon all presbyters were considered priests because they offered the Eucharistic sacrifice. To keep a distinction between them and bishops, the latter were called "high priests." For a while a beautiful custom was practiced to maintain a symbolic union between the local bishops and the priests in the surrounding area. The bishop would send a piece of consecrated bread from his Mass to these priests in the outlaying parishes who would put it in their chalice at Mass.

Our word "priest" is directly related to the Greek word *presbyteros* and the Latin *presbyter*. This latter was shortened to "prester," giving us our English "priest."

A Different Lifestyle

The first hints of a distinction between the lifestyles of clergy and laity arose already in the 200s. Clergy were expected to live differently, especially in regard to sexual expression and marriage. The apostle Paul had recommended celibacy and virginity for community leaders, or at least that bishops be married only once. The Hebrew Scriptures (see Leviticus 22:3–6) mandated that their Jewish priests refrain from intercourse before serving at the altar.

Because Christians considered the priesthood of the New Testament to be greater than that of the Jews, the call to purity was considered greater, too. And since priests served at the altar all their life, shouldn't their abstinence be permanent? Early heretics, such as Manichaeans and Montanists, added a negative influence by proclaiming that sexual expression—including that of the laity—was impure. Catholic leaders, such as St. Augustine, taught that Original Sin was transmitted through intercourse. Therefore, abstinence and virginity was the ideal life and only the weak should marry. However, most bishops and presbyters continued to marry. In fact, the only marriages that had to have any kind of blessing were those of deacons and priests.

Priests continued to live in the same style as did the people they served. They farmed and worked at trades. They did not wear distinctive clothing. Only bishops, because of their extensive responsibilities, did not do ordinary work; and they wore a distinctive insignia. Beginning in the late 5th century, priests began wearing a long tunic to distinguish them from the laity, who wore a short one. This evolved into the modern alb (white) and the everyday dark cassock.

As Christianity swept through the Germanic lands, the church adopted the feudalistic structures of culture and politics that had evolved in Europe. Precise ranking, with exact privileges and responsibilities, was determined for kings, lords, knights, and, on the bottom, the peasants. A parallel ranking made clear distinction among bishops, abbots, priests, monks, and the laity on the bottom.

Clearly determined levels of authority gave rise to elaborate investiture with distinct insignia when clerics were ordained. Deacons were presented with alb and stole; priests' palms were anointed and they were then presented with chasuble and stole, along with paten, chalice, bread, and wine; bishops received the stole, ring, crozier, and eventually the miter; deacons received the Book of the Gospels; acolytes received a candle; lectors, the Book of Epistles; porters, a key.

The tradition of celibacy continued to evolve. In some places it was expected that priests not be sexually active after ordination. When monastic spirituality became popular in the fourth and fifth centuries, it promoted the ideal of celibacy as a model for all priests. However, the crisis in Europe following the barbarian invasions made it difficult for church leaders to enforce the discipline of clerical celibacy.

One way church authority enforced celibacy was by ordaining monks, who took the vow of chastity, to evangelize large areas of Europe. Church authority continued to mandate celibacy. The First Lateran Council (1123-1153) forbade those in orders to marry and ordered all those already married to renounce their wives and do penance. Later legislation declared the marriages of clerics not only illegal but also invalid. Widespread disregard of these laws continued until a reorganization of preparation for priesthood following the Protestant Reformation and the Council of Trent in the 1500s.

Post-Reformation Priesthood

As the Middle Ages gave way to modern times, there was widespread scandalous living among priests and bishops, along with emphasis on the mere externals of worship and sacramental ministry. Consequently, Protestant reformers had little respect for the Catholic priesthood even though many of them, such as Martin Luther, were priests. They emphasized ministry rather than priesthood, except for the priesthood of all the baptized. The Catholic church responded with a Counter-reformation that included a more adequate and structured preparation for celibacy and ordination by way of seminaries, renewed discipline for those ordained, and separation from "the world." These efforts were very successful and continued into contemporary times.

Current Trends

Catholic priests do not fit any one definition. For almost 2000 years they have been at the center of the sacramental life of the church. But they have also been educators, counselors, administrators, theologians, and more.

In the *Decree on Priestly Formation* Vatican II called for more biblical, pastoral, and social science studies in seminary training. It also recommended more contact between seminarians and real society. A permanent diaconate, open to married men, was re-established.

Like so many other Catholic traditions, those surrounding the priesthood entered a crisis stage in the mid-1960s. Mandatory celibacy was challenged. Tens of thousands of priests worldwide resigned from the active ministry. Optional celibacy, the ordination of married men, and the ordination of women continue to be debated issues. A shortage of priests and vocations to religious life has encouraged the evolution of other parish ministries now filled by the laity.

Priest Garb

Until the 19th century priests wore no distinguishing clothes. The black suit and Roman collar is a more recent American custom and today is in a transition phase as clergy wear clerical shirts of different colors or lay clothes. Ironically, the traditional "turned around" collar was first worn by Protestant clergy in Europe.

19

SACRAMENTALS

It used to be easy to identify Catholics. They wore medals and scapulars. They did little rituals in the privacy of their homes, such as sprinkling holy water or burning a piece of palm when bad weather threatened. They faithfully fingered their rosary beads and prayed from prayer books and leaflets. They blessed themselves with holy water and genuflected when entering church. They knelt and prayed before burning vigil lights and votive lights. In fact, they seemed to kneel and make the Sign of the Cross often. Men tipped their hat when passing a church, and women wore theirs in church. They were faithful in attending Mass on Sunday and novena services with Benediction during the week. Holy pictures and statues were prominent in churches and homes. Parishioners were devoted to Mary, the Sacred Heart, to the presence of Christ reserved in the Blessed Sacrament, and to canonized saints. They tended to multiply religious activities and to visit grottoes and shrines.

In being faithful to these practices, and much more, Catholics believed they were in contact with divine presence and power. And they were.

Catholics have always been a people devoted to sacramentals. They clothe their religious faith and worship with a multitude of physical forms. There have been changes in the use of sacramentals since Vatican II. The principle of sacramentality, however, continues as a distinguishing feature of Catholicism.

At first glance, some Catholic practices seem far removed from the really sacred and from the heart of the church's worship and unfolding of the church year. The contrary is true. When men tipped their hats on the occasion of passing a church, they were imitating genuflections and bowing in the presence of the Blessed Sacrament. Private uses of holy water reflect the waters of purification and rebirth in the sacrament of baptism. Palms on the walls of homes and used as a sacramental were blessed and used in the Palm Sunday procession. Daily private prayer continues an ancient tradition among

Jews and early Christians. Even the rosary as a private prayer evolved out of the daily Liturgy of the Hours.

Definition

Sacramentals are associated with or imitate the church's official rituals as they unfold daily, weekly, monthly, and yearly. They include religious signs, symbols, public and private devotions, prayers, gestures, rituals, music, images, and natural or made objects. Some of them are found only in the church's official rituals, such as sacred oils. Others are common in parishioners' private lives, such as candles and holy water. In themselves they might not be religious (for example, a particular color, or form of things, or position of the human body). They become sacramentals and, therefore, sacred, in their religious purpose and use.

In one form or another, sacramentals have been part of Christian religious practice from the earliest centuries. Since the Protestant Reformation, most of them have been preserved only by Catholics.

Popular Devotions

An important category of sacramentals is popular devotions. They may be either private or public and usually support a particular religious theme. Consisting of special prayers, gestures, and rituals, they are performed to worship God, honor the saints, or to seek divine favors. They are not part of the church's official liturgy of sacraments and prayer. Praying the rosary or burning a candle in front of a crucifix are examples. So are litanies, novenas, and prayers in honor of the Sacred Heart or Precious Blood. Some devotions lend themselves to communal expression. These are called public devotions and are associated in some way with essential mysteries of Christianity. Examples are group participation in praying the Stations of the Cross in church during Lent or praying the rosary publicly in a group during October. Public devotions are practiced throughout the church and provide a great variety in Catholics' spirituality.

Private devotions, on the other hand, support an individual's needs or personal spirituality. Some Catholics pray the rosary privately or light a candle to seek some favor or give thanks for favors received. Others wear a religious medal or scapular as a testimony of personal faith or to obtain some spiritual or temporal favor. Private devotions may be only remotely related to faith, such as displaying a St. Christopher statue on the car dashboard for personal safety.

Reforms and renewal in the Catholic church since the Second Vatican Council have put sacramentals and devotional practices into a better perspective in relation to the church's sacramental liturgy. They remain, however, an important part of the church's living religious traditions. "Popular devotions of the Christian people are warmly commended, provided they accord with the laws and norms of the Church. Such is especially the case with devotions called for by the Apostolic See. Devotions proper to individual churches also have a special dignity if they are conducted by mandate of the bishops in accord with customs or books lawfully approved. Nevertheless these devotions should be so drawn up that they harmonize with the liturgical seasons, accord with the sacred liturgy, are in some fashion derived from it, and lead the people to it, since the liturgy by its very nature far surpasses any of them" (Constitution on the Sacred Liturgy, 13).

The earliest Christian sacramentals came out of the Jewish tradition where they were familiar features of religious life. They formed the sacramental core of Christians' religious life: bread, wine, purifying waters, oil, laying on of hands, etc. Ritual words were also borrowed: Amen, Alleluia, Hosanna. Rituals of feasts were borrowed and found pregnant with new meaning: Passover and Pentecost, or Feast of Weeks. Features of synagogue services and family Sabbath meals and other sacred meals would give structure to the early Eucharistic ritual.

The Hebrew first commandment prohibited the making of images of Yahweh-God. Symbolism of the presence, power, and nature of God, however, was common, and by the time of Jesus was rich in variety, decorating both the Temple and local synagogues. This symbolic art crossed over into early Christian decoration.

Principle of Sacramentality
The principle of sacramentality, found already in the Jewish religion, expanded rapidly in early Christianity. It rests on an attitude toward mediation. The invisible mystery dimension, or God dimension, of all of reality can be experienced in visible ways. The mystery of God is discovered, and God and people touch each other through the finite, through sacramentals. These might be actual events in personal or corporate history. They might also be objects, rituals, symbols, and in fact, the whole cosmos.

Early Christians scratched symbols on tombs of martyrs, walls of house-churches, and later on catacomb walls. They painted frescoes and created mosaics of those they held dear: Jesus, Mary, and the saints.

The Jewish and pagan practices of blessing lights in the evening and eating sacred meals were continued by Christians. New seasonal sacramentals were adopted as the church year evolved (for example, blessed palms and ashes).

As centuries passed, a separation occurred between the church's use of sacramentals associated with its public rituals of worship and the people's use of them in a more private way. Popular spirituality, with emphasis on the veneration of saints, gradually drifted away from a biblical-liturgical center. This was caused in part by an ever-expanding chasm between the evolving vernacular languages of the ordinary people and the Latin language of church, education, Scripture, and worship. The cause was also theological. Church leaders continued to reflect upon the great mysteries of Christianity and to develop dogmas about them. The simple folk went about celebrating their religion in more earthy ways.

The church kept a vigilant, but not always successful, eye on superstitious attitudes related to the use of sacramentals. Poorly educated priests often promoted this superstition. Sacramentals were used to ward off evil and obtain good luck. Ritual incantations were recited a specific number of times for miraculous results. The Protestant Reformation challenged the validity of sacramentals partly because of abuses. Protestant tradition today reflects a continuing suspicion about the use of them.

The Catholic church after the Council of Trent unintentionally supported a tradition of devotions and other sacramentals completely separate from the church's liturgical life. It spelled out with precision the official forms of worship. This stifled future development and change. In the future the needs of people for new rituals and creative expression of religious faith would have to evolve outside of the liturgical life of the church. Church authorities tightly controlled official rituals connected with the sacraments and church year. As a result, these gradually entered a stage of fossilization. Popular devotions, on the other hand, went their own way and were quite free of official control. They often functioned separately from, or on the fringes of, important themes of Christianity.

An accident of language also supported the proliferation and popularity of unofficial devotions. Official worship was locked into Latin. Devotions, on the other hand, allowed worship, prayer, and singing in the vernacular.

Pre-Vatican II Catholic religious identity was characterized by popular use of sacramentals and practices of private devotions. Today's post-Vatican II church continues to defend their validity. The closer a sacramental and devotion approaches the church's official rituals, however, the more valid they are. "Way out" devotions are considered spiritually damaging because they remove a person from the core truths of Christianity.

The qualities of a valid use of sacramentals are: (1) They conform to revealed truth and are rooted in sound theology, Scripture, and tradition. (2) They are not smothered with sentimentality, becoming self-centered rather than God-centered. (3) They lead people to a deeper and effective spirituality.

Rituals that make use of sacramentals, often called paraliturgies, are popular today because laypeople can preside at them. (Note: Some devotions and uses of sacramentals are found in other chapters of this book; see Index.) Contemporary devotions and rituals exist alongside traditional forms in parishes. Charismatic prayer meetings and healing rituals are popular. American bishops have recognized the importance of contemporary prayers and blessings and approved a *Book of Blessings* prepared by the International Commission of English in the Liturgy. Some blessings are designed for use within liturgy or on more formal occasions. Many others, however, may be prayed outside of it, led by laity. This resource proves that Catholics believe in blessing everything for the glory of God. Another but more simple source is *Catholic Household Blessings and Prayers*. Both are published by the United States Catholic Conference, Washington, D.C.

St. Blaise and Blessing of Throats
Some sacramentals have become very closely associated with the church year, occurring on the same day each year. An example of one such popular sacramental ritual is the blessing of throats on the feast of St. Blaise, February 3. This bishop saint suffered martyrdom early in the 4th century. Legends say that he was a physician before becoming a bishop. While in prison he miraculously cured a young boy who was choking from a fish bone in his throat. St. Blaise became one of the most popular saints during the Middle Ages, being invoked as a helper in times of sickness related to the throat. The tradition of blessing the throats of parishioners with two crossed candles has been popular for centuries. The ritual prayer is: "Through the intercession of Saint Blaise, bishop and martyr, may the Lord free you from evils of the throat and from any other evil."

Gestures and Bodily Positions

Devotional gestures and bodily positions are popular forms of sacramentals. When people gather in the presence of their God and speak with their God, it is natural that they use some posture and gesture that is expressive of their reverence. Special meaning is given to the public and private prayer life of believers through these devotional or liturgical positions and gestures: kneeling, genuflecting, standing, prostrating, bowing, striking the breast, folding of hands, and raising of the hands and eyes.

Standing

Some Catholics today complain that there is too much standing instead of kneeling during Mass. Standing, however, is the most ancient of liturgical positions. In fact, kneeling on Sunday and during the fifty days of Easter season was forbidden by the first ecumenical council of Nicaea (325). It was the ordinary position at worship for almost the first thousand years of Christianity.

Standing was a natural expression of respect, reverence, and readiness. All religions in ancient times used this position at worship. Pagans knelt only when they were adoring gods of the underworld.

Christianity spread its early roots in a gentile culture where kneeling was the position of servitude and slavery. Standing straight, tall, and free as baptized children of God had special meaning for them. Only for a brief moment before the presider's official prayer of the day did people kneel. Even this exception was canceled on all Sundays and during the Easter season in honor of the resurrection. During the Eucharistic Prayer and blessings, the posture of the people was one of deep bowing. Standing during the reading of the gospel was a tradition since ancient times because of the special dignity associated with it.

Facing East

Christians not only stood while praying, they did so with hands upraised like the priest and facing east, the direction from which the sun, the symbol of Christ, rises. This is an example of the influence of solar symbolism upon Christian spirituality. Churches were built in such a way that the congregation would always stand facing the east. This tradition faded when Roman church architecture put the altar at the west end of the nave.

Kneeling

Kneeling has been a popular devotional position only during modern times. There always was, however, a tradition of kneeling for prayer. The Apostle Paul is described as kneeling in prayer with Christians at Miletus (Acts 20:36). Kneeling was gradually introduced into the liturgy as a sign of penance, supplication, and adoration. Kneeling during Mass was influenced by a growing emphasis placed on the divinity of Christ and the unworthiness of human persons in his presence. It eventually became so common that by 813 C.E. (Synod of Tours) kneeling was considered the ordinary posture of people during Mass. An exception was always made for the reading of the gospel, when the more ancient and therefore traditional position of standing continued.

Parishioners began kneeling to receive communion about the year 1000, when the tradition of placing the communion on the tongue of the recipient became common.

Prostration

Another prayer position is prostration. It is an intense, total, and dramatic expression of adoration, penance, or supplication. It was common among ancient peoples and from them passed into Christian tradition. Jesus himself prayed this way in the Garden of Gethesemane the night before he died: "He advanced a little and fell prostrate in prayer" (Matthew 26:39). A full prostration by the priests began each Mass until after the early Middle Ages. It is still retained at the beginning of the Good Friday liturgy.

Genuflecting

A gesture peculiar to Catholics is that of genuflecting before entering a church pew. This is a sign of adoration and greeting directed toward the divine presence of the Blessed Sacrament reserved in the tabernacle in the sanctuary. Today in many churches the Blessed Sacrament and the tabernacle are located in a special chapel separated from the sanctuary. Many parishioners still genuflect out of habit, even though the Blessed Sacrament is not present.

Bowing

The gesture of bowing has always been the custom of Catholics in the Eastern church instead of genuflecting. In the Western church it was a popular tradition to bow slightly when the name of Jesus and even Mary occurred in prayer. A more profound bow always substitutes for a genuflection.

Both the genuflection (Latin, "bending of the knee") and the bow are symbolic of one's smallness, or humility, in the presence of the greatness of the Lord. These devotional gestures were borrowed from court etiquette of the Roman Empire, which in turn had borrowed them from oriental courts. They are a modified version of a prostration. People would fully prostrate themselves upon the ground or floor when entering the presence of an idol, divinized emperor, and eventually lesser princes and officials. This, along with other pagan and civil ceremonial and etiquette gestures, entered the church's liturgical rituals once the church became legally free in the early 4th century. Previously these gestures had been too closely associated with the cult of emperor worship.

Sitting
There is no particular religious significance to the position of sitting. It is a posture of receptive listening and resting. It became popular for the listening parts of the Mass only after pews were introduced into churches in the 16th century. They became popular first in reform churches where services concentrated on listening to Scripture and preaching.

The Raising of Eyes and Hands
The raising of the eyes and hands to the heavens is another prayer gesture. God traditionally has been pictured as dwelling in a heaven above creatures. It is natural, therefore, to raise one's eyes upward in prayer. Jesus is described as praying this way: "He looked up to heaven, blessed and broke [the loaves and fishes]" (Matthew 14:19).

For the same reason, it was the custom of Christians from the earliest times to raise their hands in an upward gesture, often with palms open in a gesture of receiving or giving. There is evidence for this gesture in catacomb paintings. This was always the prayer position of priests at the altar, disguised until recent times by a much curtailed and rigid form. This custom has been revived among many people today.

Laying on of Hands
Christians continued the ancient Jewish tradition of laying on of hands to signify a giving of special authority and blessing. In some form this gesture is used in all seven sacraments.

Folding Hands
The traditional gesture of folding one's hands, either with fingers

interlocked or palms flat against each other, is another borrowing from social etiquette. It evolved among the German people in the Middle Ages, during the Age of Feudalism. When people took an oath of allegiance to the local lord, they placed their joined hands between those of the lord as a sign of submission and subjection. This origin adds meaning to a very traditional prayer gesture.

Striking the Breast

The striking of the breast is another devotional gesture. It is a sign of sorrow for sin, the root of which was thought to be in the heart. This was a gesture familiar among ancient people and is found in the Christian Scriptures, in the parable of the publican (Luke 18:13). It was also used as an expression of guilt by witnesses to Jesus' crucifixion (Luke 23:48).

Sign of the Cross

The Sign of the Cross came into use as a religious gesture of blessing during the Middle Ages. It takes several forms. The big Sign of the Cross is made with the hand, touching first the forehead, then the breast, left shoulder, and finally the right shoulder. While doing it, it is common to add an expression of faith in the Trinity: "In the name of the Father, and of the Son, and of the Holy Spirit. Amen." The little Sign of the Cross is made by tracing a small cross on the forehead, mouth, and breast. In ancient times it was made with one finger only on the forehead and by the 2nd century was a popular practice in this form.

This popular gesture was introduced into the liturgy during the 4th century with the tracing of the cross on the forehead of candidates for baptism. It was also used from early centuries as a gesture of blessing over the bread and wine of Eucharist and other objects to be dedicated to God. In this way people, too, were blessed.

Music

Music and songs used in prayer and worship are sacramentals. Early Christians used the musical elements, acclamations, and responses popular in the temple and local synagogues. The Book of Psalms, the Jewish scriptural hymn book, was always available to Christians. The Christian Scriptures record several ancient Christian hymns such as the Magnificat (Luke 1:46–55), Benedictus (Luke 1:68–79), and Nunc Dimittis (Luke 2:29–32). The Glory to God (*Gloria in Excelsis*) was already used in the 3rd century, at first in the daily morning prayer service. In the 4th and 5th centuries, congregations became larger and worship was done in churches and basilicas. Music began to be used to grace the opening and closing processions of clergy. In time, it was used also during other transition times of the Mass. The most famous of church music is Gregorian chant, a plainchant, popularized first by Pope St. Gregory the Great (540-604).

Since these early centuries, church music and instruments have evolved within the culture of peoples.

Ritual Words

Ritual words are sacramentals. Some of the most common ones are the ancient Hebrew ritual words: *Amen* (So be it!), *Alleluia* (Praise the Lord), *Hosanna* (Please, save [us]), which becomes an acclamation like Alleluia.

Litanies

Litanies become a favorite method of praying in the Middle Ages. The two most popular ones are the Litany of the Saints and the Litany of Loreto, commonly referred to as the Litany of the Blessed Virgin Mary. In modern times so many litanies were composed, some with questionable content, that the church began restricting their public use. The only litanies officially approved today, besides the Litanies of the Saints and Loreto, are those of the Holy Name, Sacred Heart, St. Joseph, and the Precious Blood.

Altar

Originally the Eucharistic table, or altar, was the ordinary family table in house churches. Permanent altars, made of stone or marble, became popular only when the fixed altars of the Jewish Temple and pagan temples, with their animal sacrifices, no longer existed.

Early in Christianity altars became associated with martyrs; many churches and basilicas were built over their graves. This association with martyrs was continued in the Middle Ages with the relics of martyrs placed in a bored-out hole in the top of the altar or in the altar stone. This tradition continued until recent times.

Altars stood in the middle of the sanctuary, with priests or bishop facing the people until the 5th century. Then it became popular for the altar and priest to face east, or toward the wall. The altar was moved against the wall, with the priest presiding with his back to the congregation. Beginning in the Middle Ages, the altar could hardly be described as a table, becoming instead a display area for the relics, statues, paintings of saints, a crucifix, and finally the tabernacle itself.

Shelves were built to hold candles and flowers. Altar cards, serving as memory aids, were added in the 16th century.

An altar cloth was a practical feature of the Eucharistic table since early Christianity. It was also symbolic of the Eucharistic banquet. Gradually these evolved into permanent fixtures, made out of precious materials, eventually three in number to absorb any spilled sacred elements. An *antependium*, a large cloth "hanging in front of" the altar, was originally a part of these cloths. Churches usually had a number of these, highly decorated, often changing with the theme and color of the liturgical seasons.

In post-Vatican II times, the altar has once again become a recognizable table, close to the people, with the presiding priest facing the people and inviting their participation. Candles are usually placed nearby, with the tabernacle commonly in a special chapel. A simple altar cloth is customarily spread during the preparation of gifts.

Lights

A very common sacramental among Catholics is the use of special lights in the form of burning candles. Since ancient times, light has reminded people of all religions of divine presence, joy, happiness, goodness, purity, life, and a spirit of celebration. Darkness, on the other hand, has been symbolic of ignorance, sin, sadness, error, gloom, evil, and death.

A symbolism of light entered Christianity from Jewish customs and pagan and civil ceremonies. Jews kept a perpetually burning light in the temple sanctuary until its destruction in 70 C.E. They also burned lights before the tombs of prophets, and displayed them during their festivals. Hanukkah, which remembers the rededication of the Temple, is called the Feast of Lights. Sacred meals, such as the Seder during Passover and the weekly Sabbath meal, called for a ritual of lighting lamps.

Pagan customs included lighting lamps and candles in their sanctuaries and doorways of homes on religious festivals. They also burned lights in front of idols, images of the emperor, and in front of tombs to honor the dead. A light-bearer accompanied civil officials in public—an ancient perk!

The symbolism of light versus darkness is an obvious theme in both the Hebrew and Christian Scriptures. It describes God (Baruch 5:9; Ezekiel 10:4; Exodus 13:21; 1 Samuel 3:3). In the gospels, light becomes the symbol that describes the incarnate God in Jesus: "The light shines on in darkness, a darkness that did not overcome it"

(John 1:5), and "the real light which gives light to every person" (John 1:9). Jesus describes himself as light: "I am the light of the world. No follower of mine shall ever walk in darkness" (John 8:12) and "I have come into the world as its light, to keep anyone who believes in me from remaining in the dark" (John 12:46).

With this extensive scriptural symbolism supporting their spirituality, it is understandable that Christians throughout the centuries became preoccupied with lights. One of the pervading themes of the Christmas season is the theme of light coming into a world of darkness. The very first words of Scripture proclaimed at the Christmas Mass at midnight are: "The people who walked in darkness have seen a great light; upon those who dwelt in the land of gloom a light has shone" (Isaiah 9:1). The theme is carried out seasonally by way of religious traditions beginning with the Advent Wreath and continuing with lights on Christmas trees, in windows, and on the grounds of homes.

Candles

This theme is also obvious in the practical and symbolic use of candles. These often took the form of small terracotta oil lamps, plain or decorated with Christian symbols. The first evidence of their use as sacramentals comes from the 2nd century, an ancient daily evening prayer service at the twelfth hour (6 P.M.) in homes and house-churches. The ritual is called *Lucernare* (Latin *lux*, "light"). This practice evolved into Vespers, one of the daily Hours. It is also considered the origin of the blessing of the Easter Fire and Easter Paschal Candle.

Christians carried candles in funeral processions from the 3rd century on, burned them at the tombs of martyrs and other dead, and, from the 4th century, before relics and images of saints.

Candles continued to be a feature of public worship and churches when the church became free under civil law in 313. Only from the 7th century, however, is there evidence of their symbolic use at Mass. By then they were carried in the opening procession and gospel procession and placed around the altar. In the eleventh century they were placed on the altar for the first time. The use and number of candles at Mass were determined by church law only from the 17th century.

The symbolic use of candles at Mass was probably influenced by civil practices. High-ranking officials had the privilege of being accompanied in public by a light-bearer. This practice seemed to have been transferred to high-ranking church people, especially bishops, once Christianity obtained a privileged position in the Roman Empire. It was only natural that lights or candles eventually honor the presence of the most important person present, Christ himself, symbolized by the altar. The candle that is kept burning before the presence of Christ in the reserved Eucharist, popularly called the tabernacle light, or sanctuary light, reflects this meaning. This tradition began in England in the 13th century and was made obligatory everywhere in the 17th.

Votive and Vigil Lights

Two kinds of burning lights, which are so evident in most Catholic churches and shrines, do not seem to be part of a light vs. dark symbolism. Votive lights (Latin *votum*, "vow") and vigil lights (Latin *vigilia*, "waiting," or "watching") are symbolic of two purposes of prayer. The former is associated with seeking some favor from the Lord, Mary, or a saint in return, usually, for some promise or vow. The candle is burned as were sacrifices in ancient times. The latter, as its name "vigil" indicates, accompanies prayer of attention or waiting.

Holy Water

Another popular sacramental and religious tradition is the use of holy water. It is used to bless oneself, others, and things. "Taking holy water" before entering church is a way of remembering one's baptism with a hint of purifying oneself before approaching the presence of God. For this reason, one tradition is to have the baptismal font or pool located close to the entrance of the church. A water ritual of submersion was common in pagan and Jewish religions as an external sign of internal purification. It crossed over into Christianity from Judaism. During the first centuries, baptismal water was not blessed. Over a period of time, however, an elaborate Easter Vigil ritual was used to bless this water, called Easter water. To this day, parishioners take some of this Easter water home to use as a sacramental. Ordinary holy water is blessed by a special ritual including exorcisms and blessed salt.

A "Rite of Sprinkling" may take the place of the Penitential Rite at Mass. This ritual takes the place of the *Asperges* which was a popular tradition in pre-Vatican II times.

Vestments

Another sacramental began to grace the church's rituals—and the persons of the clergy—when vestments became popular in the 4th century. Originally, the clergy wore what was common among middle-class people. There came a time when conservative clergy continued to wear what had passed out of fashion. The alb (Latin *alba*, "white") was the basic everyday garment, similar to a tunic: white for festivals and darker color for everyday use; Eventually the clergy were distinguished from the laity by the length of this tunic. Clergy wore a long one. The amice (a scarf around the neck), the cincture (a belt), the maniple (a handkerchief or napkin), the *chasuble* (a kind of coat). Today, presiders usually wear only an alb and chasuble, or a combination, along with a stole. The stole, a symbol of authority, was borrowed from Roman civil life.

Bells

Small bells were already in use in the 6th century. Later they became much larger, needing special belfries or towers. They were used to call people to Mass, to prayer at times of the Angelus, announcing the death of a parishioner, and to inform the neighborhood that the consecration was taking place.

Medals

In popular thinking, sacramentals are often equated with blessed objects used for a religious purpose. One of the most common sacramentals in this sense is the wearing of religious medals. This has been a pious practice among Christians since the earliest centuries. A 2nd-century medal has been found, bearing the image of Sts. Peter and Paul. Others, from the 4th to the 8th centuries, bear the image of other martyrs. St. Zeno spoke of this practice as a means of purifying pagan customs.

By the 4th century, the newly baptized were given a medal as a remembrance of that event. In the 12th, it became popular for pilgrims to wear medals stamped with a sign of a particular popular shrine.

Religious medals as we know them today became popular only in the 16th century. It was then that indulgences began to be attached to them with the blessing. This new kind of medal bore the image of Jesus and Mary, events in their life, a favorite saint, or a particular devotion.

Miraculous Medal

One of the most popular medals in modern times is the Miraculous Medal, an engraved image of a vision of Mary that St. Catherine Labouré had on November 27, 1830. Mary appeared standing on a globe, crushing a serpent beneath her foot, with rays of light symbolizing graces streaming from her outstretched hands. Around her were the words: "O Mary, conceived without sin, pray for us who have recourse to thee." The reverse of the medal showed an "M" with a bar and a cross over the hearts of Jesus and Mary, one pierced with a sword and the other crowned with thorns, and surrounded by twelve stars. So many favors were reported received by the wearing of the medal that people began to call it the Miraculous Medal.

Religious medals are not magic charms and must not be considered such. The church has always been careful that such superstition be avoided. In themselves medals possess no particular power. They are symbols that remind wearers of their personal faith and religious commitment. It became tradition that medals be blessed by a priest when special indulgences became attached to wearing them.

The tradition of wearing the scapular began with St. Peter Damian (see page 127). Originally, a scapular (Latin *scapula*, "shoulder blade") was an ordinary part of religious habits, a panel of cloth worn over the shoulders to protect monks and friars from bad weather. In the 13th century, devout laypeople, called tertiaries, or Third Order members, put themselves under the spiritual direction of monks. As a sign of their connection to a particular religious community, such as Franciscans or Dominicans, they began wearing a scapular, two pieces of cloth worn on the chest and back, connected by strings or tapes. This was reduced to a mere symbol beginning in the 16th century: one or two 2-inch square pieces. It was common to decorate these with a picture of Mary or a saint, the Sacred Heart, or the passion of Jesus. Since 1910, it has become widespread to substitute a medal for the piece of cloth. Altogether, eighteen different scapulars are approved by the church for private devotion.

Incense

Burning incense as a perfume was an ancient practice in the Near East where Christianity originated. From its secular use it crossed over into pagan and Jewish worship. Among the Jews, it was often combined with burning sacrifices. It was burned on an altar of incense or in a censer when used alone. Among pagans, incense was offered to idols as an important part of worship. It was also used to keep demons away. The emperor was honored with incense as a sign of divinity. Christians often were forced to offer incense to an image of the emperor as a pledge of loyalty; there were dire consequences if one refused.

The use of incense has been part of the church's rituals since the beginning of Christianity, but it has seldom been used privately as a sacramental. Among Christians, it has been used to purify, to bless, and to symbolize the motion of prayer upwards to God. In the description of heaven in Revelation (5:8; 8:3–4), gold vessels of incense symbolize the prayers of God's people.

Early Christians used incense at funerals. At first they rejected its use in worship because of pagan overtones. When paganism was no longer a threat, the use of incense became popular to honor the altar, sanctuary, high church officials, and eventually the congregation. In the 8th century, it was introduced into the Hours of Lauds and Vespers.

Colors

During the Middle Ages, the church in Gaul emphasized those features of worship that affected the senses. The use of colors became important along with frequent use of incense. These liturgical colors, already listed in the 12th century, were standardized throughout the church in the post-Tridentine period. They remain a tradition today with little change. Purple is used during Advent, Lent, and special penitential days such as Rogation Days and Ember Days. White is the color of the Easter season, Christmas season, feasts of our Lord and Mary, non-martyred saints, and special solemnities outside these times. Red is used for Pentecost, Good Friday, and feasts of martyrs. Green, the color of hope and life, is used in Ordinary Time. Until this generation, black was the color for funerals, Masses for the dead, and originally Good Friday. Seldom used today, it has been replaced by white (symbolic of resurrection) for funerals and red (symbolic of Jesus' obedience to death and, therefore, prototype of all martyrs) for Good Friday.

The church's use of symbolic colors is sometimes influenced by cultural factors. Church authorities in early centuries objected to the use of black for funerals because it was so closely associated with the burial of pagans.

Symbols

Religious symbols have always been important sacramentals. There is no attempt at realism. In fact, their form is usually highly stylized. Symbols suggest or point to some spiritual reality beyond themselves, usually some basic theme of Christianity. The earliest Christian symbols were inherited from Jewish traditions and Old Testament imagery. The symbols of living waters and palm fronds, for example, came from the Jewish feast of Tabernacles, or Booths. They symbolized a new age which the Jews were waiting for and which Christians believed was realized in Christ.

Christians soon developed their own symbols:

Jesus: All personal names are symbolic of the person herself or himself. The name by which the Lord was known, therefore, is a precious symbol when written, printed, or engraved.

IHS: This is the name "Jesus" abbreviated into three Greek letters. Since the Middle Ages, this has been written as IHS and in this form it is often found in church decorations. In English this monogram has been popularly but erroneously rendered as "I Have Suffered."

The superimposed Greek letters, *chi* and *rho,* are the first two letters of the Greek *Christos* and form a popular acronym or Christogram for the Lord. It has been widely used with variations in shape since the 4th century.

IXΘYΣ: This is the Greek word for "fish" and is found in the catacombs as a symbol referring to the meaning and dignity of Jesus Christ. It is an acrostic made up of the first letter of five Greek titles for the Lord: I *(Jesus),* X *(Christos),* Θ *(Theou*/God's), Y *(uios*/Son), Σ *(Soter*/Savior).

The image of a fish has the same meaning as the acronym itself. It has been used since early Christianity and is still a popular symbol worn by Christians today. It is possible that it was used as a secret identification code during times of persecution.

I.N.R.I.: These letters are usually found above the image of the crucified Jesus on a crucifix. They are the first letters of the Latin title written by Pilate: *Jesus Nazarenus Rex Iudaeorum* or "Jesus of Nazareth, King of the Jews."

A and Ω: These are the first and last letters of the Greek alphabet: Alpha and Omega. Used in a Christian context, the symbol refers to the divinity of Christ who is the beginning and end of everything that is.

† : No Christian symbol is more common or speaks more clearly than the cross. It preserves the fundamental belief of Christianity: Jesus died on the cross and was raised from the dead. It is, therefore, a sign of victory even though its basic form images a common method of execution of slaves and criminals in the Roman empire at the time of Jesus.

Early Christians avoided representing the body of Jesus on the cross. The first evidence of a crucifix (cross with Jesus' body fixed on it), so popular today, comes from the 5th century. Even the plain cross was seldom displayed in public until the end of the persecutions. The reason for this is understandable. During times of persecution, association with the symbol of the cross could bring identification as a Christian with dire consequences and also possible desecration to the symbol itself. Christians sometimes disguised the cross for this reason. One disguise was to use an anchor, which also served as a symbol of hope. Another was to use combined letters from the name of Jesus Christ, especially combinations of the Greek chi (X) and rho (P) (see above).

Another reason might lie in the distaste associated with crucifixion among both Jews and pagans and possibly among some Christians.

When the Roman Empire became Christian in the 4th century, the cross became public and very popular. Emperor Constantine credited his military victory in 313 over opposing forces to the image of the cross. Religious freedom came to Christianity through his protection. In 326, his mother, Helen, claimed to have discovered in Jerusalem the cross on which Jesus was crucified. It became a precious relic, with its wood divided up, and eventually holy splinters found their way throughout the universal church.

During the 5th and 6th centuries, the cross became a highly glorified symbol. It was popular to decorate it with precious jewels to represent the victory achieved through the cross and its power. Another motivation may have been a desire to erase the ugliness associated with crucifixion.

The cross continued to take on new shapes throughout the centuries. The crosses shown on page 190 are some of the common forms.

Emphasis on the suffering Savior in the late Middle Ages led to the popularity of the crucifix over the cross. This has continued to present times.

The image of a lamb, bearing a wound and a standard of victory, lying upon a book is a symbol of the redemptive suffering and victory of Jesus Christ (Revelation, 5:6ff).

Images of four creatures: a man, an ox, a lion, and an eagle come from a vision of the prophet Ezekiel (1:1–26). They were interpreted by early Christians as symbolic of Jesus' journey of redemption: incarnation, the sacrificial death, the triumphant resurrection, and the ascension into glory. Later these symbols were used for the four evangelists because of the way each of their gospels begin.

The image of tongues of fire is symbolic of the outpouring of the Holy Spirit on the first Pentecost (Acts 2:3). Another symbol for this religious experience is that of the dove, representing the sanctifying power of God in the Holy Spirit. The symbol of the dove is hinted at in the gospel story of the baptism of Jesus in the Jordan River (Matthew 3:16).

Images of Jesus as the Good Shepherd were among the most popular symbols in early Christianity. They are found on the walls of catacombs, on tombs of Christians, on sacred vessels, and on walls of buildings used for the Eucharist. The image points to the gospel parable of the lost sheep (Luke 15:3–7). As a piece of religious art, the Good Shepherd imitates a pre-Christian tradition among the Greeks and Romans to represent the god Hermes in a similar fashion.

In religious art and decoration, sheep represent those who enjoy the fruits of salvation and belong to Christ. Other representations for Christians are deer panting after fountains of water, doves or pigeons pecking at grapes on a vine, fish swimming in baptismal water.

Christian life is represented in many ways in Christian symbolism: Christian hope by an anchor, struggle and victory by a palm branch or crown, virtue by a flower.

Stylized representations of sacraments are popular in religious symbolism. Baptism is often represented by wavy lines suggesting water, grapes and ears of wheat stand for the Eucharist, and multiplication of the loaves and fishes also for the Eucharist.

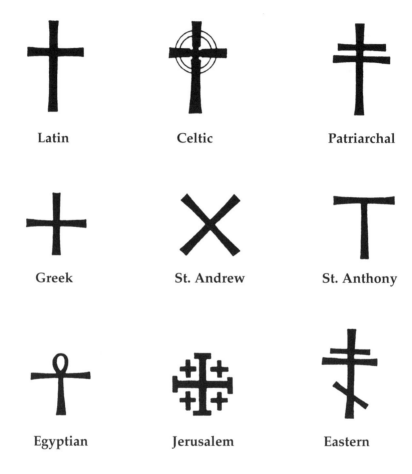

Latin Celtic Patriarchal

Greek St. Andrew St. Anthony

Egyptian Jerusalem Eastern

Maltese

PART SIX

SPECIAL DAYS

HALLOWEEN
THANKSGIVING
MEMORIAL DAY

20

HALLOWEEN

Each part of the year has its own special atmosphere. It is this atmosphere that causes traditions to arise among the people. These traditions in turn affect the atmosphere of the season. Autumn is one such time. In the cycle of the church year it occurs during Ordinary Time. There is no extraordinary theme or feast to celebrate and, consequently, no particular popular religious traditions within this part of the church year. Yet, a considerable number of traditions have evolved. Some of them are connected with the seasonal transition as summer departs and fall arrives. There is the theme of harvest or bounty as farmers reap the benefit of their spring and summer work. The fall equinox is a reminder that darkness will soon again rule. These themes introduce a seasonal reminder about the reality of death in nature and among people.

Two days in the fall have a particular atmosphere surrounding them, which has given rise to popular traditions only indirectly connected with Christianity. These are Halloween and Thanksgiving Day.

Halloween is observed the night of October 31. It takes its name (All Hallow e'en) from being the eve of the holy day of All Saints on November 1 (All Hallows Eve). Halloween has its origin in pre-Christian times and there is no direct connection between this day and any Christian tradition. Traditional practices associated with Halloween are delightful and earthy, but they are not Christian practices. There is no reason, however, why they should not be enjoyed by young and old alike.

The Celts in Wales, Ireland, Scotland, and Brittany in northwestern France celebrated New Year's Day on November 1. Among the Celts, under the influence of the religious leadership of the Druids, a festival was held the evening before to honor Samhain (pronounced "Sow'en"), their lord of death. This celebration ended harvest time and ushered in the winter season, the season of cold, darkness, death, and decay in nature. This time of the year was also symbolic of the mystery of human death.

The Celts believed that Samhain allowed the souls of the dead to return to their earthly homes during this night. Sinful souls who had died during the year, and who were imprisoned in the bodies of animals, could be freed for heaven through gifts and sacrifices. Human sacrifices were also common. Men, usually criminals, were shut up in wicker cages shaped like animals and burned. The Roman conquerors forbade this practice.

On the eve of November 1, the people would extinguish their hearth fires and the Druids built large sacred bonfires, often on hilltops. From these fires people would reignite a New Year's fire for their homes. It was hoped that these new fires would rejuvenate the sun and ward off evil spirits.

There are several possibilities for the origin of the tradition of giving treats as part of trick or treating. It was a belief among the Celts that on this night evil spirits, demons, ghosts, and witches roamed freely to greet their season of winter darkness. These would threaten, scare, and play tricks on people. The only way to be safe was to bribe them with treats or to pass as one of them by dressing and acting like them. The more probable origin lies in the pagan New Year celebration among the Celts. It was thought that the ghosts who roamed freely that night would be satisfied with a banquet table laid out in homes. For a while after Christianity arrived in Celtic lands, there was an attempt to transfer this custom to the eve of All Souls Day (November 2). Masked children would go from door to door to pray for departed loved ones in return for a treat.

Halloween customs survived into contemporary times with hardly any change. They were not widely observed in this country until the potato famine in Ireland in the 1840s caused a massive migration of the Irish, a Celtic people. The traditions include outlandish costumes, carving jack-o-lanterns, trick or treating for sweets, and ghost stories. Costumes have changed with the times, however, and some tend to be "cute" rather than "scary." Children's motives might be different than in ancient times. Instead of acting out fears connected with agents of evil, children take the opportunity to fill bags of treats with a party atmosphere.

The tricking tradition originated when Halloween was observed as "Mischief Night." Tricks could be blamed on ghosts and other similar creatures. This tradition has turned into "Devil's Night," observed the night before Halloween, in some places with harmful intent.

The ever-popular pumpkin jack-o-lantern with a fearsome face originated in the practice of Irish children to carve faces in rutabagas, turnips, and potatoes. They would place a candle inside to add a dimension of festivity to Halloween gatherings but probably originally to scare ghosts away. It is also possible that the jack-o-lantern is a leftover symbol, combining the night's traditional atmosphere of evil with the Halloween New Year fire lit by the Druids.

Some parishes have incorporated Halloween practices into their holy day eve Mass on October 31, with children attending in costume. Other parishes organize pageants at this time of the year to depict, by way of costumes, popular saints. It is also becoming popular to organize group parties for children to prevent the dangers associated with roaming the streets in the dark.

21

THANKSGIVING

Thanksgiving receives the prize for being the most earthy of celebrations in our contemporary culture. It is a day of special foods and smells, of going to a particular home and there, probably with the same people as the previous year, enjoying family ties and bonds of love. The old expression of "going to Grandma's house" says it all.

"Made in the U.S.A." is stamped all over our Thanksgiving observance. Other holidays (for example, Christmas) are just as popular, but many of them originated in religious traditions of far-off lands and peoples. Thanksgiving started here and the day still has nuances of Pilgrims and Native Americans. It evolved as a feast day that was primarily secular but adopted religious overtones as the generations passed.

Thanksgiving Day is a harvest festival, thanking God for the bounty received from God's good graces. People have always found ways of expressing thanks to their deities for favors received, usually by way of some kind of sacrifice. These sacrifices returned to the source of all life a portion of what one had received.

Thanksgiving has been a basic theme in all religions throughout history. Regardless of race and ethnic origin, all peoples have enjoyed harvest festivals. They celebrated the end of the growing season and the fruit of their hard work with feasting. Paradoxically, the Pilgrims, who were responsible for the origin of the American Thanksgiving, were much opposed to the celebration of festivals.

Jewish religious traditions included both public and private sacrifices of thanksgiving. Some of them are described in detail in the Hebrew Scriptures. The fifty days after Passover were a seven-week thanksgiving festival called Shavuot, or Feast of Weeks, ending with Pentecost. In the fall they celebrated another one, Sukkot, or Feast of Booths.

The same theme was prominent in Christianity from the earliest generations. The word chosen to describe the bread-and-cup memorial ritual of Jesus' resurrection and continuing presence, the Eucharist, was Greek for "thanksgiving."

The Aztecs of Mexico celebrated the corn harvest by beheading a young girl who represented Xilonen, the goddess of new corn. It seems that the Pawnees also sacrificed a girl. The Cherokees danced the Green Corn Dance, and began the new year at the end of the harvest.

The church has never had a liturgical feast on its calendar dedicated specifically to the theme of Thanksgiving. Since the late Middle Ages, however, most countries observed some kind of Thanksgiving, often on another feast during harvest time, for example, the Feast of the Assumption on August 15 in Hungary, and the feast of St. Martin, November 11, in Germany, France, Holland, England, and in central Europe.

The story of how Thanksgiving Day started in the American colonies is well known. It began with English settlers, called Pilgrims. They had first spent twelve years in Holland to escape persecution for their religious beliefs. Because of religious and financial problems they left Holland, by way of England, for the colonies on the famous Mayflower. They arrived on November 11, 1620 at Patuxet, afterwards to be called Plymouth. In the first year, a bitter winter and poor diet took the lives of 47 of the 100 Mayflower voyagers.

The Pilgrim's first harvest in the colonies was meager. Yet it was decided to have a thanksgiving holiday in the fall of 1621. The first Thanksgiving lasted three days. Massasoit, chief of the Wampanoage, was invited with ninety braves. There was competition in games and marksmanship. The banquet tables were filled with venison, duck, goose, seafood, eels, white bread, corn bread, leeks, watercress, greens, dessert made from wild plums and dried berries, and wine. It seems that turkey was not on the original menu, although it was plentiful as a wild game bird.

The Pilgrims were familiar with a harvest festival in their homeland. Their charter called for a day of thanksgiving on the anniversary of their arrival. Two years later, their governor, William Bradford, decreed a day of fasting and prayer for deliverance from drought and starvation. Rain fell the next day, followed by news that another ship with supplies and more Pilgrims had arrived. The governor issued a proclamation naming July 30, 1623, as a day of thanksgiving and prayer.

Subsequent Thanksgiving Days seemed to have been sporadic. The tradition, however, spread to the other colonies. The date depended on when the crops were harvested locally.

In 1789, President George Washington, at the authorization of Congress, proclaimed November 26, 1789, a day of national thanksgiving. A regular annual celebration, however, did not exist throughout the individual states. Finally, President Abraham Lincoln proclaimed the last Thursday of November as a day dedicated to praise and thanks to a gracious Father. This annual proclamation by the president was continued each year. Finally, Congress passed legislation in 1941 that the fourth Thursday of November be observed as Thanksgiving Day and a national holiday.

Thanksgiving is primarily a family celebration, a time for families and friends to feast at table with one another. Special table grace (Latin *gratiae*, "thanks") is prayed. Most churches celebrate with a special prayer service, often ecumenical in attendance. Although the day is not part of the church year calendar, a votive Mass of Thanksgiving is usually used for the Mass formula.

22

MEMORIAL DAY

Another day that began as a secular observance and took on religious overtones is Memorial Day, celebrated in most states on the last Monday in May. It began as a popular way to honor those who died in our nation's wars but has undergone many changes, some of them echoing Catholic November traditions to remember the dead.

In 1868 Major General John A. Logan, commander-in-chief of the Grand Army of the Republic, an organization of Union veterans of the Civil War, named May 30 as a day to remember dead veterans. Some southern states observed a similar memorial for their Confederate dead. Two years previously on May 5, 1866 the people of Waterloo, N.Y., first observed a Memorial Day and this place is recognized as the birthplace of the holiday.

Roots of this special day go back even further. In 1863, during the Civil War, some women in Columbus, Mississippi, decorated the graves of their Confederate war dead at a small country cemetery. Nearby were graves of Union soldiers who died in the same battles. Out of compassion, they decorated these graves, too. Because of this tradition to decorate graves with flags and flowers, the day was originally called Decoration Day.

Decorating graves of veterans with flags and flowers has continued as a popular tradition. In most communities there are patriotic parades and speeches which remember and honor veterans who served their country.

Religious observances have become an important part of this national holiday. For Catholics Eucharist is now celebrated in many local cemeteries on this day. This hearkens back to the ancient church when Christians celebrated the Eucharist at the burial place of martyrs and saints, sometimes using the tombstone as an altar. In most parts of the country weather cooperates with this tradition more than during the month of November, traditionally devoted to remembering the dead.

While this holiday continues to emphasize a remembering of this country's dead veterans, a popular remembering of all the dead, and the decorating of loved ones' graves continues to grow. For this reason the *Book of Blessings* from the American bishops has a chapter (57) which is all-inclusive: "Order for Visiting a Cemetery on All Souls Day (November 2), Memorial Day, or on the Anniversary of Death or Burial."

SELECTED BIBLIOGRAPHY

NOTE: The very nature of religious traditions is that their exact origin is clouded in the mists of history and their practice varies among people. No one source book gives an exact and adequate presentation of all of them or even any of them. Readers who wish to pursue this important feature of religion are encouraged to check, among others, the following resources to which the author is indebted:

Adam, Adolf. *The Liturgical Year: Its History & Meaning after the Reform of the Liturgy.* New York: Pueblo Publishing Company, 1981.

Catholic Household Blessings and Prayers. Washington, D.C.: United States Catholic Conference, Inc., 1988.

Catholic Encyclopedia. Washington, D.C.: Catholic University, 1967.

Chesto, Kathleen O'Connell. *Family Prayer for Family Times.* Mystic, Conn.: Twenty-Third Publications, 1995.

Cully, Iris V. and Kendig Brubaker, eds.: *Encyclopedia of Religious Education.* New York: Harper & Row, 1990.

Dalmais, Irénée Henri, et al. *The Church at Prayer,* Vols. I, II, III, IV. Collegeville, Minn.: Liturgical Press, 1987.

DeGidio, Sandra. *Enriching Faith through Family Celebrations.* Mystic, Conn.: Twenty-Third Publications, 1989.

DeGidio, Sandra. *Sacraments Alive: Their History, Celebration and Significance.* Mystic, Conn.: Twenty-Third Publications, 1991.

Hatchett, Marion J. *Sanctifying Life, Time and Space.* New York: Seabury Press, 1982.

Huels, John M., O.S.M. *One Table, Many Laws: Essays on Catholic Eucharistic Practice.* Collegeville, Minn.: Liturgical Press, 1986.

Klauser, Theodor. *A Short History of the Western Liturgy.* New York: Oxford University Press, 1969.

Martos, Joseph. *Doors to the Sacred: A Historical Introduction to Sacraments in the Catholic Church.* New York: Doubleday, 1982.

Mauck, Marchita. *Shaping a House for the Church.* Chicago: Liturgy Training Publications, 1990.

Mazer, Peter. et al. *Sourcebook for Sundays and Seasons.* Chicago: Liturgy Training Publications, 1989.

Meyers, Robert. *Celebrations: The Complete Book of American Holidays.* Garden City, New York: Doubleday and Company, 1972.

Porter, H.B. *The Day of Light: The Biblical and Liturgical Meaning of Sunday.* Washington, D.C.: Pastoral Press, 1987.

Vogel, Cyrille. *Medieval Liturgy: An Introduction to the Sources.* Washington, D.C.: Pastoral Press, 1986.

INDEX

Abstinence, 8, 34, 75, 79, 92-93

Advent, season of, 17, 42-48, 52

Advent calendar, 47

Advent colors, 48

Advent house, 47

Advent, manger, 48

Advent, origin of, 43-44

Advent theme, 43

Advent wreath, 46

Aetheria, *see* Egeria

Agape, 21, 31

Alb, 169, 183-4

Alcuin, 45, 124

Alleluia, meaning of, 180

Alleluia, lenten suppression of, 72, 74

All Hallows Eve, 115, 192

All Martyrs, feast of, 109

All Saints, feast of, 109, 115

All Souls, feast of, 134, 193

Almsgiving, 38, 75, 132

Alpha/Omega, 91, 187

Alphonsus Ligouri, St., 121

Altar, 180-181

Altar cloth, 181

Altar, stripping of, 83-4

Ambrose, St., 163

Amen, 173, 180

Angelus, 122, 125, 184

Anne, St., 114, 121

Annunciation, feast of, 69, 119

Anointing of the sick, 159-162

Anointing and the dying, 160-1

Antependium, 181

Antiphons, Marian, 123-4

Apparitions of Mary, 118, 125-6

Ascension Thursday, 100

Ash Wednesday, 34, 73-74, 156

Asperges, 183

Assembly, Sunday, 23-5

Assumption of Mary, 119, 121, 127

Augustine, St., 130, 164, 168

Baptism, 71, 146-49

Baptism, current, 148

Baptism, private, 147-8

Baptismal candle, 149

Baptismal robe, 147

Baptistries, 147

Bedtime prayer, 33

Bells, 19, 83, 184

Benediction, 102-3, 151

Bernadette Soubirous, 125

Bernard of Clairvaux, St., 120

Bethel, 6

Bishop, 167

Blaise, St., 175

Blessed Sacrament, 82, 84, 87, 102-3, 151, 171, 177

Blessing of children, 33

Blessing of Flowers and Herbs, 127

Blessing of homes, Epiphany, 68

Blessing of throats, 175

Blue laws, 27

Bowing, 177-78

Breviary, 31

Calendar, origin of, 14-15

Calendar, Gregorian, 15, 65

Calendar, Julian, 15, 38, 51, 65

Candle, Christmas, 54

Candlemas, 68-69

Candles, 182-83

Canon law, 25

Canonization of saints, 115-16

Carnivals, 73

Caroling, 58

Carols, Christmas, 53, 58

Catafalque, 128

Catechumenate, 71, 147

Catherine Labouré, St., 121, 184

Catherine of Siena, St., 114

Cecilia, St., 111, 114

Celibacy, 169

Charlemagne, 45, 161

Charles Borromeo, St., 158

Chasuble, 184

Chaucer, 140

Chapel of Adoration, 83, 85

Charismatic gifts, 21, 24, 149, 160

Chrism Mass, 84

Christmas, 9, 43, 49-69

Christmas candle, 54

Christmas cards, 59

Christmas carols, 53, 58

Christmas crèche, 53, 55

Christmas, date of, 50

Christmas lights, 9, 53, 54, 57

Christmas Man, 61

Christmas, origin of, 50

Christmas pageants, 59

Christmas theme, 66

Christmas tree, 10, 46, 53, 56-57

Christmas tree ornaments, 57

Christmas, Twelve Days of, 63-64

Chrismation, 90, 149

Christ the King, feast of, 103-4

Christopher, St., 137-38

Church, 24-25

Church building, 153

Church year, origin of, 15-16

Church year, evolution of, 16

Circumcision, feast of, 66

Clappers, 83

Clergy, ranks of, 11, 152

Colors, liturgical, 48, 186

Colum Cille, St., see Columbkille, St.

Columbkille, St., 136-37

Communion of saints, 110

Confession, 82

Confession, seal of, 158

Confessionals, 159

Confessors, 108, 109, 137, 157, 159

Confirmation, 149-51

Corpus Christi, Solemnity of, 102-3

Corpus Christi procession, 102-3

Cross, meaning of, 187

Cross, sign of, 101, 179

Cross, veneration of, 86

Cross, kinds, 190

Cross, symbol, 187

Crucifix, 187

Cycles of time, 14

Daily Mass, 34-35

Dead, Mass for, 34, 35, 128-30, 135, 186

Dead, prayer for, 129, 130

Dead, remembering, 128, 133, 198

Dead, visiting graves of, 134

Deacons, 24, 31, 64, 164, 167-68

Deaconesses, 147, 167

Decoration Day, 198

Devotional feasts, 18, 101, 103

Devotions, 172

Dies Natalis Solis Invicti, 51

Divine office, 31, 33, 123

Divorce, 162-63

Dominic, St., 123

Doxology, 101-2

Druids, 10, 58, 81, 91, 140, 192

Earthiness, 10-11

East, facing, 176

Easter, 16, 94-100

Easter bunny, 99

Easter candle, 91

Easter clothes, 97

Easter, date of, 73, 95

Easter duty, 82, 97, 153

Easter eggs, 98-99

Easter, fertility theme, 95-96

Easter fire, 22, 90-91

Easter ham, 98

Easter lamb, 98

Easter lily, 99

Easter, name of, 96

Easter parade, 98

Easter Sunday, 82, 92, 96-97

Easter, sunrise services, 97

Easter Vigil, 23, 71, 79, 89-93, 96, 115

Easter water, 89, 90, 92, 96, 97, 183

Egeria, 79

Elders, relation to priests, 166

Ember days, 34, 37-38, 43

Ember days, and ordination, 38

Endtimes, 129

Epiphany, 43, 63, 66-67

Epiphany, blessing of homes, 68

Epiphany, origin of, 66-67

Equinox, 14, 15, 51, 52, 65, 73, 95, 97, 98, 192

Eucharist, 151-55

Eucharist, renewal, 154

Eucharistic devotion, 153

Eucharistic Prayer, origin of, 33

Eucharistic sacrifice, 152, 167

Evening prayer, 29, 31, 32

Exchanging gifts, 60, 136

Exorcism, 71-73

Extreme Unction, 161

Facing east, 176

Family, Holy, 63, 65

Family prayer, 33

Fasting, 33-34, 75-76, 79, 87, 92-93

Father Christmas, 60-61

Father's Day, 124, 134

Fatima, 125

Feast days, 64, 112-13

Fertility, 96

fields, procession to, 39

Fire, *see* Candles

First Day of the Week, 20

First Friday, 9, 29, 35

Forty Hours Devotion, origin of, 84

Francis of Assisi, St., 55, 58

Friday, abstinence, 29

Friday, fasting, 29

Friday the 13th, 36

Funerals, liturgical color, 7, 135, 186

Genuflecting, 177

Germanus, St., 140

Gestures, 51, 172, 176, 178

Good Friday, 34, 85-87

Grace at meals, 33, 197

Grave blankets, 134

Graves, visiting, 134

Gregorian calendar, 15, 65

Gregorian chant, 124, 180

Guadalupe, Our Lady of, 127

Hail Mary, 123

Hallelujah, see Alleluia

Halloween, 10, 115, 192-94

Halo, 117

Hanukkah, 49, 55

Healing ministry, 160

Helen, mother of Constantine, 86, 188

Hippolytus, 129

Hispanic practices, 33, 54-56

Holly, 58

Holy Cross, see Cross

Holy days, 112

Holy Family, feast of, 65

Holy Innocents, 64-65

Holy Thursday, 82-84

Holy Saturday, 91

Holy water, 183

Holy Week, 78-88

Hosanna, 173, 180

Host, communion, 103, 151-52

Hot cross buns, 77, 87-88

Hours, Prayer of the, 31

House church, 20, 24, 31, 173

Hyperdulia, 118

IHS, 187

Images of Mary, 126

Images of saints, 113-14

Immaculate Conception, 121, 127

Immaculate Heart of Mary, 121, 127

Incarnation, 44, 46, 47, 69, 125

Incense, 185-86

Indulgences, 128, 131-33, 158

Initiation, sacraments of, 146, 150-51

INRI, 187

Isidore, St., 114

IXYTHS, 187

Jacob, 6

January 1, 65-66

Jesse Tree, 47

Jesus, 10, 106, 114, 145, 155, 160

Jesus, symbol, 186-87

John the Evangelist, St., 64

John XXIII, Pope, 36

John Paul II, Pope, 25, 28, 137

Joseph, St., 35, 54-56, 59, 110, 114, 180

Julian calendar, 15, 38, 51, 65

Justin, 130

Juan Diego, 125

Kneeling, 176-77

Kriss Kringle, 60

Kwanzaa, 55

Labouré, St. Catherine, 121, 184

Las Posadas, 56

Last rites, 146, 161-62

Latin, 33, 152, 174

Lauds, 31, 32, 186

Laying on of hands, 74, 150, 161, 167, 173, 178

Legion of Mary, 118, 121

Lent, 70-77

Lent, atmosphere of, 74-75

Lent, fasting and abstinence, 75-76

Lent, origin of, 70-71

Lights, 181-83

Litany, 39, 115, 180

Litanies, Marian, 125

Litany of Loreto, 125, 180

Litany of Saints, 39, 89, 90, 115

Little Office of Our Lady, 123

Liturgical colors, 186

Liturgical centers, ancient, 174

Liturgy of the Hours, 31-33

Liturgy of the Hours, revived, 32-33

Lord's Day, 22

Louis de Montfort, St., 120

Lourdes, 125

Lucernare, 22, 31, 91, 182

Luminaries, 54-55

Luther, Martin, 158, 170

Madonna, 126

Magi, 67-68

Mandatum, 82

Manger, 48

Mardi Gras, 73

Margaret Mary Alacoque, St., 35, 103

Marian devotion, 120

Marian devotion, cautions, 122

Marian themes, 119, 121

Marriage, 162-65

Marriage, current thinking, 165

Marriage, indissolubility, 163

Marriage, sacrament, 164-65

Martin, St., 43, 45, 196

Martyrs, 106-8

Mary, 118-127

Mary, assumption of, 32, 121

Mary, feasts of, 18, 127

Mary, images of, 126-27

Mary, Immaculate Conception, 121, 127

Mary, intercessory role, 120

Mary, Legion of, 118-121

Mary, litany of, 125

Mary, modern devotion to, 120-121

Mary, month of, 124

Mary, scapular, 127

Mass, 151

Mass, for the dead, 35, 128, 129

Mass, origin of name, 151-52

Mass, private, 34, 154

Mass, daily, 34-35, 130

Mass obligation, 25-26

Mass of Pre-Sanctified, 86

Mass stipends, 133

Massasoit, 196

Maundy Thursday, *see* Holy Thursday

May, month of, 124

Meal prayer, 33
Medals, 171, 172, 184
Medjugorje, 126
Memorial Day, 198-99
Midnight Mass, 53
Miraculous Medal, 121, 184-85
Mistletoe, 58, 81
Mithraism, 51
Monstrance, 102, 103, 151, 154
Month, division of time, 14-15
Morning prayer, 29, 31, 32, 179
Mother's Day, 124
Music, 179-80
Mystagogia, 99, 148
Mysteria, sacraments, 145
Mystery cults, 90, 145

Name days, 111
Nativity, *see* Christmas
Nativity scene, 47, 55, 56
Nero, Emperor, 107-8
New Year's Day, 63, 65-66
Nicholas, St., 60-61, 108, 136
Nine Fridays, devotion, 35
November, 134

O Antiphons, 44
O Salutaris, 103, 151
Octave of Christmas, 63, 65-66
October, month of rosary, 124
Office, divine, 31
Oils, 84
Oplatek, 56
Orders, ranks of clergy, 167
Orders, sacrament, 166-70

Ordination process, 167
Ordinations, and ember days, 38
Ordinary Time, 17, 23, 101-4
Origen, 130

Paczki, 73
Palms, 73, 80-1, 171
Palm Sunday, 80-81
Paradise tree, 10, 57
Parousia, 43
Pascha, annual, 16, 23, 71, 95
Pascha, weekly, 16, 19
Paschal Candle, 22, 182
Paschal controversy, 95
Paschal Lamb, 95
Paschal Mystery, 17, 19, 52, 80, 82-83, 107
Passover, 78-79, 85
Patrick, St., 102, 136, 140-41
Patron saints, 111-13
Paul, St., 106, 108, 111, 163, 177
Penance, books of, 157
Penance, lenten, 73-76, 177
Penance, sacrament,
    see Reconciliation
Penitents, 74, 156-59
Pentecost, 17, 100
Pentecost, novena, 100
Persecution, 11-12, 106-8, 147
Peter, St., 108, 111, 114
Peter Damian, St., 127, 185
Pews, 178
Pilgrims, 195-96
Pius V missal, 92
Poinsettia, 59

Polycarp, St., 108
Poor souls, 130
Prayer, daily, 30-31
Prayer, family, 30-31
Prayer, public, 30-31
Precious Blood, devotion to, 18, 35
Precious Blood, feast of, 18, 102
Pre-Sanctified, Mass of, 86
Presbyter, 166-68
Presentation of the Lord, 69, 119
Pretzels, lenten food, 76-77
Priesthood, celibacy, 168-170
Priesthood, current trends, 170
Priesthood, garb, 170
Priesthood, lifestyle, 168-69
Priesthood, origin of, 166
Priesthood, post-Reformation, 169-70
Prostration, 177
Purgatory, 128-30, 158
Purification, feast of, 69
Pysanki, 99

Quadragesima, see Lent
Qahal Yahweh, 24
Quarantine, Lent, 74
Quartodecimans, 95

Raising the eyes and hands, 178
RCIA, 72, 148
Reconciliation, 81, 155-59
Reformation, 132, 146, 158
Relics, 109, 110, 113
Reliquaries, 113
Requiem Masses, 129
Rest, day of, 26-27

Resurrection, *see* Easter
Ritual words, 173, 180
Rogation days, 34, 37, 39, 102
Rogation procession, 39, 102
Rosary, caution about, 122
Rosary, month of, 32, 123
Rosary, origin of, 32, 123
Rosary, mysteries of, 32

Sabbatarianism, 27
Sabbath, 14, 20
Sacramentality, principle of, 144
Sacramentals, 171-90
Sacramentals, abuses of, 173-75
Sacramentals, definition, 172
Sacramentals, Jewish origin, 173
Sacraments, 148-170
Sacred Heart, devotion to, 35, 103
Sacred Triduum, 79-80
Saint Martin's Lent, 43
Saints, abuses of devotion to, 110
Saints, canonization, 115-16
Saints, communion of, 110-11
Saints, devotion to, 18, 109
Saints, Feast of All, 115
Saints, feasts of, 112-13
Saints, images of, 113-14
Saints, Litany of All, 115
Saints, medals of, 113
Saints, patron, 111-12
Saints, praying to, 114-15
Saints, relics, 113
Sanctoral cycle, 17-18, 106-141
Santa Claus, 60-62
Saturday, Holy, 91-92

Saturday, Mary's day, 124

Saturday evening Mass, 28

Saturnalia, 44, 51, 60

Scapegoat, 10, 145, 155

Scapular, 122, 127, 171, 172, 185

Seal of Confession, 158

Seasons, 37-39

Sebastian, St., 114

Second coming, 156

Seder, 21, 33, 85, 95, 98

Servile work, 27

Sex, 164

Shamrock, 102, 141

Shrove Tuesday, 73

Sign of the Cross, 179

Simon Stock, St., 127

Sin, mortal and venial, 157

Solstice, 10, 14, 22, 50, 51-2

Souls in purgatory, praying for, 3, 128, 130-31, 158

Spring cleaning, 82

Sprinkling, rite of, 183

Standing, as posture, 176

Stations of the Cross, 76

Stephen, St., 64, 106-7, 111, 112

Stipends, 35, 133-34

Striking the breast, 179

Stripping the altar, 83-84

Sunday assembly, 23-5

Sunday, day of rest, 26-27, 152

Sunday, first day of week, 14, 20, 90

Sunday, obligation, 25-28

Sunday, origin of, 19-20

Sunday themes, 22

Sunday, contemporary observance of, 27-28

Sunrise service, 97

Superstition, 12

Symbols, 186-190

Tabernacle, 154

Tabernacle light, 183

Temporal cycle, 17, 42-104

Ten Commandments, 26

Tertiary, 185

Tertullian, 129-30

Thanksgiving, 10, 195-97

Theotokos, 119

Thomas Aquinas, St., 121

Thomas à Becket, 109

Three kings, 68

Throats, blessing of, 175

Thursday, Holy, 17, 82-86

Traditions, earthiness, 10-11

Traditions, origin of, 6

Traditions, subject to change, 7-8

Traditions, Jewish origin of, 10-11

Traditions, nature of, 6

Trent, Council of, 150, 158, 161, 165, 169

Tre Ore, 87

Triduum, Easter, 72

Trinity Sunday, 101-2

Trinity, symbols, 102

Twelve Days of Christmas, 63-4

Valentine, St., 139-40

Valentines, 136, 139-40

Vatican Council, Second, 1, 8, 27, 106-7, 110, 112, 114, 122, 130, 154, 165, 173

Veiling of statues and crosses, 75

Veneration of cross, 86

Veneration of saints, 7, 54, 110, 114, 174

Vernacular, 174

Vespers, 22, 31, 32, 182, 186

Vestments, 183-84

Viaticum, Holy, 160-162

Vigil lights, 171, 183

Votive lights, 171, 183

Votive Masses, 34, 35

Washing of feet, 82, 83

Water, holy, 33, 68, 161, 171, 172, 183

Wedding banns, 165

Wedding cake, 163

Wedding ring, 163

Wedding traditions, 162-64

Week, division of time, 14-15

Weekdays, names, 30

Weekdays, themes, 35-36

White baptismal robe, 147

Wreath, Advent, 46-7, 54, 182

Year, division of time, 14-15

Yule, relation to Christmas, 56

Zeno, St., 184

OF RELATED INTEREST...

CATHOLIC SYMBOLS: *Our Rich Spiritual Heritage*
MIKE DALEY

Michael Daley offers a fascinating and informative overview of our symbolic language, breaking these down into core symbols of Catholicism, symbolic persons from Scripture, saints as symbolic persons, virtues, Christian symbols, and symbols of the Mass. A must-have resource for anyone who teaches about the faith—or just wants to know more about it.
120 pages | $12.95 | order 957538

WHAT CATHOLICS BELIEVE: *Exploring Our Faith Today*
JOAN PAHL MORRIS

An experienced religious educator presents key topics of Catholic belief in an informed and accessible style. In particular she looks at some of the ways our understanding of the Catholic faith has been enriched since Vatican II. An excellent resource for catechists and teachers, for senior high students and RCIA catechumens and candidates, and for adult Catholics who want a Catholic faith refresher.
112 pages | $10.95 | order 95263X

BASICS OF THE CATHOLIC FAITH
BILL, PATTY, AND LISA COLEMAN

Readers can refer to this handy resource for a wealth of information about Jesus and his teachings, the customs and traditions of the church, Catholic prayers, saints, and devotions, and much more. This is a great "refresher course" for catechists and other parish ministers, as well as for the RCIA catechumens and candidates.
144 pages | $12.95 | order 951099

THE HUMAN QUEST FOR GOD: *An Overview of World Religions*
JOSEPH STOUTZENBERGER

This is a fascinating journey for anyone who wants to learn more about the search we humans share: the search for an almighty, loving, and universal presence in our lives. It covers the history, major themes, underlying philosophy, and components of the principle religions of the world and includes an overview of minor religions as well.
272 pages | $24.95 | order 955663

ORDER ONLINE AT
23RDPUBLICATIONS.COM